Long Walk Home

Long Walk Home

REFLECTIONS ON
BRUCE SPRINGSTEEN

✧

Edited by Jonathan D. Cohen
and June Skinner Sawyers

RUTGERS UNIVERSITY PRESS

New Brunswick, Camden, and Newark, New Jersey, and London

Library of Congress Cataloging-in-Publication Data

Names: Cohen, Jonathan D., 1990– | Sawyers, June Skinner, 1957–
Title: Long walk home: reflections on Bruce Springsteen /
    edited by Jonathan D. Cohen and June Skinner Sawyers.
Description: New Brunswick: Rutgers University Press, 2019. |
    Includes bibliographical references and index.
Identifiers: LCCN 2019002452 | ISBN 9781978805262 (cloth)
Subjects: LCSH: Springsteen, Bruce—Criticism and interpretation.
Classification: LCC ML420.S77 L66 2019 | DDC 782.42166092—dc23
LC record available at https://lccn.loc.gov/2019002452

A British Cataloging-in-Publication record for this book is available
from the British Library.

www.rutgersuniversitypress.org

Manufactured in the United States of America

CONTENTS

Part VI: Springsteen and Aging

Part VII: Springsteen beyond Borders

Long Walk Home

Introduction

✧

Why Springsteen?

JONATHAN D. COHEN AND
JUNE SKINNER SAWYERS

In 2014, almost sixty years after he first picked up a guitar, Bruce Springsteen reflected on his legacy. "When you're playing," he noted in an interview with *NPR*, "you hope that somebody hears your voice, is interested in what you're doing and then gathers whatever they think might be of value in it and then moves it down the line." Just as Springsteen was influenced by the songs of Elvis Presley, Bob Dylan, and many others, he expected that those who came after him would draw from his own work. And Springsteen has made clear that his legacy will not be purely musical. He hopes his work will be moved down the line by songwriters and also by the millions of fans who have heard his albums, seen him perform, and pored over his lyrics. As he writes in the final pages of his autobiography, "I work to be an ancestor."

Springsteen will turn seventy in 2019, and while he has retained a creative energy unique among septuagenarian rock stars, this milestone offers an opportunity to reflect on his career and what he will leave behind for future generations. Springsteen has been a major musical figure and cultural icon for over four decades. He burst into the public consciousness in 1975 with *Born to Run* and cultivated a fanbase with unbeatable live performances and a collection of songs that offered both joyous celebration and a class-conscious examination of life at the end of the American postwar boom. In 1984, *Born in the U.S.A.* catapulted

Springsteen into international megastardom, and in the span of a decade he brought his show from small clubs to cavernous football stadiums. Following over a decade of personal introspection and musical experimentation, he reemerged in the public arena in the aftermath of 9/11. In the years since, he has thrilled audiences all over the world, brought his music to Broadway, and offered stark commentary on the direction of American society. While he continues to produce new work, the music that he will be remembered for has proven an enduring, impactful feature of American and international culture for decades.

However, it proves difficult to assess the legacy of one musical artist. Countless musicians have been influenced by Springsteen and his albums represent tangible objects that will endure for years to come. But other aspects of his career are more ephemeral. Consider, for example, Springsteen's legendary live shows. Biographers, scholars, music journalists, and fans often compare Springsteen concerts to church meetings, especially since he reunited with the E Street Band in the late 1990s. Around that time, Springsteen began relying increasingly on performance techniques associated with African American preachers, particularly the raising of hands, gospel-themed monologues, and ritualized audience call-and-response. Yet, unlike the pastors whom he emulates, Springsteen is a religious leader without a formal institution. Attendees report feeling transfixed, transformed, and spiritually awakened at his shows, but the Church of Springsteen has no mailing address, no set gathering place. It relies entirely on Springsteen himself. When he is not touring it does not meet, and when he is gone it will cease to exist. There is no line of succession for the Boss.

So what will remain when Springsteen's career comes to a close? What will it look like when his work is moved down the line? What will be his legacy?

Long Walk Home endeavors to answer these questions, illustrating that Springsteen's legacy must be measured at the personal level. Over the past fifty years, millions of people all over the world, from Bergen, Norway, to Bergen County, New Jersey, have been touched by his music. This impact is difficult to assess and impossible to quantify, but, as the essays in this volume make clear, Springsteen's greatest legacy will be the ways his music has affected individual listeners. Springsteen helps his audience cope with hard times, both personal struggles and tumultuous political periods. His music reflects his listeners back onto themselves, challenging their assumptions and helping them make sense of their messy, chaotic lives. He writes what musicologist John Sheinbaum calls "healing music," music that can "make difficult times better."

Springsteen often describes his work as a conversation with his audience, a dialogue back and forth between songwriter and listener. He has done most of the talking, to be sure, but audiences make their own meaning from music and draw whatever value they need for their own lives. Some songs fade away. Others endure because they continue to resonate. In a 2005 conversation with novelist Nick Hornby, Springsteen speculated that two of his signature songs, "Born to Run" and "Thunder Road," have remained popular for decades because "people took that music and they really made it theirs." Springsteen's songs do not belong to him. They belong to his listeners, all of whom can extract what they need from his music. As he told the *New York Times* in 1992, "I've always believed that people listen to your music not to find out about you but to find out about themselves."

Springsteen's work resonates with audiences in part because he writes music designed to connect with people and to help them address the issues they are facing. "When I started out making music, I wasn't fundamentally interested in having a big hit right away," he recalled in an interview with *Guitar World*, slightly romanticizing the early history of the E Street Band: "I was into writing music that was going to thread its way into people's lives. I was interested in becoming a part of people's lives, and having some usefulness." Springsteen's songs—from "Streets of Fire" to "Streets of Philadelphia," "My Hometown" to "My City of Ruins," "Jackson Cage" to "Jack of All Trades"—indicate that he didn't just want to make music. Springsteen wanted to make "useful" music. Music that engages listeners. Music that touches on timeless questions about what it means to be human, about faith and friendship, about hunger and humanity, about love and loss. Music premised on the simple assumption that rock and roll can change lives.

And indications are that Springsteen's music *has* changed lives. Testimonials from fans recorded in ethnographic studies as well as the 2013 documentary *Springsteen & I* demonstrate how people from all walks of life and from all over the world have found meaning in his music. Similarly, the sheer amount of written material about Springsteen reflects the number of people who have spent their lives engaging with his work. This growing library includes over a dozen biographies, theater performances based on his lyrics, fiction inspired by his songs, and scholarly studies of nearly every aspect of his career. Memoirs, too, have been dedicated to accounts of growing up with Springsteen's music, including one by journalist Sarfraz Manzoor about his relocation from Pakistan to England, *Greetings from Bury Park*. Manzoor describes how Springsteen's music helped him understand his traditional, withdrawn, and frustrated father. "Independence Day," Manzoor writes, "opened my mind to the pain that my father was feeling," particularly the embarrassment of unemployment and the growing cultural separation between him and his son. Like Manzoor, all fans have the chance to incorporate Springsteen's songs into their own life in their own way. The power of his music lies in its ability to serve many functions, to provide each of his listeners with what they need.

But what allows Springsteen's music to feel so personal for so many people? One of the goals of this book is to find out. The answer cannot be found by analyzing his album sales or his long list of awards and accolades (most of which he received years after the peak of his popularity). Rather, the usefulness of Springsteen's music is best illustrated through personal reflections and personal stories. To that end, *Long Walk Home* is composed of essays from musicians, authors, academics, music critics, and others, all of whom answered a seemingly simple question: "Why Springsteen?" Contributors considered what attracted—and continues to attract—them to Springsteen and the ways they have been moved, shaped, and challenged by his music. As a result, these essays vary in subject matter, from recollections about walking with Springsteen in the backwoods of New Jersey in 1982 to the story of how "Growin' Up" helped a lonely Indian girl adjust to life in the American South. One essay follows a budding Irish writer who saw working-class life in Dublin expressed in Springsteen's lyrics, and another examines Springsteen as a model for the role of artists in a democratic society. Two essays reveal the ways Springsteen represents a forgotten dream of rock-and-roll racial integration, while one piece describes how *Born to Run* helped a group of young Australians cope with their country's 1975 constitutional crisis. Taken together, these essays illustrate the usefulness of Springsteen's music and demonstrate the value he has provided to millions of fans over the course of his career.

Our contributors were chosen not simply because many of them are avowed Springsteen fans. The essayists featured in this collection represent influential individuals notable for their writing, their music, their activism, or their contributions to the arts. Their work illustrates how Springsteen's music has influenced novels, music, photography, politics, and academic scholarship, and they are actively engaged in moving his work down the line. Springsteen fans will see themselves reflected in these fans' experiences of his music, and the essays in this book will help bring fans closer to answering the question "Why Springsteen?" for themselves.

However, this collection does not claim to represent every Springsteen fan. Due to unforeseen changes to our list of contributors, this volume is composed largely of essays by middle-aged American straight white men, although it also does include Australian, Canadian, English, Irish, and Welsh contributors as well as nonwhite and queer voices. While the white male demographic embodies the stereotypical image of a Springsteen fan—and the stereotypical rock critic interested in Springsteen—it does not account for such a large percentage of his overall audience. Similarly, most of the contributors who write about Springsteen's political beliefs admire him for his outspokenness and his open support in recent years of Democratic candidates, though indications are that sizable portions of his fanbase do not share Springsteen's liberal politics. Nonetheless, rather than offer just one author's experience, this collection of twenty-six reflections offers twenty-six distinct perspectives on the power of Springsteen's music.

Among these essays, certain recurring themes speak to features of Springsteen's music that explain his special resonance. Fans were drawn to Springsteen by the power of his performances, his probing lyrics, and his musical borrowing from a range of styles and influences. Many felt empowered by the youthful dreams of his early material but also connected with his acknowledgment of the ties that bind, the problems and possibilities that accompany growing up. In recent years, many have remained Springsteen fans because of the creativity of his latest albums, his commitment to social justice, his openness about his struggles with depression, and his candid embrace of the aging process.

Running through this collection is the often-unstated understanding that Springsteen has the unique gift to write music that is universal in scope. Whether drawing from material about his own life or singing from the perspective of a working-class woman, a Mexican migrant, or a New York City firefighter, Springsteen's music reaches into the heart of the human condition, articulating feelings that everyone experiences. This has allowed fans, regardless of their background, to feel that a Springsteen song is about *them*, that Springsteen knows *them*, that he wrote a certain song for *them*. Take, for instance, "The River," a song Springsteen penned in 1979, inspired by his sister and brother-in-law and the struggles they faced in their first years of marriage. The ballad is one of the most discussed songs in this collection not because our contributors have met Virginia Springsteen but because they saw their own lives reflected in this story. "Is a dream a lie if it don't come true / or is it something worse?" the narrator wonders. The song resonated for many of our authors because they felt it described their lives, that they intimately understood this tale of regret, the downsizing of dreams, and the toil of the working life. Springsteen uses small stories to ask big questions, and, by doing so, he has helped his listeners come a little closer to finding the answers they are looking for.

On the occasion of Springsteen's seventieth birthday, this volume offers a new type of consideration of his career. Between the flood of biographies, a growing body of scholarship, and his recent memoir, there are few lingering mysteries about Springsteen's music, career, or personal life. What remains to be examined is the impact he and his art have had—and will continue to have—on audiences in the United States and across the globe. Just as Springsteen's music draws the universal from the personal, his legacy is best assessed by examining universal experiences through personal stories.

Released on the album *Magic* in 2007, "Long Walk Home" describes a character who returns to his hometown to find that while familiar structures remain standing, longtime inhabitants have moved on. Nonetheless, certain values endure, and the narrator recognizes the long journey to come but also acknowledges the ideas and ideals that will light the road ahead. So too this collection records the journeys that members of Springsteen's audience have taken with him, how his music offered them something they couldn't find anywhere else. Springsteen's legacy will be as an artist who provided inspiration, comfort, and healing. He has helped his listeners on their own journeys, and this book shows how, in return, they have already begun the long walk to move his work down the line.

Works Cited

Holden, Stephen. "When the Boss Fell to Earth, He Hit Paradise." *New York Times*, August 9, 1992.

Manzoor, Sarfraz. *Greetings from Bury Park: A Memoir*. New York: Vintage, 2007.

Powers, Ann. "A Long Road to 'High Hopes': An Interview with Bruce Springsteen." *NPR*, January 15, 2014. www.npr.org/sections/therecord/2014/01/14/262485987/a -long-road-to-high-hopes-an-interview-with-bruce-springsteen.

Sheinbaum, John J. *Good Music: What It Is and Who Gets to Decide*. Chicago: University of Chicago Press, 2018.

Springsteen, Bruce. *Born to Run*. New York: Simon & Schuster, 2016.

———. Interview with Neil Strauss. *Guitar World*, October 1995. In *Talk about a Dream: The Essential Interviews of Bruce Springsteen*, edited by Christopher Phillips and Louis P. Masur, 170–181. New York: Bloomsbury, 2013.

———. Interview with Nick Hornby. *Guardian*, July 17, 2005. In *Talk about a Dream: The Essential Interviews of Bruce Springsteen*, edited by Christopher Phillips and Louis P. Masur, 292–299. New York: Bloomsbury, 2013.

Part I

Springsteen Stories

"Nite Shirt #2." (Frank Stefanko)

1

Growing Up with Bruce Springsteen

A Fan's Notes

ERIC ALTERMAN

When Bruce played in Barcelona in 2012, a group of Spanish kids held up a sign that read "Bruce, Thanks for Making Our Lives Better." I've spoken to Bruce exactly four times in my life, if you include handing him his guitar in the green room of the *Charlie Rose* show in 1998 and posing for a photo with him at Barnes & Noble in 2017. Otherwise it was only twice. (Well, I also gave him directions once, in college.) I have strong feelings, naturally, about what I said and what I wished I had said. But I actually feel pretty powerfully that Bruce, the person, does not really matter to me. He could be just as dickish as any famous rock star and it wouldn't matter. The music is what matters. And though I've written a great deal about Bruce the musician and public figure, I've never gone to a lot of trouble trying to interview him, nor imagining him coming to dinner or renting a movie theater so he could show me *The Searchers* the way John Ford meant it to be seen. I just go to the concerts and listen to the CDs. I do admit that I sometimes try to think about what my life would be like had there been no Bruce in it. To be honest, I can't do it. It sounds ridiculous, but it is literally too terrible to contemplate. There have been greater and more admirable men and women in public life than Bruce Springsteen, but none have ever meant so much to me. That sign did a pretty good job of saying it all.

To be honest, I don't know how to sum up the role Springsteen has played in my life so far or even give it a coherent structure. Part of the problem is that I discovered Bruce when I was fifteen and I'm now fifty-nine. My understanding of the world and my relationship to music and the artists who make it have naturally changed quite a bit over that time. But I have to say a big problem with summing up Bruce is Bruce himself. Both the man and the artist—and I distinguish between them whenever possible—present a package of frightful contradictions. I'll leave the complicated questions about the effect of his extremely bizarre upbringing on both his psyche and his artistry to his therapist(s). I'm interested in the music. But that too is impossible to generalize about. Think about all the different artists you've heard (or seen) Bruce channel. Way back when he was the "New Dylan," he was already fourteen other things. Remember, he was fronting a kind of jazz band and had already been through at least six musical incarnations before that. Pick a moment in Bruce's professional career—after, I would argue, the dreadful Steel Mill heavy metal mush—and you hear someone repeatedly challenging any number of iconic musicians in a remarkable array of genres. There's the Dylan / Woody Guthrie / Pete Seeger Bruce, of course. But there is also Elvis Bruce. There's Hank Williams Bruce. There's the Ronettes / Swingin' Medallions Bruce. There's the Sam and Dave Bruce. And there's definitely the James Brown Bruce. What am I missing? Well, there's supposedly a hip-hop Bruce in an album he decided against releasing. There's that Suicide, "Dream Baby Dream" Bruce and even a Clash Bruce. I could go on, but my point here is that, dammit, they all work. I recently read heartfelt appreciations about Bruce from Emmylou Harris and Joe Strummer. Can you even imagine two more different artists? Yet both saw Bruce as important influences; inspirations, even. The apparent contradictions between Bruce's various musical personas somehow remain within a zone of authenticity. And each speaks to different parts of us in different ways with an honesty and power that eludes mere language; at least they have to me. I taught a class last year on Springsteen and Dylan. What I found most interesting was how different they were. Dylan repeatedly assumed new identities throughout his life, beginning with the character "Bob Dylan." Bruce just spoke with different parts of himself.

Anyway, what follows are some personal notes about what it's been like to "grow up" with Bruce. I wouldn't be the man I am without him.

1975

I was in ninth grade. I had missed *Greetings from Asbury Park, N.J.* and *The Wild, the Innocent & the E Street Shuffle* somehow, even though I loyally read the record reviews in *Rolling Stone* beginning—I swear this is true—with the David Cassidy-smoking-a-joint-and-showing-pubic-hair issue, which I still recall bringing to summer camp. I hated disco, there was no punk yet, and I was stuck in what I still think of as the "Life-Sucks-So-Who-Gives-a-Shit" decade. I smoked a lot of pot in those days, but my parents didn't sweat it too much because my mom worked in a school system where kids sometimes shot one another. What's more, I got good grades, so, really, what was the big deal? The Allman Brothers were awesome, and so were the Grateful Dead. And hey, Pink Floyd still holds up. But those bands were largely passive experiences. Everyone at their shows was stoned to the point of nearly passing out. That's what it was; music to pass out to.

I still remember walking around those garbage-strewn streets of about-to-almost-default New York City that summer and seeing Springsteen on posters hung up on the sides of dumpsters and at abandoned construction sites like he was a modern-day Russian icon, except in sneakers and a leather jacket with a guitar on his back. WNEW-FM—the station that, loser that I was, actually provided me with a serviceable substitute for friendship—had gotten the Bruce bug before *Born to Run* was released and was playing the first two albums all the time. They were fucking great, as I would have said then, but were difficult to understand ("Cat long sighs holding Kitty's black tooth"? What the hell was that?). When the Bottom Line gigs finally arrived, I tried to get in but my fake ID got me nowhere. (Years later, the owner's wife advised me that in 1974, when nobody cared about Bruce, the fake ID would have been fine.) But when WNEW broadcast the August 15 show on the radio, I was betting on Bruce to deliver something I could never have defined. And damned if he didn't do it. Listen to the bootleg of Bruce singing "And Then She Kissed Me" if you doubt my word. It's as great a three minutes of rock and roll as you will ever hear. And Bruce stopped playing it for thirty-three years because, well, he had about a million of those up his sleeve and didn't even need that one.

I bought the album ten days later, August 25, 1975, the day it came out. I got my sister, Marcia, to drive me to E. J. Korvette's on Central Avenue in Yonkers, a chain of discount department stores named after eight Jewish Korean War veterans. I don't remember what I bribed her with, but it remains the best $3.33 I ever spent. I later wrote that *Born to Run* "exploded in my home, my mind and changed my life," just as Elvis and the Beatles had done for Bruce a decade earlier. Springsteen's music pierced this misplaced teenage soul exactly where he was aiming. I could never have articulated it at the time, but *Born to Run* offered me an alternative context for my life, one in which it was okay to try and fail, rather than just appear too cool to care. What had previously felt ridiculous was endowed with dignity and, no less important, solidarity. Most of my life was beyond my control, but my reaction in the face of it would be my own. Fuck Scarsdale, ripping the bones off my metaphorical back like a metaphorical death trap. One day I would pull out of there to win.

1976

Every Thursday during my sophomore and junior years of high school I would head to the school library at lunchtime and grab that week's *Village Voice* to see if Bruce was playing somewhere where they would finally let me in. I didn't know about the lawsuit. I didn't know what was holding him up. I devoured the cover stories in *Time* and *Newsweek* and fought back, in my head, against the backlash. (Peter Frampton? Billy Joel? Give me a break.) But I felt like a fraud because I had never seen him live. And with Bruce, that was the thing. See the guy live. There was no substitute. I heard he had been offered a million bucks to do a TV special and had turned it down. Goddamn artistic integrity.

I didn't understand it at the time, but the library got the *Voice* a day late. So when the ad finally showed up for six nights at the Palladium, most of it was already sold out. I had a girlfriend at the time who was always in and out of the hospital. It turned out later that she had been given some bad medicine or something and this gave her all kinds of terrible reactions that nobody could diagnose. So it wasn't as psychosomatic as everyone assumed, but still, it was a pain in the ass for her boyfriend. Half of our relationship took place in hospitals; a not terribly convenient place for a sixteen-year-old kid, if you get my drift. I remember that morning, she was being tested for cancer. Thing was, she had a car and I didn't. I needed that car to drive to Macy's in White Plains and get those tickets. She was like, "Don't you want to hear about my cancer tests?" And I was like, "Not now, goddammit, this is serious." ("At least as serious as cancer," I might have added, but I didn't.) That relationship didn't last much longer—surprise, surprise—but I brought two other girls to the three shows I saw (in nosebleed seats) and I married one of them and had my daughter with the other. (I think I'll save the story of my marriages for my memoirs.) Anyway, the band came out and broke into "Night." I was worried that nothing could possibly live up to the hype and yet one more supposedly great thing was going to suck. I put my worries away. It was like an electric bolt traveled from Bruce's guitar into my teenage heart. There was magic in those nights.

1978

I was supposed to go to college a week early for one of those Outward Bound–style bonding trips. So, I didn't use the coupon in the *New York Times* Arts and Leisure section to buy tickets for Bruce's first-ever Madison Square Garden shows. I gave them to this friend of mine named Danny. (We worked at the Bronx Zoo together. I was supposed to interview random visitors for a membership survey. It ended up being heavily weighted toward pretty teenage girls.) My parents were away when the shows rolled around so I said "fuck it" and went anyway. I don't know whether we got a refund for the trip. But I made Danny take me to at least one of the concerts. (I was out touch with him for the next thirty-eight years, but when I asked on Facebook if anyone had a U2 ticket for me, Danny, now a big macher who used to be COO of Yahoo and who is friends with Bono, answered and said he owed me for Bruce, back in 1978. It was their last show at the Garden that tour, and hey, guess who showed up for "I Still Haven't Found What I'm Looking For" and "Stand By Me"? But I get ahead of myself, yet again.)

I got "arrested" at that first Garden show. I've been actually arrested once or twice since, always for comically stupid reasons, but this one was the stupidest of all. I rushed up to the stage because, as I explained to a rather bemused member of New York City's Finest, I was trying to give Bruce my old high-top Chuck Taylors as a symbol of how much "Born to Run" had meant to me. I had to explain it fast, though, because I was missing "Spirit in the Night." "Bruce Springsteen doesn't want your ugly old sneakers, you dumb kid," the cop rather wisely observed, before letting me off with a warning and a ripped ticket, meaning I'd get thrown out if I was caught again too close to the stage for my ticket. I got back to my seat and traded tickets with my girlfriend. Ha, cop!

Also in 1978, when I was a freshman, Bruce played my school and I carried out an elaborate and brilliantly choreographed plan to leave a short story I had written in his dressing room. The plot involved the death of my entire family in a traffic accident because my parents had forced me to leave the previous year's New Year's Eve Southside Johnny concert before Bruce appeared onstage. (I am still furious about this, as my poor parents, ages eighty-four and eighty-nine, well know.) I had snuck into the hall to watch the sound check, but, tragically, was discovered and kicked out the back door. Just as I was making my involuntary exit, the band's bus pulled up and Bruce got out. He was a scrawny little guy in a leather jacket that made him look like any old greaser from Eastchester. He walked into the gym and spoke to nobody (except me, alas) and said, "What a dump." Then he asked where they could go and play some pool. I suggested somewhere, but they never made it. The venue apparently sucked so much the band never did do a soundcheck. And Bruce, it was later reported in my college newspaper, did not eat the steak the concert rider called for. But yes, they were fucking terrific. I caught him when he fell backward during "Spirit." I had never held a guy before (or since, I might add). But Bruce was beyond gender. He was the music itself. During the encore, I was pushed up against the stage by the entire crowd, and I actually worried I might be being forcibly sterilized. Bruce was trying to talk and people were all screaming at him. I turned around and said, "Shut up. That's the Boss talking." Miraculously, they did. Bruce looked down and said, "Hey, thanks a lot, there," and went back to screaming. "Jenny, Jenny, Jenny. . . ." It was, and still is, one of the greatest moments of my ridiculous life.

1979

In September 1979, Bruce caused a major rift in my family. In what turned out to be his only announced appearance during the more than two years he spent recording *The River*, Springsteen played a benefit with a group of laid-back Los Angeles rockers at Madison Square Garden to oppose nuclear energy. Because the Clash and the Who would also be in town the same week, I decided this rare astrological constellation outweighed the importance of any classes I might miss by going home. My parents, who viewed college in terms of the tens of thousands of dollars they paid in tuition, room, and board, begged to differ. Bruce and his fellow "Musicians United for Safe Energy" made matters a million times worse by scheduling the first of Springsteen's two shows on Kol Nidre, the holiest night of the Jewish calendar. First my education, next my immortal soul. I remember getting picked up hitchhiking to the train that night by the mother of an old JV basketball teammate. She thought she was giving me a ride to meet my parents for Yom Kippur services. When I told her the real story—I was going to see a Springsteen concert—she made me get out of the car and walk.

Rarely in history has a cause gone less recognized by those ostensibly assembled to support it. Nuclear power? Sure, it sucked, whatever. We were there to see Bruce. The performers who preceded him on the bill either rode the Springsteen wave or were swept under by it. Jackson Browne smartly joined the crowd in chanting "Broooce" in between his own songs. Chaka Khan ran off the stage in tears. ("Broooce" apparently sounds a lot like "boo" when you're onstage.) "Too bad his name isn't Melvin," quipped Bonnie Raitt by way of meager consolation.

The fifty or so minutes it took the crew to set up the E Street Band's equipment after Browne finally left the stage were the longest minutes of my then-nineteen-year life. It was more than just the weight of the wait, though that was considerable. While the other acts played for about forty-five minutes each, that was inconceivable for Bruce. The longer Bruce took to come onstage, the greater the likelihood I would miss the last train home and end up sleeping outside Grand Central Station when they swept out its permanent denizens between one thirty and five o'clock in the morning. If he didn't get started by ten, I figured I was sunk.

I was. Springsteen came on late, played a magnificent ninety-minute set, and forced me to pass Yom Kippur morning with the bums, none of whom looked to have been anywhere near High Holy Day services in quite a while. Yet if the point of prayer is to inspire spiritual epiphany in the company of religious community, as the founder of Reconstructionist Judaism—and, I would argue, the most important influence on contemporary American Jewish practice—Rabbi Mordecai Kaplan claimed, then I had been in the right place on Kol Nidre. This was not just music anymore. It was something bigger, more powerful; more like a religion.

Springsteen introduced "The River" that night and dedicated the song to his sister, who had gotten pregnant and married at seventeen. It was a sad and beautiful moment. "Mary," who we left driving rapturously to nowhere in "Thunder Road," was now pregnant and married—at nineteen—to the boy who had been forced to grow up and put away all his dreams as childish stuff. Her husband, the narrator, would return over and over to the banks of the river where all those dreams took place, only to feel them mocked by his "union card and wedding coat." The song, inspired by the old Hank Williams moan "Long Gone Lonesome Blues," ends with a question as frightening and haunting as any rock musician had ever asked his audience: "Is a dream a lie if it don't come true / or is it something worse?" Were we idiots for believing that we could build different lives than our parents? Were we really born to run or merely born to delude ourselves for the brief adolescent moment when such things seemed possible? It was a question that would not go away, but in the meantime, we were at a Bruce Springsteen concert. That show ended, as I recall, with Bruce singing Mitch Ryder's "Detroit Medley," followed by Gary U.S. Bonds's "Quarter to Three." Bruce did the James Brown cape thing, followed by a little "Jailhouse Rock" dance offstage. It was an ur–rock and roll moment I'll never forget. Later, this show became famous because Bruce was kind of a bully to his ex-girlfriend from the stage; another kind of ur–rock and roll moment, one supposes. This upset a lot of people, but not me. It's not that I think it's cool to bully women. It's just that I already understood by then that it didn't matter whether Bruce was a great guy or not. Greatness had been thrust upon him; we are all fallen, but Bruce, like nothing else in my life before or since, picked us up. He could have been an axe murderer for all I cared. Just download the *No Nukes* movie and you'll see what I mean.

No Nukes occurred during another of Springsteen's "I'm going to make the perfect rock and roll record if it takes me the entire decade" phases, which now tended to separate releases by approximately three years. While these waits felt interminable, it was considered bad form to complain. Our guy was a perfectionist. How he knew perfection when he saw it was a mystery beyond our collective comprehension. He left great songs off albums in place of only okay ones that somehow fit his idea of the record's literary thrust. He already had a backlog from *Darkness on the Edge of Town* that would have made a terrific set of three or four albums, and he still refused to release "The Fever." But all we could do was sit tight and play our four records until we wore out the grooves in the vinyl. Ours was not to question why. When the album finally came out, I was spending the semester in London, miserable. My girlfriend at college, now my ex-wife, had started dating someone else while I was away. I had two roommates, and I played the cassette on my boom box rather a lot. Both swore that they never wanted to hear that thing again as long as they lived.

December 31, 1980

I flew home from London by way of Boston to catch two Bruce shows there; don't tell my parents. I then took a really long bus to Ithaca to try to win my girlfriend, now ex-wife, back (I swore I'd drive all night . . .). It worked. We saw the band welcome in the New Year 1981 at Nassau Coliseum; they played thirty-eight songs in four and a half hours. And it was not as if anyone coasted during any part of the show. They played, Nils Lofgren would later observe, as if "someone said 'You've got four hours left on earth. What are you going to do with it?'" Springsteen explained the incredible physical exertions of his show in matter-of-fact terms: "If you start rationing, you're living your life bit by bit when you can live all at once. . . . That's what rock and roll is: a promise, an oath. It's about being true to a particular moment." But he would also note, in later interviews, that part of what drove him was the fact that he had little in the way of an emotional life off the stage.

Years later, my girlfriend—the same one—and I went to an inn in West Virginia and I played "I Wanna Marry You" on the boom box and took out my mom's ring. She said "no." She should have stuck with that, all things considered. Not too long afterward, I spent a lot of time with *Tunnel of Love*, the world's second greatest divorce album (after Dylan's *Blood on the Tracks*, but ahead of Richard and Linda Thompson's *Shoot Out the Lights*). I didn't really "get" the album, I'll admit, when Bruce first released it; the first time that ever happened. But I sure got it after the divorce. Try it, if you've been divorced.

1984–1985

I was in Paris, doing a pathetic Hemingway imitation, when *Born in the U.S.A.* came out. I was living in the "writer's room" of the bookstore Shakespeare and Company, which was a pretty sweet deal, since it was free and it gave me a certain *je ne sais quoi* with the girls traveling through town; though I had to use a public shower and the bathroom was beyond gross. Thing was, I had nothing to play music on. So when the album came out, I had a real problem. In France, in those days anyway, all the record stores had listening booths. I went in every day. One day when they were closing early, the female clerk saw me come in and started to yell "No Bruce, No Bruce." Imagine a world. . . .

The following year, the world broke open for Bruce and he became the most popular white man in the world. What's more, he started to gain a little confidence politically. At No Nukes he had left his portion of the program empty, save for photos, unlike every other artist. He had shown up at the nuclear freeze rally in Central Park on June 12, 1982— my first ever surprise Bruce showing. But he had let Jackson Browne do all the talking before playing "The Promised Land." He made a few comments on *The River* tour, but now he was out front on Reaganism, on Central America, on nukes, and on what was then the beginning of America's burgeoning economic inequality crisis. I was starting my career as a political writer at the time and, lo and behold, Bruce's politics were my politics. Okay, that wasn't supposed to matter; it's the art not the artist, remember?

As it happens, however, my Bruce mind-meld only confused me more. It still sort of does. I got a ticket to a Giants Stadium show way up at the top of the place because my girlfriend/ex-wife's little brother camped out all night at Ticketron. I can remember watching the amazing sight of sixty thousand people (on each of six nights, if you're counting) and recalling those shows, nine years earlier at the Palladium when I was thinking things like: "What if the rest of the world could understand how great this was? What if Bruce became the most popular performer in the world? Would the power of his music change everyone? Would manual labor acquire dignity in the eyes of the bourgeoisie? Would parents start all of a sudden being cool?" On the other hand, if I didn't know better, didn't this scene look a bit like the old newsreels of those awful Nuremberg rallies in Hitler's Germany? Bruce would put his fist in the air. We would put our fists in the air. Bruce would shout nonsense syllables while standing atop a piano or a bank of speakers and so would all sixty thousand of us. "Isn't this how it all begins? By giving over your power of independent thought to a charismatic individual who seems to have it all figured out ahead of time?" What if someone evil, like, say, Donald Trump, suddenly had this power?

1992

I was actually fine with Bruce breaking up the band. An artist has a right to try new things. I had just gotten married and felt like those were "better days." They weren't; not for me, not for Bruce. I had become friends with Bill Moyers, and he deputized me to approach Bruce about doing an hour-long special interview for PBS. Bruce chose *60 Minutes* instead. This was all to the good, as it turned out, because I would have had to drop out of my doctoral program to help, and that would look very dumb today. Still, as a result, I was given front-row seats to see the "Other Band" at Shoreline in Mountain View. The "Other Band," I know. But still, I lack the words. . . .

1995

That summer, I received a tip that Springsteen would be joining Joe Grushecky at a gig scheduled at a Jersey Shore bar called Tradewinds. I called up the club, and the guy who answered the phone admitted that Bruce had practiced with the band the night before. He sold me a ticket for all of ten dollars—including the service charge—and I borrowed a car and drove to Jersey, trying not to get my hopes up. I remembered all the plane, train, and automobile trips I had taken in years past because some bar had announced a show by a performer who was said to be a friend of Bruce's; or had recorded one of the songs he gave away; or had been an oldies act whose career he had revived; or sounded a lot like Bruce, and he was said to approve; or had been in the E Street Band once, and the two were said to still be in close contact. I had seen some wonderful shows by Southside Johnny, Beaver Brown, Gary U.S. Bonds, Steve Earle, Steve Van Zandt's Disciples of Soul, and Clarence Clemons & the Red Bank Rockers, but almost all of them had been marred by the phenomenon of drunken louts shouting "Broooce" in between every song. Not only was it cruel to the performers, it made the rest of us feel like even bigger schmucks for believing he might show.

Even this trip did not feel like a sure thing. Such tips had never been reliable in the past, and the guy who sold me the ticket might just have been having a fine time at my expense. Grushecky and his band came on about midnight, which was already pretty late in my aging opinion. (Here is some free advice for the lovelorn. There were three warm-up bands scheduled that night, and I had expected a long wait, so I brought the novel I was reading at the time, Norman Rush's *Mating*. Hovering over the book in the back of the bar, I made an amazing discovery much too late in life for it to do me any good: Reading a book called *Mating* in a bar full of early twentysomething women works pretty well as a babe magnet. A steady parade of young women came up to me all night, asking my feelings about "marriage" and "mating issues." Big tough guys with Springsteen-sized muscles approached me after a while asking me if this technique always worked so well. I told them I never left the house without it, and they seemed duly impressed.) Never mind that, though. There was no sign of Bruce and I was getting that sinking feeling in my stomach that had become so familiar by now, magnified by my advancing age. Then I noticed Tim Robbins and Susan Sarandon bopping to the recorded music in a corner near the stage. Immediately, I felt a little worse but a lot better. Worse, because Bruce really should not be hanging around with movie stars, even talented, lefty ones, but better because well, you know why. He was here! After twenty years of trying, I was finally going to see Bruce Springsteen in a bar! On the Jersey Shore!

It may have been the simplest, most uncomplicated moment of unadulterated joy in my life. I have had a few great things happen to me—some ultimately far more significant than this one—but I am the kind of person who can see the problem with everything. Almost every happy moment I can remember has had at least a potential downside to it. But not this. I was seeing Bruce in a Jersey Shore bar. And hell, there was Steve Van Zandt right next to him, exactly where he should be. They were singing "Lucky Town," which would not even place among the songs I would have chosen, but hey, I'm not complaining. Max Weinberg showed up a little while later to play drums. For the next two hours, they alternated between Bruce songs, songs from Grushecky's *American Babylon*, and great old stuff like "Gloria" and "Mustang Sally," "Doo Wah Diddy Diddy," and "Down the Road Apiece." They closed with the "Ramrod" to end all "Ramrods." The police even lifted the local curfew in celebration of this Blessed Event. The big stupid football player behind me kept yelling "Thunder Road" and spilling beer on my back, but what could I do but forgive the dumb bastard?

Also in 1995, a friend in the White House asked me to help out with Bill Clinton's speech celebrating the opening of the Rock and Roll Hall of Fame in Cleveland. I agreed on the condition that it close by quoting Bruce and that the president refer to him simply as "the man." He said okay. And that's what happened. You can look it up. You can also look up Bruce and the E Street Band's performance that night. It was the worst one I've ever seen, no contest. I was working at *Rolling Stone* at the time, and, given my experience there, I blame Jann Wenner.

1998

Tracks had just come out. I read somewhere that Charlie Rose was taping a Springsteen interview that day. I had been on the show a few times to talk about politics and called Charlie to ask if I could come over and watch. Charlie said, "It'll cost you fifteen questions." I wrote them right away. I sat in the green room with Jon Landau and company as they cheered when Bruce gave the answers they wanted him to give. (Charlie used almost all of my questions, but I did not give them to Landau in advance.) One was "Why the hell haven't you released 'The Fever'?" And another, "Why the hell haven't you released 'The Promise'?" Charlie asked them both, but nicer. *18 Tracks* came out a little later with both songs. You're welcome, everyone.

Also 1998

I had a kid in part because of Bruce. More on that below.

1999

Reunion tour. I wrote a book about Bruce called *It Ain't No Sin to Be Glad You're Alive*. Read it—it's good. Bruce wouldn't talk to me for it, though, and his people took forever to give me permission to quote the lyrics. It was crazy-making. Finally, a guy who worked for Bruce's lawyer called me and said I could have the lyrics for twenty-five hundred dollars but I was not allowed to use the title. But they had waited so long that the book was already in production with that title. Now this was a real crisis. I called everyone I could think of to try to get help. The lawyer called me back. He spoke to me in comically tough-guy language as if he lived his life in a David Mamet play. He was really pissed that someone had told him he had to give in to me. So he said I could have my title for another five hundred. I said, "great, but one question: What does Bruce Springsteen need with my lousy three grand? I mean it's real money to me, but not to him." And he was like, "You little shithead. Bruce doesn't even know about your stupid three grand and never will. We have to protect his position in the marketplace, you are getting a special deal you ungrateful little pisher, Why I oughtta. . . ." Blah blah blah. Listening to this, I thought, well, cool. I'll just keep the money. I did. Bruce, you know where to find me if you still want it.

July 2003

Getting Bruce tickets had always been the bane of my life. (This does not apply to me, but I always felt it was unfair to religious Jews that Bruce's people released tickets on Saturday mornings. They should have put aside a decent set for the Shabbat-observant, of whom, I have no doubt, there are tens of thousands.) Even when I started getting press tickets, back in 1992, I still needed more tickets, because one show was never enough. (I am up to somewhere around two-hundred-fifty shows. While I realize this is the whitest of "white people's problems," press tickets are always for the first night of the run. That's the "A show" with all the greatest hits for folks who've maybe never seen him before. I've seen enough "Thunder Roads" and "Promised Lands." I want deep cuts. I want "Frankie," "Shut Out the Light," and, of course, "The Fever.") Springsteen tickets were often impossible to get in New York City, unless you were paying more money than I had in those days. So I scrambled and usually got them, but it took up a hell of a lot of time and energy.

One of the existential questions I've often wondered about is what would happen if Bruce just sold as many tickets as people wanted to buy. In the summer of 2003, Bruce wanted to know the same thing and also to make gazillions of dollars finding out. The answer, as of 2003, anyway, was ten outdoor shows at the Meadowlands, or somewhere between five and six hundred thousand tickets. This is, I'm pretty sure, the most tickets any one performer has sold in any one place at any one time. And it's appropriate that the greatest performer in the history of humankind is the guy who did it. I went to six of them. But shit, Bruce, that's a lot of money. What are you doing with all that cash? It's a real question I also often wonder about. I mean, I know about the donations. And I know there are still secret donations. And I know that people actually write articles about how Bruce does not charge enough for his tickets to clear the market like a good capitalist. This was true even of the insane prices for the Broadway show. But still. I find it weird that Bruce still wants to make more money from his fans. I find it weird that he even wants to cover his costs. I think every show should be played for a different charity; both to give the money to that charity but also to give it publicity. Bruce is either the most successful single performer in history, moneywise, or number two, depending on what Madonna has done lately. I don't expect this charity from Madonna, I should add. Or of Bob Dylan or Mick Jagger or Paul McCartney. And ultimately, it doesn't matter for the music. But still . . .

2004

That year, Bruce became a kind of president of an Alternative America, one that would never think of reelecting George W. Bush. He finally invested some of that working-class cred to try to win over some voters to the Democrats. John Kerry clung to him like, well, something very clingy. I have no doubt Bruce could have done better in an election against

Bush than Kerry did, but nobody knows how many people who showed up at Kerry rallies or Vote for Change concerts committed themselves to Kerry's victory. The money was no doubt helpful. But the whole thing was weird. I remember Bruce being interviewed and telling a reporter that he thought Kerry had given one of his best speeches so far, like he was a CNN talking head. I wrote a *Nation* cover story about this political Bruce at the time, and I tried to think of a precursor in American history to this guy. There isn't one. Woody Guthrie was a communist. Bob Dylan lost interest in politics in his early twenties. Nobody tried to claim either of them the way Ronald Reagan, Walter Mondale, Chris Christie, Joe Biden, and many others all tried to claim Bruce. Bruce got more and more political as he got older. And although his politics matched those of, say, Elizabeth Warren, he also grew more and more comfortable with the political Democratic establishment / gazillionaire types like David Geffen—on whose yacht he often sails. A decided rich man in a poor man's shirt, he wore it well, if not in perfect comfort.

2012

I made a close friend when I was writing my Springsteen book. He was a college student at the time, and nobody he knew liked Bruce. So he wrote me and asked if he could be my volunteer research assistant. He knew lots of stuff I didn't and vastly improved the book. Then he went into the TV business and had Steve Van Zandt's show about the gangsters in Norway pitched to him. He turned it down. So when I got invited to the premiere, he didn't want to go. He just wanted to have dinner that night instead. So I said, "Okay, but let's have dinner near the screening, just in case we want to go to the party."

We had dinner and then stopped by the hotel where the screening was happening downstairs. When we got there, I did the kind of thing you're never supposed to do but I try to do all the time, which was to ask to see the list and see who was there before I decided whether to stay. The young woman let me see it, and there were two amazing things about it. It was tiny, maybe twenty-five people tops. (What was I doing on it?) And one of them was Bruce!

This was a kind of existential crisis for me, given the hard line I had always taken about not really caring about Bruce, the guy. (I had never heard one word about my book.) But when was I going to get another chance like this?

So we went downstairs and waited for the screening to end. Steve was hanging around too, and we talked but didn't say much. Then it ended and the people in the room came out. I watched Bruce do some chit-chat with David Chase and then Tony Bennett and I forget who else. Finally, after like forever, I went up to Bruce and introduced myself. He said something like, "Hey, thanks for all your great work in the *Nation*," making this one of the greatest moments of my life, right off the bat. I was tempted to walk away right then, but I had recently presided over my daughter's bat mitzvah (sort-of) ceremony and I thought Bruce might be touched hearing about his role in it.

I explained to him that he was the only gentile who made it into the program. This was because it was one of his lyrics that, in my thirty-eighth year, convinced me that maybe I did want to have a kid after all. You guessed it: "In a world so hard and dirty so fouled and confused / searching for a little bit of God's mercy / I found living proof." Back in the year she was born, I wrote:

> I can't say that I decided to change my mind about not wanting to have a child purely on the basis of hearing this song. But the lyric haunted me over time, and forced me to rethink and reconsider and turn the matter over and over in my mind. "Living proof of God's mercy," huh? That sounded pretty compelling. This is song so powerful it could redeem an entire career. Hell, I sometimes listen to it, holding my own beautiful daughter, and think it justifies the whole history of rock and roll. It certainly felt that way when I brought her home from the hospital, barely seventy-two hours old, and turned on the stereo so she could start appreciating the music that helped inspire her existence.

After telling him about "Living Proof," Bruce hugged me. Now I'm not a hugger, but I let this one happen. We talked a little more about our kids and then, at about the twelve-minute mark, I told Bruce I was going to have to cut things short. I couldn't take the risk that he might say something that might, somehow, interfere with my relationship with the music. He put his arm around my shoulder and said something like "See you down the road, friend." Amazing. I had wondered about how such a meeting might go for nearly forty years and here it had come and gone nearly perfectly. How often is life like that?

2015

I talked to Bruce again. This time wasn't so great. It was at a party in East Hampton for a movie starring Bill Murray and directed by Barry Levinson. Bill Clinton was there. Paul McCartney was there. Roger Waters and Jon Bon Jovi and Jimmy Buffett were there. I said hello to Bruce but, again, was worried about screwing things up. Most of the evening I spent eavesdropping on Bruce and McCartney (the latter is a much better musician than he is a talker, take my word for it). There was one cool part, when I got to talking about the election with Bill Clinton. Jann Wenner, who had fired me at *Rolling Stone* decades earlier—well, let my contract go—came over and pretended we were best friends. Then, lo and behold, so did Bruce; not pretending anything, just listening. Okay, so it was mostly Clinton doing the talking and me asking questions, but still. I told Bruce that I had downloaded his answering machine message from when he was recording *The River*. I think this made him put me on the weirdo side of things. I also told him that his best unreleased song was "The Losin' Kind" should he do a *Tracks II*. He thanked me for my sage advice. When Bruce and Jann left, I walked out to the parking lot at the same time. I showed Bruce the bumper sticker I had on my 2006 Corolla. I got it from *Backstreets*. It read: "My Other Car Is a '69 Chevy with a 396." He laughed, and that was that.

2016

I read *Born to Run* and then met Bruce at Barnes & Noble. I was annoyed that, in addition to being Bruce, he was also a better and far braver writer than I am. (I would never have the courage to write about mental illness, therapy, and becoming a parent the way Bruce did. These reminiscences, I feel certain, constitute the most confessional work I've ever published.) But I didn't say any of that. I told him about bringing my kid to see him at the Meadowlands. I had just had a knee replacement and was barely able to walk (and was fighting a brief morphine addiction). Also, it rained a bit. But Bruce was great, of course. The kid left for college the next day, just as I had done in 1978. On our way out the door, during "Jersey Girl," I put my arm around her and said, dad-like, "Honey, I'll remember this night for the rest of my life." She replied, "Well, at least until you get dementia."

It's not far off, I suppose, but Bruce has been with me now for forty-four years. And I actually shudder when I try to think about what those years would have been like without him.

Works Cited

Alterman, Eric. *It Ain't No Sin to Be Glad You're Alive: The Promise of Bruce Springsteen*. Boston: Little, Brown, 1999.

Remnick, David. "We Are Alive: Bruce Springsteen at Sixty-Two." *New Yorker*, July 30, 2012, 38–57.

2

How Bruce Springsteen Made a Middle-Aged Woman Believe in the Magic of Rock and Roll

✧

NANCY S. BISHOP

I believe in rock and roll. I believe in serious things too, like the First Amendment, the democratic process, deep-dish pizza, and free Wi-Fi. And I always had faith that, some day, the Chicago Cubs would win the World Series—and they did, after 108 years. But this is the story about rock and roll and how I came to be a believer.

For many years, I loved other kinds of music. Most people become rock fans when they're young, but when I was in high school, my friends and I listened to soft pop, songs like Kay Starr's "Wheel of Fortune" and "You Belong to Me" by Jo Stafford. Buddy Holly and Elvis Presley came along when I was in journalism school at the University of Missouri in the 1950s. I remember working in the darkroom in the basement of Neff Hall and listening to Elvis sing "Hound Dog" and "Blue Suede Shoes" on the photo lab radio.

Among my friends in college, jazz was the only cool music. We were all really serious about West Coast jazz and bebop. The guys who owned all the records were two brothers nicknamed Hollywood and Pasadena.

(I have no idea what their real names were. My nickname was Crow because of my short-cropped black hair.) We'd hang out at their apartment, listening to jazz and drinking beer. They had stacks of vinyl by artists like the Modern Jazz Quartet, Dave Brubeck, Miles Davis, Stan Kenton, and Gerry Mulligan.

My love for jazz was cemented years later after my younger son Steve took up the tenor saxophone in high school and played in a succession of jazz bands. I went to his concerts whenever I could and later, when he played gigs at Chicago clubs, I was his biggest fan. He played with the Déjà Vu Big Band and at the iconic Green Mill Jazz Club. At one point he was playing with a Latin jazz band (he blended in with his dark hair and beard). My friends and I went to hear him at a second-floor club near Lincoln Square one Saturday night and were sternly searched before entry. "No knives. We don't want any fights tonight," the security guy admonished us. Did I look like I was going to start a fight? The Crow's hair was turning gray.

My love for jazz endured, but things changed when I discovered Bruce Springsteen. One day in 1984, I hooked up my television set to cable for the first time and stumbled onto MTV. I had just moved from Chicago (where high-rises had antennas but no cable TV) to Louisville to work in the corporate offices of Kentucky Fried Chicken. Those were the days when MTV programmed music videos day and night. I was mesmerized—by Michael Jackson, the Police, Prince, and, most of all, Springsteen. *Born in the U.S.A.* was a huge hit, and the title track as well as "Dancing in the Dark" played in regular rotation. When I got home at night from long days at the office, I'd pour a glass of wine and dance by myself in my Louisville living room. I remember thinking, "I'm a forty-five-year-old professional woman. I have a serious job. All of a sudden I'm mad about rock and roll. But hey—how did it take me so many years to discover this stuff?"

When I first stumbled onto Springsteen's music, I loved the rhythm and beat of "Born in the U.S.A." But as I listened to it, I realized that this was not some mindless arena anthem. I read the lyrics in the liner notes and began to gain a deeper understanding of Springsteen's music and his beliefs. After all, a man who starts a song, "Born down in a dead man's town / the first kick I took was when I hit the ground" wasn't exactly celebrating his birth in the U.S.A. And on the same album, "Working on the Highway," "Downbound Train," and "No Surrender" told similar stories masked by similar upbeat rhythms.

When I discovered *Darkness on the Edge of Town* several years later, I found a well of meaning in the lyrics. "Badlands," "Racing in the Street" (always one of my favorites), "The Promised Land," and "Factory" told hard stories of working-class people in a country that devalued them. "Factory," clocking in at just over two minutes, has the most telling lyrics, as a simple drumbeat drives home the grimness of a father walking through the factory gates every morning: "The working, the working, just the working life."

When I found him on MTV, Bruce Springsteen fascinated me because of his charismatic, energetic performances and his guitar work. In the months and years that followed, my appreciation for him deepened because his music spoke to human values and because of his ability to tell important stories—political and social stories, not just tales of love and sex that abound in popular music.

Even after I bought *Born to Run* and the rest of the Springsteen albums on vinyl, and then on CDs when that revolution came, seeing a live Springsteen concert never entered my mind. I did not attend my first Springsteen show until fifteen years after I discovered his music. My nephew Brad, a lifelong fan, was pleased that I had become a fan too, and he invited me to see the reunited E Street Band at the United Center in Chicago in September 1999.

It was a life-changing, magical experience. The lyrics to Springsteen's songs had always spoken to me, but now his voice, his movements, and the keyboards, drums, guitars, and saxophone of the E Street Band spoke to me too. I was caught up in the experience with thousands of other fans, singing, dancing, clapping, and, yes, sometimes crying. Live rock-and-roll concerts are loud, emotional, cathartic, exhausting, and exhilarating. Recorded music is important, but, I realized that night, it's a placeholder for the real thing. My reaction was similar to Linda Randall's description of a Springsteen concert in her 2011 book *Finding Grace in the Concert Hall*: "My response was completely visceral, emotional, nonintellectual and absolutely unexplainable in the moment. I felt in unison with all those around me. . . . To feel a part . . . of this joyous, raucous celebration of life, love, friendship and music was an extraordinary encounter."

Even more rewarding about my love for Springsteen was the beginning of a new, deeper relationship with my nephew (the son of my late sister who died when Brad was three). Since 1999, we've made many road trips together to see Bruce; sometimes just the two of us, sometimes with friends, and once with Brad's daughter who fell asleep sprawled across the bleachers at Scottrade Center in St. Louis. It was August 2008; Karissa was only seven and already a fan.

Sharing the music with Brad has been one of the most treasured parts of my Springsteen journey. Recently, Brad's father died and we all gathered in Hot Springs Village, Arkansas, to remember him and tell stories about his life. Brad was one of the speakers during the service, even though he knew it would be emotionally difficult. He told about the things he had learned from his dad: passion for the Chicago Cubs and Wrigley Field, love for fishing, and love for music, even though they didn't share musical tastes. And Brad told about how this passion for music had enabled him to bond with his Aunt Nancy in so many ways—attending concerts together all over the Midwest, listening to bootleg recordings, and sharing a love for barbecue as well as Bruce. Fortunately, I had plenty of tissues in my purse because my eye makeup was in danger. Springsteen had brought Brad and I together and had helped both of us forge family bonds.

Now, twenty years after Brad brought me to my first Springsteen concert, I've attended thirty-three more, six of them in 2012. I celebrated my retirement that year by traveling around the country to visit friends who lived near Springsteen concert venues.

By this point, I consider myself an expert in comparing Springsteen shows. One measure of a good concert is how the fans respond. Is the audience around you staying in their seats or are they standing, fist pumping, and singing along? Are butts out of seats?, as Bruce would say.

I've attended a number of concerts in Greensboro, North Carolina, where my son Andy lives and where the fans are extraordinarily responsive. When you're at a concert in Greensboro, everyone is on their feet for the entire show, perhaps sitting only for a few ballads. (Being one of the oldest fans present at these concerts, I need to rest now and then.)

After a May 2009 concert, the Greensboro *News & Record* reported, "Springsteen and the E Street Band were received like conquering heroes" during a show "that repeatedly drove the adoring, near-sellout crowd into fist-thrusting, sing-along frenzies." The paper tied Springsteen's performance to the audience reception, and Springsteen himself acknowledged, as other musicians had in the past, that "Greensboro is consistently one of the best audiences in the United States."

My son, an economist, and I have speculated about what it is about Greensboro fans that make them so enthusiastic. It's an old industrial blue-collar city. Is that part of the mystique? They're Springsteen's blue-collar base. At a concert in Charlotte, in comparison, there are a lot of suits—it's a banking center, after all. The audience is much better behaved. I've attended shows in both cities, and there is a huge difference in crowd response, no matter what the fans are wearing.

My friends ask, "How can you go to so many concerts? Aren't they all the same?" No, I tell them again and again, each one is different. Each one is full of surprises. And the crowd at each one forms a one-night-only community that moves, sings, and celebrates together. At many concerts, Springsteen comments on the political issues of the day (his PSA, he calls it). Although not all of his fans agree with his politics, his remarks are usually greeted with supportive cheers. And so have his appearances in support of political candidates, like John Kerry in 2004 and Barack Obama in 2008 and 2012.

Beyond my relationship with Brad, my love for Springsteen's music has helped me form friendships with other Springsteen fans from around the United States and across the globe. I feel like a part of Springsteen's community whenever I go to a concert and strike up conversations with fans sitting near me or when I hang out near the driveway where we think Springsteen's black SUVs will arrive. (Will he stop for photos? Will he open the window and wave?) And I've gotten that same feeling when I've bought or sold concert tickets through BTX, a fan forum run by *Backstreets*, the Springsteen fan magazine. Sometimes I've met the buyer or seller for coffee and exchanged tickets and money in person and sometimes the exchange is by mail. But no matter how the transaction takes place, there's a feeling of trust among buyers and sellers because we know Springsteen fans wouldn't cheat other Springsteen fans. That's why the BTX policy is that tickets can be sold only for face value. The community he creates believes in the power of his music and shares his belief in fairness and equality.

Another aspect of the Springsteen community is the group of fans who spend time writing about him and presenting their thoughts to fellow writers and scholars. In April 2018, the fourth Springsteen Symposium was held at Monmouth University in Long Branch, New Jersey. I've been to all four of these conferences, and I enjoy the sessions and the opportunity to visit Springsteen's home territory: to explore Asbury Park and to walk along the boardwalk on the Jersey Shore. But the most important part of these conferences has been the chance to meet other Springsteen fans from Chicago and around the world.

Today, I'm in post-retirement mode, and my belief in the power of rock and roll hasn't changed. I read everything I can about the genre and listen to it almost every day, and I still go to concerts as often as possible. Most of the time, I go with friends or relatives. But even when I go alone, I still feel the power that joins us in the spirit of rock and roll. In this divided world, that's no small achievement.

Decades ago, Don McLean wrote "American Pie," a classic song about "the day the music died"—the day a plane crash killed Buddy Holly, Richie Valens, and J. P. "the Big Bopper" Richardson. McLean sings, "Do you believe in rock and roll? Can music save your mortal soul?"

I'm not sure about the soul part. It took me a long time to learn this, but Springsteen has made me believe there's magic in rock and roll. You can find that magic in his music, in the new friends you make, and in the communion with old friends and relatives who are also believers.

Works Cited

Puterbaugh, Parke. "3-Hour Show Rocks 'Steensboro.'" *News & Record* (Greensboro, N.C.), May 3, 2009.

Randall, Linda. *Finding Grace in the Concert Hall: Community and Meaning among Springsteen Fans.* Long Grove, Ill.: Waveland, 2011.

3

From the Backstreets
to the Badlands

✧

My Springsteen Journey

DEEPA IYER

1984

My Springsteen story begins in 1984, the year of *Born in the U.S.A.* I was twelve years old that summer. My family had moved to the quiet suburbs of Louisville, Kentucky, from the urban landscape of Kerala, India. Everything in America felt confusing, overwhelming, and scary. I entered sixth grade in September with an "I can do this" attitude that evaporated within hours of my first day at school. It became painfully obvious that I was different from everyone else and that I stood out because of my skin color, my accent, and my status as an immigrant.

In school, I had just one goal: to be invisible. I feared being asked to read aloud in class, knowing that my strong Indian accent would elicit snickers. I dreaded class activities because no one would choose me to be part of their sports team or study group. I avoided conversations because I had no points of reference for the television shows and songs that animated the childhoods of my peers. Many times the bullying and isolation reduced me to tears in school bathrooms and hallways. I felt like an outsider and an outcast, looking into a world that I couldn't penetrate.

Music and books became my only refuge. When I listened to my Sony boom box—my own "jukebox graduate for first mate"—it didn't matter where I came from or how I looked. One day songs from *Born in the U.S.A.* echoed from my favorite radio station and the music video for "Dancing in the Dark" played on MTV. At first I was ambivalent. But it was impossible to not hear a Springsteen song on the radio at least once an hour in 1984 and soon I was persuading my parents that *Born in the U.S.A.* belonged in my small yet growing cassette tape collection. As I became familiar with the record, I didn't just revel in the peppiness of "Glory Days" or "Dancing in the Dark." The songs I played and replayed were "Downbound Train," "Cover Me," "No Surrender," and "Bobby Jean," songs about lifelong friendships (which eluded me), about dislocation and solitude (which were familiar), and about escape and freedom (which were possible?). The lyrics were small portals to a place where I could feel at ease, at home with myself despite the hostility of my immediate environment. What else did Springsteen write about, I wondered, and could he get me to that place?

That curiosity led me down a path of discovery, an exploration of Springsteen's broader oeuvre, especially *Darkness on the Edge of Town* and *The River*. When Springsteen released *Live/1975–85*, I felt like an adventurer uncovering a treasure trove. Songs like "Badlands" secured my faith in rock music salvation; "The River" subtly sounded the alarm that the journey of life includes unexpected curves and corners around the bend; and "The Promised Land" reflected my own desire to transcend the daily grind that makes your eyes go blind and your blood run cold.

But it was "Growin' Up" that touched the wounds of childhood and adolescence that had begun to fester. *Rolling Stone* describes "Growin' Up" as embodying "coming-of-age swagger and wonderment," and for me it is a deeply personal song. It recognized me and gave voice to the range of emotions I grappled with during my immigrant adolescence in Kentucky. What was my masquerade?, I asked myself. Why was I trying so hard to fit into an environment that didn't welcome me to the point that I began to neglect and hide my own culture, background, and history?

"Growin' Up" also provided alternative responses to the deception I had begun to develop. "I broke all the rules, strafed my old high school,

never once gave thought to landing," Springsteen sings triumphantly
in the middle of the song. Perhaps it was possible to actually accept my
outsider status? Besides, I wasn't the only one on the outside; apparently, Springsteen was too, and he definitely made it sound a whole lot
more interesting. And just maybe, it was *better* to be on the outside
anyway, to navigate the "fallout zone" and still emerge with my "my soul
untouched."

All I had to do was figure out how.

Those lessons weren't in Springsteen's lyrics, but he provided me with
a point of entry, with the possibility that I could define my own outsider
status instead of reject it and struggle against it. Over time I stopped hid-
ing the markers of my difference. I looked forward to the visits back
home to India where I reconnected with my family and friends and
immersed myself in Indian dance, history, food, and language. I even
introduced some of this in my Kentucky classrooms, and I wrote stories, essays, and poems about my difficulty fitting in. I participated in
speech and debate competitions with my Indian accent in tow and performed Indian dances publicly. Slowly I began to make peace with my
complex hyphenated identity as an Indian-American.

The lyrics of "Growin' Up" gave me, an adolescent immigrant dislo-
cated in the American South, the permission to accept myself. Maybe I
too could be "the cosmic kid in full costume dress," even as a mixed-up,
confused, accented, ignored, mocked, cold-shouldered, passed-over,
rejected Indian-American girl in Kentucky with a head full of impossible dreams.

2001

On the morning of September 11, 2001, I was seated at my desk at a federal building in Washington, D.C., when my supervisor notified us that
we had to evacuate immediately. I had a few moments to pull up CNN
on my computer where I saw the headline: "Two planes collide into the
World Trade Center."

I had no idea what had happened, but I knew instinctively, as I made
my way through the streets of D.C. with my colleagues, that everything
had changed. As news emerged slowly about the horrors of what had
occurred in the skies over New York City, the Pentagon, and Shanks-

ville, Pennsylvania, I was shocked. When I finally reached my home in Arlington, Virginia, I could see the smoke billowing out of the hole in the Pentagon.

In the twenty-four hours after 9/11, I moved into a state of double grief that lasts to this day. I grieved for those who lost their lives and for their families, and I read every *New York Times* obituary thoroughly to imprint them in my memory. And I grieved for my own community, which was immediately scapegoated and subjected to backlash. In the wake of 9/11 and in the decade and a half since, South Asians, Muslims, Arabs, and Sikhs have reported alarming rates of discrimination, profiling, deportations, and hate violence.

By the time Bruce Springsteen released *The Rising* in 2002, I was deep in my work to help address the post-9/11 backlash targeting my community. It was a painful period, one that in many ways reminded me of my adolescence and my feelings of not belonging. Despite the South Asian community's long history in the United States, many of us felt that the country had turned against us. Knowing that *The Rising* was Springsteen's response to 9/11, I took my time to listen to the record. There was a part of me that was wary of how Springsteen, a New Jersey–bred white man, might treat the aftermath of 9/11. Would he have reactions of jingoism, blame, and criticism?

When I finally let *The Rising* in, I experienced an emotional catharsis. Every song in the album reflects the tremendous and inexplicable fear and insecurity that so many of us experienced in the wake of 9/11. In "Empty Sky," Springsteen captures the grief of waking up not only to an empty Manhattan horizon but to the absence of a loved one: "I woke up this morning / I could barely breathe / just an empty impression / in the bed where you used to be."

For me, it was also important that *The Rising* did not depict a vengeful America. There is no call to war, no fuel for reprisal. There is no anger masked by false patriotism. There is no call to target Muslim, South Asian, or Arab communities. Instead, *The Rising* invites us to take steps toward individual and collective healing. In "Worlds Apart," for example, Springsteen's guitar merges with the vocals and musical rhythms of Asif Ali Khan, a Pakistani singer who sings in the style of Qawaali, a musical expression of Sufi devotional poetry. Let's build bridges, Springsteen urges, across assumed differences.

That theme of collective redemption continues in "Mary's Place," in which Springsteen invites us to a neighborhood block party, perhaps the epitome of normalcy at a time of community crisis. Can we find joy amid such despair? Yes, Springsteen reminds us, and he does so by setting an inclusive tableau. He invokes the Buddha, the Prophet, and the eleven angels of mercy in the first verse, and he demands a "shout from the crowd" to bless the party. In response, the audience is asked to "turn it up, turn it up, turn it up."

Many of the songs on *The Rising* contain similar chants and incantations, phrases to be repeated over and over. When Bruce sings "Lonesome Day" at concerts and launches into a stream of "It's alright / it's alright / it's alright," it's no wonder that the audience, arms aloft, repeats that mantra back to him. *The Rising* gives lost and weary travelers a roadmap to navigate their own cities in ruin.

2016

I woke up the morning after the 2016 presidential election feeling shaken and afraid. When my six-year-old son asked who won, and then followed up on my answer with "Will everything be okay?" I didn't know how to respond. "Yes, because the people in America—all of us—will make it okay," I told him tentatively.

In the days after the inauguration, the new administration swiftly released a number of executive orders that targeted communities of color and immigrants. The Muslim and refugee bans, the crackdown on immigrants, and the rollbacks on civil rights protections became realities. These weren't abstractions; there were real-life consequences. A classmate told my son that Donald Trump would deport his parents. Schools in our area were vandalized with swastikas. An Indian-American engineer named Srinivas Kuchibhotla was killed in Kansas by a man who harassed him about his immigration status and questioned his right to be in this country.

In the nearly two years since Trump became president, as the assaults on the rights and bodies of people who look like me and my family have intensified, I have returned again and again to Springsteen's music for refuge, solace, and hope. In particular, I have revisited songs in which Springsteen openly and candidly addresses race, class, and immigration status, especially as we continue to face crisis moments in this country related to police brutality and the mistreatment of immigrants at the border.

"American Skin (41 Shots)" is one of those songs. Springsteen wrote the song after the death of Amadou Diallo, a twenty-three-year-old unarmed Guinean immigrant who was shot forty-one times by New York Police Department officers in 1999. It is a song that has taken on even more resonance in the context of the uprisings in Ferguson and Baltimore, and it captures the conversations taking place in the homes of Black families around the nation, that African American children need to "understand the rules" that are different for them, that they need to be especially cautious around police officers, always keeping their hands in sight.

Springsteen has performed the song many times on his tours, often shushing the audience so that they listen carefully to the words. In 2013, after a jury handed down a not-guilty verdict in the trial of George Zimmerman, Springsteen performed the song at a concert in Ireland with this introduction: "I want to send this one out as a letter back home. For justice for Trayvon Martin." I heard Springsteen perform the song on a September night in Washington, D.C., in 2016, following a summer of tremendous pain that saw the murders of Philando Castile and Alton Sterling. Springsteen didn't have to explicitly say "Black Lives Matter." It was abundantly clear from the lyrics themselves and the use of his international platform that he hoped to send that message.

Springsteen has also written and performed songs that describe the difficult circumstances of immigrants and refugees in America. At a time when the Trump administration is separating children from families and placing them in deplorable conditions in detention centers, Springsteen's songs about the border can give all of us a nuanced understanding of the reasons people flee their countries to come to ours. Lesser known songs like "Across the Border" (from *The Ghost of Tom Joad*) and "Matamoros Banks" (*Devils & Dust*) recount the ways in which migrants searching for a better life face danger in the form of detention, deportation, and even death as they cross the southern border. In "Matamoros Banks," Springsteen writes about a character who dreams of crossing the river to the shores of Brownsville, Texas, one of the places where, in the summer of 2018, the American government separated children from their parents who were seeking asylum: "Your sweet memory comes on the evenin' wind / I sleep and dream of holding you in my arms again / the lights of Brownsville, across the river shine / a shout rings out and into the silty red river I dive."

Often, when I feel helpless about the situation in our country, I listen to these songs. They reflect the realities of the lives and experiences of migrants. And they also speak to the resilience and strength of people who struggle on the margins for a better life. Springsteen's songs about brown and black immigrants share many characteristics with his earlier work focused on working-class white communities like "Johnny 99," "Atlantic City," "Born in the U.S.A.," and "Seeds." These are all songs about people striving to improve their circumstances only to find that the system, whether it is a cop or a judge or an arbitrary geographic border, is conspiring against them. These songs remind me that perhaps we are not all so different and that we can find common ground if we take the time to listen to each other's stories and understand our shared hopes and dreams.

In the wake of Trump's election, Springsteen openly expressed his concerns about the direction of the country. At a June 2018 performance of *Springsteen on Broadway*, Bruce broke from his usual set list to sing "The Ghost of Tom Joad," prefaced by these remarks and a call to action: "There's the beautiful quote by Dr. King that says the arc of the moral universe is long but it bends toward justice. Now, there have been many, many days of recent when you could certainly have an argument over that. But I've lived long enough to see that in action and to put some faith in it. But I've also lived long enough to know that arc doesn't bend on its own. It needs all of us leaning on it, nudging it in the right direction day after day. You gotta keep, keep leaning." Bruce Springsteen might not describe himself as a political poet, but the arc of his music tells a different story, with messages that appeal to those of us on the margins of American society. In "Jungleland," Springsteen sings: "And the poets down here don't write nothing at all / they just stand back and let it all be." Thankfully, Bruce—a community poet who has not lost his compass—refuses to sit back in apathy and complacency.

Often, as I'm raving about the Springsteen concert I have just gone to, my friends will ask, "How is this successful white man's music giving you such life?" It's a fair question. And it's likely true that my connection to Springsteen's music would have ended after my initial exploration at the height of adolescent confusion if it hadn't been for his openness to addressing social justice. What is remarkable about my Springsteen journey is that his music has helped me—as a young immigrant then, and now a woman of color—reconcile my own complicated place in a country whose policies and narratives often exclude me and people like myself. Springsteen's music reflects my own belief that America is a place where people like me can and do belong, and, when I listen to his music, I believe that, together, we can make this promised land a possibility.

Works Cited

Danton, Eric R. "Bruce Springsteen Dedicates 'American Skin (41 Shots)' to Trayvon Martin." *Rolling Stone*, July 17, 2013. www.rollingstone.com/music/music-news /bruce-springsteen-dedicates-american-skin-41-shots-to-trayvon-martin-75928/.

Hiatt, Brian, et al. "100 Greatest Bruce Springsteen Songs of All Time: 'Growin' Up.'" *Rolling Stone*, December 11, 2018. www.rollingstone.com/music/music-lists/100 -greatest-bruce-springsteen-songs-of-all-time-32486/growin-up-41934/.

Sanneh, Kelefa. "Rock Review: From Springsteen, a Call to 'Rise Up.'" *New York Times*, August 8, 2002.

Springsteen, Bruce. "Bruce's Remarks before 'The Ghost of Tom Joad.'" *Brucespringsteen.net*, June 20, 2018. http://brucespringsteen.net/news/2018/bruce-remarks -ghost-tom-joad.

4

The Ripple Effect

✦

FRANK STEFANKO

On a hot Memorial Day weekend in 1982, I found myself walking with Bruce Springsteen through a wooded area at Hopkins Pond in Haddonfield, New Jersey. Bruce was familiar with Haddonfield, as we had spent several days there in 1978 while we were shooting photographs for *Darkness on the Edge of Town*. This time, however, we were working on *Nebraska*.

As we hiked through the woods, I could hear the strains of "Born to Run" filtering from a portable radio through the trees. There appeared to be a group of teenagers having a picnic nearby, just off the path.

I thought to myself, "Wouldn't it be cool if Bruce would walk towards the music, and pop in on those kids, and make their day?"

Bruce chose not to do that, and I have never asked him why. Did he think it would have been an imposition? Did he think it would have compromised our photo shoot? It still haunts me to this day: What chain of events, what ripples, would have been put into play, if Bruce had chosen to surprise those kids?

The singular event in the woods led me to reflect on the broader version of the "ripple effect": how one stone, thrown into the water, leads to ripples that spread farther than one can know. The idea was triggered while working on my second Springsteen book, a monumental opus entitled *Further Up the Road*.

Because of my childhood interest in photography, and then my college friendship with Patti Smith, I began photographing her during her early years in New York.

Because I photographed Patti in New York, and because of my interest in new music, I told her to keep an eye (and ear) out for Bruce Springsteen. I thought he would be famous someday.

Because Bruce and Patti Smith worked together, Bruce saw the portraits I took of Patti. Because Bruce liked those photographs, he asked me to shoot for *Darkness on the Edge of Town*. Because I shot for *Darkness*, I also got the cover for *The River*.

Because of *Darkness*, these ripples have radiated out, allowing me to work with Steve Van Zandt as well as Southside Johnny for *Hearts of Stone*.

I have had the honor of seeing my work chosen to be on the cover of Bruce's autobiography, *Born to Run*. I have traveled the world to see and photograph concerts, and I have been invited to speak about my work.

But more than that, I have met and heard the stories of fans in tears (with me crying as well), telling me how much my photographs positively affected them, along with Springsteen's words. Who would have imagined such a thing?

Because of these ripples, I have been able to help and mentor other talented photographers and artists. I have been able to give back in ways I'd never imagined in 1982, when I walked through the woods with Bruce. Because back then, we were both struggling young guys filled with hopes and dreams.

As another eminent photographer named Al Wertheimer once told me, "The work takes on a life of its own." You never know how far the ripples will travel.

Part II

Springsteen, Politics, and American Society

"O Mary Don't You Weep," Tweeter Center, Mansfield, Massachusetts, May 27, 2006. (Rocco S. Coviello)

5

The Role of the Popular Artist
in a Democratic Society

✦

JEFFERSON COWIE AND JOEL DINERSTEIN

A Springsteen concert is a forum for epiphanies: his objective is to have each person walk out of the show asking, wanting, and expecting more of him or herself—as well as society. He wants you to leave with a self-in-transition. The purpose of a rock concert "is to pull you up out of that despair, to shine a light on new possibilities," Springsteen claims. "Regardless of what's going on externally, those are the powers that you [must] find within yourself to keep going and change things. To try to make some place for yourself in the world." The concert offers a spring-board for new powers from within to manifest.

This is an artistic objective beyond individual uplift, mere entertainment, or Dionysian revelry, and it even bleeds into the realm of political theory. Philosopher John Dewey understood that a thriving democratic society depended upon a social circuit between the individual and the collective. "In the realization of individuality," Dewey wrote, "there is found also the needed realization of some community of persons of which the individual is a member." *Earned* individuality requires an actual, identifiable community. "Conversely," he continues, "the agent who duly satisfies the community in which he shares, by that same conduct, satisfies himself." The circle is then closed as the meaning of individuality is secured in the creation of community.

Can a popular artist serve a democracy in this manner? This question is rarely asked of artists anymore. But we believe Bruce Springsteen's lifework allows for such an analysis based on what we call the "soul circuit," our name for Dewey's "social circuit."

The first time the two of us met, we quickly descended into "Bruceology," as fans are wont to do, measuring our lives to the cadence of Springsteen releases and tours. Over drinks in dive bars and on drives to catch numerous different tours—including to *Springsteen on Broadway*, which triggered this essay—we've continued this intellectual partnership. We each carried a distinctive revelation borne of Springsteen's great seventies albums, whose bright promise has never quite died out for either of us.

At that first encounter, we each confessed to an extant belief—if battered, ravaged, and increasingly tenuous—in the American project and how Bruce helped keep faith afloat in the dark hours of the Reagan era, the needless war in Iraq, and the poisonous political environment of the Trump administration. We began to see how Springsteen could be a case study of the popular artist in a democratic society.

When Springsteen claims that a rock concert should be "part political rally, part dance party, and part religious revival," he reaffirms his allegiance to the stagecraft of the soul revues where he learned his trade. In the soul ritual, the performer is a social artist: he or she offers him- or herself up as a sacrifice to the audience to revitalize, radicalize, and exhaust the congregation through physical, spiritual, emotional, and intellectual means. Think James Brown's *Live at the Apollo*. When Jon Landau first wrote in 1974, "I saw rock and roll future, and its name is Bruce Springsteen . . . he made me feel like I was hearing music for the very first time," it was in response to his thunder-quaking, earth-shaking, stage-breaking concerts.

As it worked for Landau, so it worked for us.

It happened to Dinerstein in 1978 at a four-hour performance in the middle of nowhere—St. Bonaventure's five-thousand-seat gym in Olean, New York—during the peak concert period that produced the legendary Capital Theater and Winterland shows. "This is the greatest night of my life," he told his friends on the two-hour drive back home to the University of Buffalo dorms, and thought to himself, "I want to be as free as

Bruce is." (He did not then know, of course, that this free-spirited Bruce was a stage persona.) Dinerstein was already an acolyte in 1975—*Born to Run* was the work of art that changed his life. But it was that four-hour, four-encore show—including "Point Blank" and "Sherry Darling" two years before *The River*, the James Brown death act ("Can you stand one more?"), the Detroit medley and "Quarter to Three" for the finale—that blew the doors off of his self-perception. Even Springsteen seemed surprised by the fires he set off in that upstate audience. "Where the hell am I?" he asked.

Cowie, in contrast, rued the lost opportunity the day his friend TJ returned on the train from the 1978 show at the intimate Uptown Theatre in Chicago, his eyes ablaze with the fire of the converted. That stadium rock shit is out, explained this fifteen-year-old aesthetic guru, and Bruce was in. Cowie surrendered his copy of *Quadrophenia* to be taped over with his friend's vinyl copies of *Born to Run* and *Darkness on the Edge of Town*—aesthetic objects of a newly fueled desire. Springsteen then entered Cowie's world as an aural lifeline dangling in the darkness of the bedroom. By the time he saw him in 1981 on *The River* tour—in a big arena in the burbs—he figured he had missed his moment, given the proof of those brilliant 1978 shows he heard regularly on a lo-fi Winterland bootleg. Turns out Bruce could blow out an arena, too. Cowie walked out of that show both exhausted and revived, pledging to seize control of his life. Soon after, he peeled out of his claustrophobic Midwestern town with "Thunder Road" as the soundtrack. To Cowie, little of Springsteen's lyrical world was metaphorical: *It* was *a town full of losers*, he thought then, and *he was pulling out of here to win* (himself back).

One thing was clear: Springsteen does not simply entertain. He demands things of his audience—but only so far as he feels they can be led. This is rare. Dylan, for all of his staggering lyrical genius, cares for the art more than the audience. The Grateful Dead, the Woodstock-era bands, even Phish and Widespread Panic—these bands offer their fans an alternative community outside of America, but not one that challenges the audience to work within the mess as it exists. Bruce embraced neither the music-in-amber purity of Pete Seeger nor the overt political radicalism of Woody Guthrie. He is not didactic, but when he does preach, it is literally in the idiom of the American preacher: "Faith will be rewarded."

Deliverance through collective performance—the promise of another world realized temporally in the concert hall—lasts in the soul, as fans will tell you. This is Bruce's calling. Popular music is more often entertainment and spectacle than redemption and uplift (even twenty-first-century Springsteen shows, if we are being honest). For all of its democratic promise, this commitment to his audience has blocked him from artistic experimentation—like, say, Neil Young or Joni Mitchell, Stevie Wonder or David Bowie—because he believed his job was his calling. Long ago he traded the right to creative freedom for his commitment to three audiences: the New York/New Jersey axis of home; his nightly audience; and an imagined America he still believes in.

Springsteen is among the few American musicians to take up the artist's role in a democratic society in an explicit, constructive, hopeful way. But it is a form of cultural work, not just rock joy or communal angst. He may mesmerize his audiences but he is not a mesmerizer. The democratic artist has to speak to and for the audience with respect but does not have to share its worklife—Bruce being, of course, "a rich man in a poor man's shirt." He or she must validate their labor and suffering, their tamped possibilities and crystalline hopes, their emotional parameters and experiential world. That is and has been Springsteen's *job*: he has done it well and with his own artistic twists-and-shouts.

The motivation for such a pragmatic utopian ideal is obvious: this is what rock and roll did for Springsteen. "Rock and roll came to my house when there seemed to be no way out," he has said. "It just seemed like a dead-end street, nothing I liked to do, nothing I wanted to do, except roll over and go to sleep." Then he began his self-conscious apprenticeship to American sound, rhythm, and songcraft. He took his early local stardom from Asbury Park, amplified it through a crack rock-and-soul band, and upstaged any band not working for audience transcendence. He built his wall of fans on the old-school R&B method of thrilling live shows and word of mouth. This explosive, interactive combination of charisma, intimacy, and musical horsepower generated the Springsteen matrix: Bruce's cult of personality, the bonds of community in the band's fandom (onstage and off), and the convincing performance of his authenticity.

With his songs and the E Street Band, Springsteen made his geographical postage stamp of central New Jersey a microcosm of splintered hopes and values, then expanded the vision into a medium for the dispersed dreams of three hundred million people. Like Emerson and Whitman with poetry, like Duke Ellington and Aaron Copland with their long-form compositions, like Johnny Cash and Ray Charles, like Sam Cooke and Aretha Franklin—Springsteen put on the historical mantle and claimed the struggle. In 2004, Springsteen made his project overt—possibly clearing it up for himself as much as for his audience: "A nation's artists and musicians have a particular place in its social and political life. Over the years I've tried to think long and hard about what it means to be American: about the distinctive identity and position we have in the world, and how that position is best carried. I've tried to write songs that speak to our pride and criticize our failures."

"The country we carry in our hearts," he claimed, "is waiting."

Being a popular artist in a (small-d) democratic society means working for evolutionary rather than revolutionary change. There must be something to believe in, to save, to build on, to revive. It means creating a secular congregation for a spirit-raising that is not simply a spectacle. It means being a social artist rather than a romantic or a modernist. The modernist works on a model of self-*against*-society: he or she assumes the corruption of society and the excavation of self from an artist's ethical core as a model for change. The artistic work itself follows an "art-for-art's sake" model: there is certainly no dialogue with an audience and there is certainly not an identifiable audience to begin with. Such an audience would be in conflict with artistic experimentation, the essential quality of modernism. Consider, for example, that Faulkner wrote about his own reimagined postage stamp yet was barely read by his fellow Mississippians in his lifetime.

The popular artist in a democratic society faces a twofold challenge: First, is the audience connected by a set of values and ideas that the artist can draw out in songs and onstage? If so, then second, can the artist challenge these beliefs with new ideas? The artist must have a sense of cultural leadership and there needs to be a shared culture. (And we fear that the latter may not exist anymore.) Springsteen embodies the oldest promise of rock and roll as melting-pot messianic revivalism in concert form. Resonance is the self-measure of Bruce-worth.

Riffing off Ralph Ellison's work, Dinerstein coined the term "innovating traditionalist" for those swing-era musicians who raised the collective spirit in Depression and wartime dancehalls across the country. Ellison explained that the jazz musician's personality fits into the big band such that his or her "eloquent expression of *idea-emotions*" strikes a balance between musician, band, and audience. To play on the Basie or Ellington bandstand, any musician had to "learn the best of the past," Ellison wrote, "and add to it his personal vision." To be an innovating traditionalist also assumes a cultural heritage, a society worthy of critical engagement, and a tradition worthy of affirmation. We believe this is what Springsteen does.

A democratic artist honors value through his or her own mastery, synthesis, and stylistic inflections; he or she later becomes an elder within it (as when Springsteen inducts bands into the Rock and Roll Hall of Fame). Springsteen invented no new songforms, no new rhythmic idioms, no new rebel cries against The Man. By way of contrast, punk is (was) participatory, but it has no affirmation; mainstream country singers ply the mythic fields of Americana with uncritical patriotism.

The liberatory avatar is revealed in Springsteen's songs and, especially, onstage. His objective melds with Walt Whitman's in "Song of the Open Road," except through musical power rather than mobility and introspection: "I and mine do not convince by arguments, similes, rhymes,/we convince by our presence." This declaration is more existential than political. The presence of such an artist is meant to exude the potential of happiness, as it might kickstart any person away from closed minds and roads of repression. In the same poem, Whitman captured the elevation of spirit Springsteen seeks in a response to a new fan's first concert: "I am larger,/better than I thought,/I did not know I held so much goodness." Artists of the co-present kind convince by example—rather than rhetoric, rebellion, or fantasy.

Despite his underdog narrators, Springsteen has never sent his characters on the road to a simplistic political consciousness. Despite his performances at benefits from No Nukes to Vote for Change, Springsteen does not get on a soapbox except to ask for donations to charitable organizations. Despite the Dionysian excitement of his concerts, he has never called for punk resistance or gratuitous rebellion. He is working for *your* personal independence of mind and soul and that of the congregation gathered in the hall—he presents an audience with political possibilities but is not an overt dissident. The occasional leaden political metaphors of 2012's

Wrecking Ball, for example, subvert his usual narrative power. In fact, with a few successful exceptions—such as the profoundly moving "American Skin (41 Shots)"—he eschews protest songs and overt preaching.

We cannot think of a single American artist who thinks of audiences in this manner. Springsteen is better understood as an authentic cultural worker rather than a rock star.

In effect, Springsteen is a *social artist*. By way of example, *The Rising* is not great art, but it was a social act of spiritual revitalization for his community. After 9/11, an anonymous citizen of New Jersey rolled down his window and yelled, "Bruce, we need you now!" In response, with *The Rising*, he remained true to an old-school definition of art: *to comfort the afflicted and afflict the comfortable.* Let the healing begin: "Come on, rise up!" Which is more important, after all, the art or the community? Does an artist have to choose? Springsteen chose community. He still takes it as a challenge to bind together his nightly audience with resonant songs, his (now mellowed) free-spirited persona, the band as family, and the deepest of American rhythmic grooves.

Starting with *The River* tour, he began his artistic move from the local to the national. He often announced he was reading *Woody Guthrie: A Life* before playing "This Land Is Your Land." In the next five years, he released *Nebraska* as his dark spin on that tradition in the early years of Reagan's America, then a record entitled *Born in the U.S.A.*, and sealed the deal with two stunning tracks on *Folkways: A Vision Shared—A Tribute to Woody Guthrie & Leadbelly.* These recordings represent his proof paid to enter and inhabit a national tradition.

But this was not the soundscape—or even the class-scape—of his upbringing. Springsteen grew up immersed and enmeshed in a musical universe more accurately called rock-and-soul (Dave Marsh's term) than rock and roll. He was a white soul man, and his explosive covers of Eddie Floyd's "Raise Your Hand" and Wilson Pickett's "In the Midnight Hour" were once part and parcel of a pluralistic music kingdom we have since lost. His debts to Phil Spector, the girl groups, Dylan, Elvis, Motown, the Byrds, New Orleans, and James Brown are obvious. His synthesis is not.

Yet his commitment at times risks becoming his trap.

The whiteness of his fan base—and of the E Street Band—started to be problematic and then became something of an artistic cul-de-sac. In the arena shows of the *Born in the U.S.A.* tour, Springsteen at first managed to maintain an authentic feel, but he nonetheless lost something—maybe even a bit of himself—in some stagey concessions to the red-white-and-blue spectacle. No matter what the social politics of those concerts, the pumping fists and flying flags generated more than a whiff of a Nuremberg rally. When he tried to right the situation by touring with a largely African American R&B ensemble in the early 1990s, his fans rejected this artistic path along with the new band members. For Springsteen, his music was an American synthesis, but race remained an insurmountable issue for his audience much as it has (and does) in the nation outside of the concert hall.

Recoiling from his own fame and fortune, Springsteen came to wonder about his place as a fabulously wealthy artist in the 1990s. True to form, he turned inward and updated the search of Steinbeck and Guthrie for a New World Order that included the Latinx immigrant experience. "The premise of *The Ghost of Tom Joad*," he once explained, came from asking the question "What is the work for us to do in our short time here?" His citation of Steinbeck, by way of director John Ford's *The Grapes of Wrath*, speaks for his lifework. "I'll be all around in the dark, I'll be everywhere—wherever you can look," Tom tells Ma as he emerges as the spirit of the people. "I'll be there." With the help of Tom Morello of Rage Against the Machine, this song morphed from meditation to performance anthem.

Coming off a long series of entertaining tours that felt more like "the Bruce Review" than his soul revue model, Springsteen sometimes seemed caught, as if performing "Bruce Springsteen" rather than convincing audiences by his presence and the band's power. If "Land of Hope and Dreams" is his contribution to the dream of democratic society, "Working on a Dream" seemed overwrought and overly optimistic, particularly in its short-lived parallel to President Obama's promise. The best moments of his twenty-first-century albums are more often of the acoustic variety ("Devils & Dust," "Long Walk Home") than rock-and-soul, even if he sometimes sends sonic telegrams home to his New Jersey fans, such as "Radio Nowhere" or "Girls in Their Summer Clothes."

We would suggest that the artist's recent need for confession—his memoir and Broadway show—has come from a rebellion of his interior landscape, requiring subjective psychological ventilation and separation from his audience. In revealing his lifelong experience with depression, Springsteen turned his most iconic title on its head, making *Born to Run* a title about escape from self, yet still resonant with his solitary motorcycle trips across desert landscapes. His nightly revelations on Broadway were a form of therapy, his new narrative revised, told and retold: it was a landscape cleared with new vistas revealed. Certainly we can read "My Beautiful Reward" as an early attempt at this kind of reckoning or "The Wrestler" as a metaphor for hitting the wall of his stage persona.

Perhaps this was an inner rebellion (an internal "rising up," if you will) against a performance persona he could no longer inhabit so it manifested in new forms. It is all the more fascinating that Springsteen effected self-renewal *not* in song but in literary and theatrical form; this, too, we believe, reveals his commitment to being a social artist. For a cultural worker who gives his all for audience, community, and country—for an artist who regularly reassesses the state of the nation—it only makes sense that a period of self-reassessment was overdue. Out of such a period of clearing ground, a social artist can come back renewed to the democratic fight.

It's worth asking why American intellectuals and musicians stopped speaking about the role of the artist in a democratic society after the 1960s. Perhaps more than anything, it was the post-sixties despair over the redeemability of America itself. In terms of artistic streams, there were several reasons: the privileging of interior life over abstract social commentary for singer-songwriters; the split between art and commerce that made any popular artist a skeptical source of resistance; the equivalence of "America" with capitalism, consumerism, and global oppression. As testosterone-spiked capitalism dissolves the social fabric and as racial divides shatter dreams of solidarity, Springsteen struggles mightily against the prevailing winds to keep the congregation together. *It's his job.*

Between the loss of his African American musical taproot and the decline of a viable American imaginary, Springsteen's musical kingdom of rock-and-soul drifted in the twenty-first century. His turn to Irish music seems to appeal more to a white racial solidarity and the new tribalism than any authentic broader American solidarities. Certainly Irish music is foundational to all American musics, but Springsteen's musical biography does not reveal any deep connection to this musical tradition. First explored in *The Seeger Sessions*, fully resonant throughout *Live in Dublin* (including new arrangements of classics), and continuing through the live stomp of "American Land," the Irish turn reveals Springsteen surrendering his American synthesis to the whiter shades of Americana. A more generous read might frame this move as one in solidarity with the broader American immigrant story, but, in any case, his audience has enthusiastically greeted this ethnic engagement on their side of the color line.

Springsteen may have been our last working-class musical hero with national resonance simply because the nation has fragmented beyond repair. There have been other liberatory avatars who took on the raiment of nation and protest—Pete Seeger, Johnny Cash, Curtis Mayfield, Patti Smith, Dylan, Prince, George Clinton, Eminem, even Beyoncé and Jason Isbell in different, new ways—but none who self-consciously claimed both to speak to a tradition of national values and the right to voice a nation's dissent. Yet as we have seen, serving the country as a kind of national conscience has its own parameters, history, and artistic limitations.

Even more than his memoir, *Springsteen on Broadway* might pave the way to a new artistic phase, some kind of post-E-Street rejuvenation. The premise of his theatrical memoir was Bruce's two-hour confession of his *in*authenticity, the hustle of his musical worklife. He created a musical persona built to reflect the white working-class experience and claims the irony of never having endured a normal workweek—until his regular gig at the Broadway show. Yet this confession misreads his artistic achievement: it is precisely Springsteen's mediating of that experience in song that makes him an authentic cultural worker. And, ironically, his workweek on Broadway has produced some kind of change. With this long break from blues-shouting and arena rituals, his singing voice is more confident and nuanced than it has been in some years. He has captured a new intimacy and his guitar strumming again seems like an extension of his voice and physical gesture. We saw and heard his stage persona finally converging with his present-day psychology and the teen-aged Springsteen.

So Springsteen may turn out to be the swan song of the American dream as defined by its artistic branches: the-writer-and-his-nation works of Herman Melville and Frederick Douglass, the social realist dreams of Richard Wright and Dorothea Lange, the swing hopes of Duke Ellington and Count Basie and Benny Goodman, the soul liberation theology of Martin Luther King Jr. as embodied in Aretha Franklin's music. The hopeful politics of the shuttered factory and the dream of interracial solidarity so clear in the early incarnations of the E Street Band are gone. Who is left that Springsteen can speak to and for?

Springsteen still plays three-hour shows at seventy. He still musically conducts the band and the audience like a secular congregation; he still finds ways to let the audience into the show (as when he leaves a half hour for call-outs of cover songs); he still plies his now-haunted American gospel around the world. If the country is split, there is Springsteen in Sweden or Ireland or Japan trying to hold a vision together all by his lonesome, performing a version of America that others outside of the national boundaries wish still existed.

"Standing in the shadows of love . . . he gave his heart and soul to us, now didn't he?" This is what we can give back: our understanding of his perseverance, that he convinced by his presence. Should a pluralist musical vision emerge from the muck of our current political overlords of misrule, those cultural workers will have as one model the songcraft and stagecraft of Bruce Springsteen's musical worklife.

Works Cited

Dinerstein, Joel. *Swinging the Machine: Modernity, Technology, and African American Culture between the World Wars.* Amherst: University of Massachusetts Press, 2003.

Ellison, Ralph. *Shadow and Act.* New York: Vintage, 1964.

The Grapes of Wrath. Directed by John Ford. Twentieth Century-Fox Film Corp., 1940.

Hagen, Mark. "Meet the New Boss." *Guardian*, January 17, 2009. www.theguardian.com/music/2009/jan/18/bruce-springsteen-interview.

Springsteen, Bruce. "Chords for Change." *New York Times*, August 5, 2004.

Tucker, Ken. "Bruce Springsteen: The Interview." *Entertainment Weekly*, February 28, 2003. www.ew.com/article/2003/02/28/springsteen-interview/.

Whitman, Walt. "Song of the Open Road." www.poetryfoundation.org/poems/48859/song-of-the-open-road.

6

Starting a Fire

✧

Bruce Springsteen's Political Journey from "Born in the U.S.A." to "American Skin (41 Shots)"

GILLIAN G. GAAR

In 1984, Bruce Springsteen was hardly the outspoken activist and advocate that he is today. But that was the year he suddenly found himself thrust into the political arena. Previously he'd been the kind of artist who let his songs do the talking. But now he had to specify exactly where he stood, if for no other reason than to prevent his message from being hijacked.

The turning point came on September 19, 1984, when President Ronald Reagan was in the midst of his campaign for reelection. During a stop in Hammonton, New Jersey, he gave a nod to Springsteen, one of the state's most famous residents, in his speech: "America's future rests in a thousand dreams inside your hearts; it rests in the message of hope in the songs of a man so many young Americans admire: New Jersey's own Bruce Springsteen. And helping you make those dreams come true is what this job of mine is all about."

Reagan had been inspired to make his remarks by a recent column written by fellow conservative George Will in which Will wrote approvingly of a Springsteen concert he'd attended, singling out the song

"Born in the U.S.A." in particular. Will called it "a grand, cheerful affirmation" of the good life in the land of the free and the home of the brave.

It was a complete misinterpretation of the song that would become
one of Bruce's signature compositions. Far from being celebratory, "Born
in the U.S.A." was meant as something of an indictment, a bitter depiction of how someone could be made to feel they had nothing left to live
for, even in the wealthiest country on earth. What was most surprising
was that this statement came from a performer who for years had largely
kept his political views to himself.

Springsteen had never been much interested in politics. In the late 1960s,
he'd fought the draft, but not out of any political convictions; he simply
didn't want to be sent off to some strange foreign country and get killed,
as he'd seen happen to fellow Jersey Shore musicians. On July 5, 1972,
the Bruce Springsteen Band played a fund-raiser for presidential candidate George McGovern, but Springsteen issued no accompanying
statement of support. Nor did he do so when he played two concerts
benefitting Musicians United for Safe Energy (MUSE) in September
1979 at Madison Square Garden. "Bruce felt that a statement wasn't
appropriate—the music was enough," his manager, Jon Landau, told
Rolling Stone.

But his sensibilities were beginning to change. The MUSE concerts
were put together in response to the partial meltdown of a nuclear power
plant at Three Mile Island in Pennsylvania the previous spring. Springsteen might not have referenced the incident in performance, but he did
write a song inspired by the event, "Roulette" (not released until 1988).
And just over a year after Landau told the press that Springsteen was
interested in speaking only through his music, he was forthright about
Ronald Reagan's ascent to the presidency in 1980. The evening after election day he told an audience in Tempe, Arizona, "I don't know what you
guys think about what happened last night, but I think it's pretty
frightening."

The onetime draft dodger was also becoming increasingly interested
in veterans' issues. While traveling through Arizona, he'd picked up a
copy of Ron Kovic's searing memoir about his experiences in Vietnam,
Born on the Fourth of July, and fortuitously run into Kovic soon after
reading it. Kovic introduced him to veterans' groups, and Springsteen

found their stories very moving. Wanting to help in a more substantial way, he donated all the proceeds from one of his August 1981 shows in Los Angeles to the Vietnam Veterans of America, inviting the organization's founder, Bobby Muller, onstage to make a few remarks to the audience at the start of the show. It was the start of a long-term relationship that would develop between Springsteen and many veterans organizations.

He also began seeking a deeper meaning in his writing. The characters in his songs were largely on the fringes of society, lost souls burdened with life's struggles. But what made life such a struggle for people? What external factors seemed to stack the odds against these outcasts? In considering his 1978 album *Darkness on the Edge of Town*, Bruce writes in his autobiography that "the political implications of the lives I was writing about began to come to the fore and I searched for a music that could contain them." The personal was becoming political.

In December 1981, Springsteen had his guitar tech, Mike Batlan, set up a four-track cassette recorder at his house in Colts Neck, New Jersey, allowing him to record demos at home. It was during this period—late December 1981, early January 1982—that he recorded the first version of "Born in the U.S.A." It was actually a commissioned song; he'd been asked to write the title song for an upcoming Paul Schrader film of the same name (Schrader's film was eventually retitled *Light of Day*, with Springsteen writing the title song).

"Born in the U.S.A." was sung from the perspective of a Vietnam veteran and was partially drawn from an earlier, unreleased song he demoed in 1981, "Vietnam." The original demo for "Born in the U.S.A.," later released on the 1998 compilation *Tracks*, is stark and edgy, featuring just Bruce and his guitar. It's the story of a man whose life has been an endless cycle of defeat; a petty crook sent off to Vietnam instead of jail who returns to find no job or Veterans Administration assistance waiting for him. The loss of his brother in the same war only adds to his bitterness. There's a hint of bravado in the fade out, as he sings of being a "cool rockin' daddy," but the real truth lies in the last line of the last verse. This is a man at a dead end, making the painful admission that he "ain't got nowhere to go."

If this acoustic version of the song had been released first, there would've been no doubt as to what it was trying to convey. But Bruce had other ideas. A number of the songs he demoed at the same time wound up in similarly unadorned arrangements on his 1982 album *Nebraska*, but he saw "Born in the U.S.A." as a hard-driving rock song. During sessions held April 27–28 and May 3, Bruce re-recorded the number with his full band.

This version is a strutting anthem from the start, opening with Roy Bittan's chiming keyboard line (which Bruce felt reflected the sounds of Southeast Asia) backed by Max Weinberg's no-nonsense drum beat, the full band joining in after the first verse. Bruce's raw, scraped vocal adds a sense of desperation. By the time he reaches the chorus, he sounds defiant, but the chorus—simple repetitions of the song's title—means that defiance can be read two ways. Does the narrator think being born in the U.S.A. is a blessing, or a curse? Therein lies the song's ambiguity.

Bruce wanted a song that matched his artistic vision, and this was a song he wanted to rock out to. "If I'd tried to undercut or change the music, I believe I would've had a record that would've been more easily understood," he wrote in his autobiography, "but not as satisfying."

The *Born in the U.S.A.* album was released on June 4, 1984, and the title track made its live debut four days later, in a warm-up show at the Stone Pony in Asbury Park, prior to a national tour. By the time George Will caught Springsteen in Largo, Maryland, on August 25, the album had topped record charts in the United States and ten other countries and was on its way to selling thirty million copies worldwide. In Will's syndicated piece, first published on September 13, he described Springsteen not as a troubadour singing about oppression and lost dreams but as a pragmatic voice offering his audience "homilies" that directed them "to 'downsize' their expectations." A worse misreading of what Bruce's songs were trying to say can scarcely be imagined.

Springsteen made no public comment about Will's column. But in the wake of Reagan's comments, he fired back two days after the president's speech, during a show in Pittsburgh. "The president was mentioning my name the other day, and I kind of got to wondering what his favorite album must've been," he wryly observed. "I don't think it was the *Nebraska* album," a pointed reference to one of his bleakest works. He told biographer Peter Ames Carlin that he resented being name-dropped in such a fashion, reduced to just another item on Reagan's "shopping list of things that needed to be done for the six o'clock [news]." He felt used.

Yet he didn't shy away from publicly defining who he was and what his values were. He began introducing "Born to Run" by saying, "Let freedom ring—but it's no good if it's just for one. It's got to be for everyone," giving a political cast to a song about the joy of escape. Supporting political causes (anti-Apartheid, voter registration, workers' rights) through charity recordings and benefit shows gradually became a significant part of his career. He made sure that groups working on local issues (for example, food banks, veterans' rights) could set up booths at his shows.

Still, though his work continued to focus on the plight of the underdog (especially on his 1995 album *The Ghost of Tom Joad*), he largely refrained from making explicit political statements in songs. But that was due to change.

Just after midnight on February 4, 1999, a twenty-three-year-old immigrant from Guinea named Amadou Diallo was returning to his home in the Bronx. He was confronted by police (dressed in street clothes, not uniforms; whether the officers identified themselves or not remains disputed), and was shot dead when reaching for his wallet, the officers mistaking it for a gun. There was an immediate outcry, especially when the police officers involved were acquitted.

The following year, when Bruce's tour was in its final stages, he wanted to have a new song on hand when he closed in New York City. He chose to write about Diallo's death, which he felt brought to light the nation's continued struggles over race. "American Skin (41 Shots)" made its debut in Atlanta on June 4, 2000. Bruce knew it was a hot-button issue, but he was still surprised by the vitriol that descended on him from some quarters who accused him of writing a song that was "anti-police."

With the title referring to the number of shots the police fired at the unarmed Diallo and the lyrical reference to a wallet, it was quite clear exactly what incident Bruce was talking about. Yet he also addressed both sides of the divide. In one verse, a mother begs her son to be polite and respectful around the police. But in the opening verse, he addresses the distress of the police officer, praying for the life of the man he's just shot. Diallo's death is viewed as a tragedy—not a blame game. It's one of Springsteen's most heartfelt works.

That didn't stop the criticism (at one show, the police refused to provide an escort when the band left the building). But Bruce now viewed the controversy with equanimity. Once he released a song, it took on a life of its own; it was certainly fair for his work to become the subject of debate. Over time, his political convictions also became clearer. In 2004, he endorsed a presidential candidate for the first time, Senator John Kerry, saying the election was too important not to take a stand. "How Can a Poor Man Stand Such Times and Live?," performed with the Seeger Sessions Band, addressed the lack of government response to Hurricane Katrina; after Donald Trump's inauguration, Bruce proclaimed himself a member of "the new American resistance" during a show. It wasn't a surprise to hear him denouncing Trump as a "con man" in his friend Joe Grushecky's song "That's What Makes Us Great."

Decades after starting his career as a scruffy teenage rocker, Bruce Springsteen had finally claimed his political voice. The former draft dodger had picked up the banner carried by such champions of progressive causes as Woody Guthrie and Pete Seeger, and he now carried it with pride. "Songs do have the capacity to translate and to communicate, and to sustain and serve," he said in a talk at Monmouth University in 2017. "And in a certain moment, the right song can start a fire." And Bruce was ready to light the match.

Works Cited

Angermiller, Michele Amabile. "Bruce Springsteen on Musical Activism: 'The Right Song Can Start a Fire.'" *Billboard*, January 11, 2017.

Carlin, Peter Ames. *Bruce*. New York: Touchstone/Simon & Schuster, 2012.

Gaar, Gillian G. *Boss: Bruce Springsteen and the E Street Band—The Illustrated History*. Minneapolis: Voyageur Press, 2016.

Graff, Gary. "New Glory Days." *Oakland Press*, April 1, 2001.

McLane, Saisann. "M.U.S.E.: Rock Politics Comes of Age." *Rolling Stone*, November 15, 1979.

Nightline, August 4, 2004.

Springsteen, Bruce. *Born to Run*. New York: Simon & Schuster, 2016.

Will, George F. "Bruce Springsteen's U.S.A." *Washington Post*, September 13, 1984.

7

Springsteen's American Dream

✧

LOUIS P. MASUR

A rocker at seventy. The idea might once have seemed ridiculous. Rock and roll always flaunts its youthfulness, rebelliousness, and self-awareness. It is filled with songs that celebrate the genre (Chuck Berry's "Rock and Roll Music" and scores of others). Some of those tunes also speak of mortality. The Who declared, "I hope I die before I grow old," but Pete Townsend and Roger Daltrey are still touring in their seventies. And Neil Young wrote "It's better to burn out than fade away," but, at age seventy-four, how much fire can he have left? Other icons from the 1960s and 1970s continue playing around the world: Bob Dylan (seventy-eight), Paul McCartney (seventy-seven), Ringo Starr (seventy-nine), Mick Jagger (seventy-six), Van Morrison (seventy-four). In 2018, Paul Simon (seventy-seven) did a farewell tour, but he has also said he will continue to perform. Not only is a rocker at seventy not ridiculous, it is now standard fare.

Springsteen differs from some of his septuagenarian peers in that he continues to take chances and develop new material. He spent 2017–2018 on Broadway performing a one-man show that united narrative and song to tell his story, a story of appearance versus reality, escape versus homecoming, sin versus salvation. As with all his work, it is a story about love. Whether with the full E Street Band or alone onstage, he delivers a show that transcends the moment and leaves audiences feeling hopeful and uplifted even as he carries them across pits of darkness and despair. He is a self-described magician and conjurer who will not reveal his tricks but continues to hone his craft as he enters his seventies.

A great artist requires a great theme and Springsteen's is the American dream. "I have spent my life," he said in 2012, "judging the distance between American reality and the American dream." The American dream has never been easily defined, but it centers on a cluster of ideals that promise a better life for those who work hard and seek the opportunity to prosper. Democracy, freedom, equality, and justice are the high-concept pillars that support it. When he first ran for president, Barack Obama sought to "reclaim the American dream" from those who advanced a politics of inequality, exclusion, and division. "America," Obama declared, "is the sum of our dreams."

Springsteen's story personifies the American dream. A working-class kid who resented his Catholic school education and dropped out of community college, who survived an abusive father (diagnosed late in life as schizophrenic) and was nurtured by a loving mother, Springsteen found salvation in rock and roll and the dream of escape that it offered. Elvis Presley first embodied the seismic shift represented by rock music and rock fame, and the revolution ushered in by Presley marked Springsteen at an early age (he was seven years old when he saw Elvis on *The Ed Sullivan Show*). It is no accident that in Eric Meola's cover photograph on *Born to Run* (1975), Springsteen is wearing an Elvis fan club pin. Several years after Elvis's death in 1977, Springsteen rewrote the Presley song "Follow that Dream":

> Now every man has the right to live
> The right to a chance, to give what he has to give
> The right to fight for the things he believes
> For the things that come to him in dreams

That is as keen an account of the meaning of America as has ever been written. As for many other figures in American history, self-education guided Springsteen's path to understanding the country. On *The River* tour in 1980–1981, Springsteen often spoke onstage about a book he was reading—Allan Nevins and Henry Steele Commager's *A Pocket History of the United States*—and how "I started to learn about how things got to be the way they are today, how you end up a victim without even knowing it, and how people get old, and just die after not having hardly a day's satisfaction or peace of mind in their lives." Springsteen kept reading. In his autobiography, he namechecks Flannery O'Connor and John Steinbeck and alludes to *Moby-Dick* and *Death of a Salesman*. Film, too, shaped his vision of America, whether the work of John Ford or Terrence Malick.

It is the dark side of the American dream that first preoccupied Springsteen: broken promises, lost opportunities, failed relationships, dead lives. "If dreams came true, oh, wouldn't that be nice," he sings in "Prove It All Night." It is a dream fueled by hunger—a hunger for more, a feeling that one deserves better. To reach for it, he tells us, is to "pay the price," a phrase he also uses in "Badlands" and unpacks in "The Price You Pay" ("caught up in a dream where everything goes wrong"). We can strive to make it in America, but to do so we often leave behind the wellsprings of our identity and we suffer for our transgressions. We can "talk about a dream / try to make it real" ("Badlands"), but in the end the striving and waiting are a waste.

In "The River," a story about a young couple trapped by circumstances, the narrator asks, "Is a dream a lie if it don't come true / or is it something worse?" Believing in the American dream and not having it come true makes the dream worse than a lie—it becomes a cancer that consumes individuals and leaves them hollow. If only, as in "The Promised Land," we can "Blow away the dreams that tear you apart / blow away the dreams that break your heart / blow away the lies that leave you nothing but lost and brokenhearted." But we can't. We are trapped between the desire to get away, to remake ourselves, and to define our own terms in a society that dangles the promise of success for those who play along.

As Springsteen dissected the underside of the American dream, he began to address the social conditions that oppressed people and prevented them from achieving any semblance of the nation's promise. In doing so, he shifted from dream to reality. The problem wasn't the myth itself, it was the economic forces that made it unattainable: "ain't been much work on account of the economy" ("The River"), "debts no honest man can pay" ("Atlantic City"), "went out looking for a job but he couldn't find none" ("Johnny 99").

Born in the U.S.A. announced that Springsteen would offer both a critique and a defense of America. That his meaning was misunderstood made the work all the more powerful. This was not the blind patriotism praised by Ronald Reagan, who was running for reelection; Reagan said America's future "rests in the message of hope in the songs of a man so many young Americans admire: New Jersey's own Bruce Springsteen." Instead, Springsteen was offering the patriotism of a loyal son calling on the nation to live up to its highest ideals. He responded to Reagan in concert by playing "Johnny 99," a song about an unemployed auto worker who kills a night clerk and tells the judge "the bank was holdin' my mortgage / they takin' my house away."

On *Born in the U.S.A.*, Springsteen continued his critique of a society that limited the chances for upward mobility for the working class: "I got laid off down at the lumber yard" ("Downbound Train"), "closing down the textile mill across the railroad tracks" ("My Hometown"), "the times are tough now, just getting tougher" ("Cover Me"). As always in Springsteen's work, there are conflicting themes that appear both musically and lyrically: there are verses cast as the blues and choruses that ring as gospel; there are good times and there are hard times; and the narrator who declares "no retreat, no surrender" ultimately submits to packing up and leaving town. Hope and despair, freedom and fate, connection and betrayal are the features of Springsteen's American landscape.

Over a long career, Springsteen has embodied multiple personas, and he soon abandoned the hypermasculine working-class American hero for the voice of conscience, the singer-songwriter in the tradition of Woody Guthrie, Pete Seeger, and folk Bob Dylan. In 1995, he resurrected "The Ghost of Tom Joad," forever fighting for justice on behalf of the downtrodden. He would return to the song time and again, and, in 2008, he performed it alongside Tom Morello, who had recorded a version with Rage Against the Machine in 1997. Springsteen and Morello exchanged verses, and Morello delivered two blistering guitar solos that made the song explode with revolutionary zeal. In the aftermath of the financial crisis, it would become a staple for portions of the 2012–2013 *Wrecking Ball* tour. In June 2018, Springsteen changed the set list of his Broadway show for the first time in 146 shows and included "The Ghost of Tom Joad." He sang it after delivering a message about American democracy and justice in the face of the Trump administration policy of separating immigrant children from their parents at the border. People of conscience, he said, cannot and will not stand by in the face of scenes that are "so shockingly and disgracefully inhumane and un-American that it is simply enraging."

Since the 1990s, Springsteen's direct engagement with social justice and political action has grown ever more robust. In 2000, he performed "American Skin (41 Shots)," inspired by the police shooting of Amadou Diallo. In 2004, he campaigned for John Kerry and participated in Vote for Change, and four years later he participated in rallies for Barack Obama. At Obama's inauguration in 2009, he played "This Land Is Your Land," a song he first performed on *The River* tour, along with eighty-nine-year-old Pete Seeger (eighty-nine!). They sang all the verses, including the usually omitted ones about private property and public relief.

The rock star who made his fame singing about the dream of escape and getting out while young now found himself at the center of American power: he had the ear of the president of the United States who agreed with him about renewing the American dream for all. In 2006, Springsteen wrote about taking a "Long Walk Home," and it is telling that he chose to include the song in his initial Broadway set list. In one of the verses a father speaks to a son:

> Your flag flyin' over the courthouse
> Means certain things are set in stone
> Who we are, what we'll do, and what we won't

Springsteen has reclaimed American patriotism from those who would use it for partisan purposes. The flag is a proud symbol, and America offers a promise that stands the test of time and cannot be shaken by adverse political winds. Returning home is as much a key component of the American dream as getting away (think *Wizard of Oz*), and, in the song, Springsteen invites us to walk the road back to where we began.

What he discovers on his return turns out to be painful, and a few years later in *Wrecking Ball*, a musical, lyrical, spiritual, and confrontational masterpiece, Springsteen offered a searing indictment of the broken American promise. In 1975, Springsteen had engaged "the runaway American dream." But in 2012, it was not just that the dream proved elusive; ordinary Americans were being trampled. New resources and weapons were needed to fight back. Springsteen's diagnosis of the problem is clear: the world of "fat cats" ("Easy Money") and "robber barons" ("Death to My Hometown") has destroyed the dignity of work and the sanctity of home. "The banker man grows fat / the working man grows thin," he sings in "Jack of All Trades." In "Shackled and Drawn," "it's a world gone wrong."

Springsteen summons the past in a new battle for the present and future. He samples tunes recorded long ago ("I Am a Soldier in the Army of the Lord" from 1949, on "Rocky Ground"), and while many of the songs offer prayers and references to enduring faith, they also encourage anger and violent resistance. On the final song, "We Are Alive," he resurrects the dead who fought in the strikes of 1877, the civil rights battles of 1963, as well as those who have perished in recent attempts to cross the border. Sampling the country classic "Ring of Fire," Springsteen places the countless dead within its ring and makes them allies, available "to fight shoulder to shoulder and heart to heart." By invoking the past, Springsteen becomes a lyrical historian, reminding us that the struggle to make America live up to its promise is as old as the promise itself.

On *Wrecking Ball*, Springsteen also affirms that the United States remains a "Land of Hope and Dreams," a song first debuted live in 1999. Similarly, "American Land" begins with a seemingly simple question, "What is this land America, so many travel there?" and celebrates those immigrants who gave their lives to build the country and make it their home. Springsteen's musical palette embraces folk, country, blues, gospel, soul—the wellspring of sources that birthed rock and roll. For Springsteen, the music itself underscores themes central to our identity: love, faith, work, and community.

Springsteen understands that the American dream, which he has lived, critiqued, and defended, can be kept alive only through continuous engagement and action. Performance is a form of action and Springsteen loves to perform. He once said he felt alive only onstage. Hopefully, decades of therapy and treatment for depression have allowed him to find life as rewarding off the stage as on. One of the great gifts he offered in his autobiography was to confess to a lifetime struggle with unhappiness and a need for antidepressants. How can that be?, we wonder. Isn't he famous? Isn't he wealthy? More than ever, in this culture that vaults celebrity and fortune, we need to be reminded that the real American dream includes rather than excludes, nourishes rather than famishes, satisfies rather than disappoints.

"So you're scared and you're thinking that maybe we ain't that young anymore." He was twenty-five when he wrote that line. I was eighteen when I heard it. I'm still scared, and I'm definitely not that young anymore. But I listen to Springsteen, savor the past, and feel inspired to dream about the future.

Works Cited

Obama, Barack. "Remarks in Bettendorf, Iowa: 'Reclaiming the American Dream.'" November 7, 2007. American Presidency Project. www.presidency.ucsb.edu/node /277481.

Reagan, Ronald. "Remarks at a Reagan-Bush Rally in Hammonton, New Jersey." September 19, 1984. American Presidency Project. www.presidency.ucsb.edu/node /261502.

Springsteen, Bruce. "Interview at International Press Conference in Paris, February 2012." In *Talk about a Dream: The Essential Interviews of Bruce Springsteen*, edited by Christopher Phillips and Louis P. Masur, 406–420. New York: Bloomsbury, 2013.

8

At the River

PAUL MULDOON

Now the eighteen-wheeler of state has flipped
and blocked what we took for an exit-ramp
and our legislative gears have been stripped
and the '69 Chevy's red tail-lamp
glows in Kentucky, in Wyoming glows,
our mines having seen a build-up of fire-damp
that threatens one of these fine days to blow,
and politicians, of course, still decamp
for any side on which their bread is buttered
while our food-workers make do with food-stamps
and our President stars in his own gutter,
the time has surely come to turn up the amp,
the Great Blue Heron taking a firm stand
on the mudflats as in the meadowlands.

9

The Ties That Bind

✦

A. O. SCOTT

On February 4, 1999, on Wheeler Avenue in the Soundview section of the Bronx, Amadou Diallo, an immigrant from Guinea, was killed by four plainclothes members of the New York Police Department's Street Crimes Unit. Diallo, who was unarmed, was standing on the front stoop of the building where he lived and reaching for his wallet when the officers started shooting. They fired forty-one bullets, nineteen of which hit Diallo, whose name was added to the seemingly endless, endlessly updated list of black and brown residents of the United States killed by law enforcement. Patrick Dorismond, Sean Bell, Michael Brown, Walter Scott, Freddie Gray, Tamir Rice, Philando Castile—all those deaths were still in the future. "Black Lives Matter" was not yet a slogan or a movement. Football players were not taking a knee during the national anthem to call attention to the slaughter.

But of course the polarized public discourse—and the deep fracture in the body politic it exposed—was not so different back then. Protests against racial injustice were taken as attacks on the police; criticism of the police was answered with non sequiturs about the pathologies of the ghetto, absent fathers, and "black-on-black" crime. Some songs never get old.

In response to the shooting, Bruce Springsteen released "American Skin (41 Shots)," a minor-key ballad, more anguished than angry, which applied the balms of empathy and narrative economy to a raw social wound. The central verse dramatizes what African American families call "the talk." As a mother, Lena, prepares her son, Charles, for school, she reminds him: "You've got to understand the rules / if an officer stops you, promise me, you'll always be polite / and that you'll never ever run away / and promise mama you'll keep your hands in sight."

The following summer, I managed to score seats up in the rafters of Madison Square Garden for one of the last shows in the E Street Band's epic reunion tour. The show was long and generous. Springsteen has never been grudging about playing the old favorites. He loves how much people love those songs—"Thunder Road" and "Born to Run"; "Two Hearts" and "Dancing in the Dark"—and he implicitly, graciously acknowledges the possible divergences between the audience's agenda and his own. The party, the "rock and roll bar mitzvah" as he has been known to call it, might be punctuated by a sermon or a civics lesson. He might feel called to get political, and we won't mind too much.

A few rows ahead of me at that show, there were two guys who did mind. I would have guessed that they were bigger Bruce fans than I was, or at least fans of longer standing and purer pedigree. When I was in high school and "Born in the U.S.A." dominated top forty radio, my thing was post-punk, and that album didn't strike me as nearly aggressive or ironic enough. (I was pretty dumb back then, as only a teenage intellectual can be: the fury of the title track and the mordant knowingness of "Glory Days" seem obvious to me now.) It took the belated discovery of *Nebraska* during my undergraduate Woody Guthrie phase to awaken me to Springsteen's bardic genius, and while I like to think I made up for lost time and earned a measure of credibility, I've always been haunted by intimations of inauthenticity. That's rock and roll, I guess. Or at least the predicament of my own perpetually belated, morbidly self-conscious generation.

But this isn't really about me. It's about those other guys, who I might not have noticed, and would never have remembered nearly twenty years after the fact, if not for what I'm about to describe. They looked a little older than I was: closer to forty than thirty. They were meatier, louder, probably drunker and having a great time—dancing, pumping their fists, exchanging high fives with strangers, singing along to every chorus and most of the verses. They were not self-conscious at all.

At least not until the first mournful notes of "American Skin." I don't remember if Bruce introduced it with a reminder of the Diallo case, or if anyone needed reminding. The officers had been acquitted four months earlier, in February 2000. Diallo's mother, Kadijatou, had filed a suit against the city in April. Maybe he said something about that, or maybe everyone remembered when he sang the line "forty-one shots." As soon as he did, the two men turned their backs to the stage, clasped their hands in front of them and bowed their heads. They didn't boo and they didn't walk out—there had been booing at other shows, picketers and empty boycott threats at others—but stood silently, registering their protest at the Boss's protest.

Once the final chorus began to fade, he shifted—without pausing for breath—into the familiar harmonica riff that leads into the first verse of "The Promised Land." Having made their point and enacted their displeasure, the two guys turned back to face the music, and when Bruce stopped singing after the first chorus and turned the microphone toward the crowd, they sang along with everyone else, belting out a stanza that expressed a different kind of protest: "Sometimes I feel so weak, I just wanna explode."

For a long time I held onto that moment as a complicated symbol of civic promise, a testament to the inclusiveness of popular music in general and Bruce Springsteen in particular. Of course he didn't have the power to fix racism, to resolve the contradictions of class and ideology, to move the world toward justice. But the reach of his empathy was wide enough to extend to both Amadou Diallo's family and, if not to his killers, surely to their families and supporters. The politics that would take any criticism of the police as a moral provocation, while far from Springsteen's own beliefs, is in no way alien to his imagination. He might not have agreed with those guys standing with their backs turned (and even if he couldn't see them, he must have known they were out there), but he understood them. And their understanding of *him* was what authorized their protest. The concert created a civic space in which two antithetical sentiments could coexist and communicate with each other.

Feelings might be hurt, but the bond between performer and fan was stronger than politics.

Something like this idea defined the public career of Barack Obama, in some ways (though not in others) the most Springsteenian political figure in American political history. The speech at the 2004 Democratic National Convention that set Obama on course to capture the presidency four years later wove a shimmering dialectic of unity and diversity. Obama rewrote historical conflict—about race, power, money, religion, and culture—as common struggle. He tried, to the consternation of allies as well as foes, to insist in particular that America's racial wounds could be salved by the mutual recognition of good will, by appreciation of the varieties of American skin we all inhabit.

"Is a dream a lie if it don't come true?" As I write this, Obama's liberal ideals—and their cultural cognates, including Springsteen's ecstatic, cathartic, ennobling vision of rock and roll—have fallen on hard times. Maybe they were illusions to begin with, each fatally underestimating the depth and jaggedness of the fissures, the intensity of the fury, the tenacity of the tribal ties that bind. And maybe too, some of us invested too much faith in the charisma of our leaders, and rested too comfortably in the conviction of our own goodness.

Or maybe we were listening wrong, missing the overtones of irony, the notes of tragedy, longing, and defeat that sounded through even the most ringing and rousing choruses. The liberal Springsteen has been a comforting fantasy, but the radical Springsteen—the poet of work, violence, futility, and all-in existential revolt—needs to be recovered, just as we are being forced to recall that the character of our common civic life has always been a matter of life and death. "You can get killed just for living in your American skin."

Part III

Springsteen Live

"Hungry Heart," HSBC Arena, Buffalo, New York, November 22, 2009, Clarence Clemons's last performance with the E Street Band. (Rocco S. Coviello)

10

Live at the Roxy

✧

GREIL MARCUS

On 7 July 1978 Bruce Springsteen and the E Street Band played a show at the Roxy in Los Angeles. KMET-FM broadcast it—from "Rave On" to "Raise Your Hand," twenty-three long songs in all—and bootleg LPs and off-the-radio tapes have been circulating ever since. I got hold of third-generation cassettes well over six months ago; since then, I've played them often enough, but in the last weeks a few performances have come off those tapes and taken me over. It's not the only music I've listened to this late spring, but it is the only music I've felt scared to play, and scared not to.

If you're lucky, at the right time you come across music that is not only "great," or interesting, or "incredible," or fun, but actually sustaining. Through some elusive but tangible process, a piece of music cuts through all defenses and makes sense of every fear and desire you bring to it. As it does so, it exposes all you've held back, and then makes sense of that, too. Though someone else is doing the talking, the experience is like a confession. Your emotions shoot out to crazy extremes; you feel both

Note: This piece was originally published in *New West* on July 2, 1979. It has not been altered in any way. One annotation, inserted by the editors, is marked with an asterisk.

ennobled and unworthy, saved and damned. You hear that this is what life is all about, that this is what it is *for*. Yet it is this recognition itself that makes you understand that life can never be this good, this whole. With a clarity life denies for its own good reasons, you see places to which you can never get.

Such a thing happens when it has to. Springsteen's Roxy performances of "Prove It All Night" and "Racing in the Street" (one followed the other in his set) stood out the first time I heard the tapes, but they mainly confirmed what I'd heard at the Berkeley Community Theater a few nights before the Roxy show: onstage, these songs exploded the limits of their recorded versions. It was only after the verdict in the Dan White trial came down*—a verdict so shameful and corrupt it cheapened the lives of all who were involved, including those who only paid attention—that this music became undeniable. Every thought was suddenly vulnerable to a loathsome ugliness, and as I played the tape, the music absorbed that ugliness, took it into account—had, it seemed, been ready for it—and had more to say.

I listened again and again. Once, the songs made me think of a story Maxim Gorky told about Lenin's love of Beethoven. Edmund Wilson quotes it in *To the Finland Station*:

"I know nothing [Lenin said] that is greater than the *Appassionata*; I'd like to listen to it every day. It is marvelous superhuman music. I always think with pride—perhaps it is naïve of me—what marvelous things human beings can do!" Then screwing up his

---

* Dan White had resigned from the San Francisco Board of Supervisors when he asked Mayor George Moscone to reappoint him to the seat he had left vacant. On November 27, 1978, after he was told the mayor had made another choice, he entered City Hall and shot and killed both Moscone and fellow supervisor Harvey Milk—the first openly gay elected official in California and one of the first in the nation. On May 21, 1979, six weeks before this review was published, White was, as his attorneys had recommended, found guilty of voluntary manslaughter rather than first-degree murder, thanks in part to what became known as the "Twinkie Defense." His lawyers argued that his diminished mental state and struggles with depression—as indicated by an increased consumption of sugary foods—were the cause of his actions. The verdict sparked outrage in San Francisco, especially in the city's gay community, which engaged in a series of riots the day of the verdict. After five years in prison, White was released in 1984, and in an interview that year he confirmed that the killings had in fact been premeditated and that he had planned to kill two other city politicians as well. He took his own life in 1985.

eyes and smiling, he added, rather sadly: "But I can't listen to music too often. It affects your nerves, makes you want to say stupid nice things and stroke the heads of people who could create such beauty while living in this vile hell. And now you musn't stroke anyone's head—you might get your hand bitten off. You have to hit them on the head, without mercy, although our ideal is not to use force against anyone. Our duty in infernally hard."

Springsteen's music made me think of that story; it also made me think that Lenin didn't have it quite right. Exactly what is right, I don't know.

The Roxy show came at the start of a tour that would carry Springsteen and his band through the next six months. Unlike most live broadcasts, which are produced by radio station crews and come off blurred and unbalanced, with two instruments drowning out the rest, this one was handled by Springsteen's producer, Jon Landau, and his engineer, Jimmy Iovine. The result is one of the most vivid pieces of sound in the recorded history of live rock 'n' roll. There's nothing you can't hear; even when the band goes after its harshest, most brutal rave-ups, every note stands out. When Max Weinberg brings his stick down on the rim of his snare drum near the end of "Racing in the Street," you think you can feel the grain of the wood; the thump of the bass drum has slammed doors in my house. The band isn't playing to you, you're inside it, catching cues passed from one musician to another, understanding for the first time the way Roy Bittan's piano leads the music, the way Danny Federici's organ supports it, drawing out a story that would be meaningless without Bittan's frame. Bittan, Federici, Weinberg, bassist Garry Tallent, second guitarist Steven Van Zandt, and even sax man Clarence Clemons on triangle read each other's minds; their sympathy is absolute. They give Springsteen the freedom to cut loose, to send out vocals and guitar that sound heroic, but which, you can now hear, are as much as anything the product of friendship, of trust. Even on the best live albums, the musicians often sound like hired hands; here, they sound like mentors.

The Roxy was a special date on the tour, and the club was packed with music business people (Glenn Frey and Eagles manager Irving Azoff stalked out after the fourth song; Jackson Browne ended the night

standing on a table, screaming). The sounds of the crowd are sometimes as exciting as those of the band: even they are preternaturally
clear, and the thrill that takes over the audience—a woman's wail as the
band drops back in the middle of "Prove It All Night," a whoop that
seems to anticipate and then ride a line from Springsteen's guitar—is
not like anything I've come across before.

If most of the Roxy performances escaped the limits of their recorded
versions, emotionally the Roxy "Prove It All Night" and "Racing in the
Street" don't seem to have any limits at all. Both are songs of desperation: "Prove It All Night" is about seizing the last chances life offers,
"Racing in the Street" about facing its final defeats. With the first, the
band rolls into the melody, stretching it over chorus after chorus, leading you through an instrumental buildup so lovely and painful you don't
care if Springsteen ever starts singing. The song seems to have said everything it can possibly say before the first word is sung. The music traces
a great circle, widening, moving out—but then Springsteen takes the center and claims it.

A kiss to seal
My fate
Tonight

That this performance should be followed by anything seems strange;
that it is topped, taken past itself, is absurd. That's what happens. I know
why I had to listen to "Racing in the Street" after a jury told Dan White
he was better than the men he murdered; the story this song tells is just
as bad.

There has never been an artist so aware of the rock 'n' roll heritage as
Bruce Springsteen. In its structure, "Racing in the Street" is Van Morrison's "Tupelo Honey"; in its theme, it is a bitter inversion of Martha
and the Vandellas' "Dancing in the Street"; in a very specific lyric reference (the odd construction "you'd best keep away" transformed into
"out of our way buddy you'd best keep"), it is Jan and Dean's "Dead Man's
Curve." Most of all, it's the Beach Boys' "Shut Down," "409," "Little Deuce
Coupe," and "Don't Worry Baby." Springsteen took the Beach Boys' teenagers with their easy, obvious freedom, and dumped fifteen years on
them; he made those teenagers grow up. He imagined that they would

never really outgrow the freedom they found in their cars and on the road. He made them drive forever toward a dead end that, as a curse, they would always see, that they could never wish away, but that they would never quite reach.

Springsteen finishes the story; he is singing in the first person, and he has understood exactly what has happened to him. The music falls off; then Weinberg begins to tap his stick, and very slowly, the band comes in. After two choruses, Springsteen's guitar, tuned to the soft, high tone that opens "Backstreets," joins the dirge and makes it an elegy. There's no ending. After a time—each change staggering you with a force that is truly awful—Springsteen simply begins to tell a story to introduce the next song, and as the band drops off, Roy Bittan just keeps playing "Racing in the Street" on his piano. You never really hear him stop.

There will, of course, be more shows. Springsteen is twenty-nine, with four albums behind him; that's not many, and I think it's only *Darkness on the Edge of Town* that is mature work. The scary thing about Bruce Springsteen is that he's just starting. Given what his music has done for me these past days, that's also the most positive statement I can summon up, about rock 'n' roll or anything else.

11

The Magic Circle

✧

WESLEY STACE

On October 1, 2004, Bruce Springsteen played Philadelphia in a cavernous arena, then called the Wachovia Center. Bright Eyes, John Fogerty, and R.E.M. made up the rest of the bill, part of the Vote for Change tour, designed to encourage people to register to vote in an election that ultimately saw Democrat John Kerry fail to become president. Springsteen closed the sold-out show (19,353 tickets), which made $1,552,750.

Springsteen blew everyone else away, as he had years before on the similar Amnesty International tour, which also featured Sting, Peter Gabriel, Tracy Chapman, and Youssou N'Dour (which I saw in London on September 2, 1988). It takes all sorts, so this doesn't reflect badly on the other performers (R.E.M. was particularly good but played only three or four crowd-pleasers in their twelve-song set). But the concert made me wonder why Springsteen is so good—the best—at what he does. Yes, he's a great songwriter and lyricist; but how does he also manage to provide the best rock-and-roll show of all time, almost *every* time, in the same inhospitable arenas that regularly dwarf other performers?

It's easy to conclude that he's a natural: a born performer. None of the other singer/songwriters I liked when I first saw Springsteen were incredible *musicians*; they simply strummed while the rest of the band did the music, so it blew me away when I realized he played the solos (I had naturally assumed it was Steve Van Zandt, the show-offy guy with the headband). But Springsteen is not only a great guitarist, a great bandleader, a great songwriter—none of this is news. He's also a great mover. You don't often see his moves analyzed in print but whether he's grinding the mic stand, swaying his head as he plays a solo, or presiding over one of his religious revival routines, it all seems effortless and unembarrassed. The way Springsteen moves is the way everyone wants to move on a stage: joyously, unselfconsciously.

This is the key. Bruce does not wink at you; he gives you the truth straight. His smile is open. The show is not ironic, though there is always humor. It *seems* entirely honest. That is its appeal. The most remarkable thing about this honest rock-and-roll show is not only that, being so much fun, it can easily embrace any number of rock-and-roll chestnuts (and my recent favorite was at a concert at MetLife Stadium on August 30, 2016, when Bruce followed his own "Blinded by the Light"—a hit single for the group Manfred Mann—with "Pretty Flamingo" a few songs later, Manfred Mann's 1966 hit). The truly remarkable thing is that these shows are primarily showcases for Springsteen's own catalogue, which, lest we forget amid all the good times, comprises songs of intense lyrical seriousness and musical complexity, set in what might in anyone else's hands seem a bewildering array of styles, indicative of Springsteen's generous musical tastes.

Despite the sponsored arena, the insulting parking situation, the overpriced drinks, the popping of popcorn, the punitively uncomfortable chairs, and the massive troubles associated with getting into the venue and then extricating yourself again (and this was before the days of security checks), Springsteen will make you believe in rock and roll once more. Whatever it was you liked about it to begin with, before it was dirtied by the horrid smirk, the knowing wink, and Ticketmaster presales, Springsteen will help you recover. His show is good for anything that ails you. He'll take you back to the prelapsarian world, and yet, the whole way there, he'll tell you in detail about the fall.

No one will tell you better.

But back to that Thunderdome near Philadelphia, formerly known as the Spectrum, then CoreStates Spectrum, then First Union Spectrum, then the Wachovia Spectrum, and now, finally, the Wells Fargo Center, which goes to show that it's only the names of the banks that change, a reminder that they're all otherwise identical, that they own both you and rock and roll, that there will be another crash and, despite being its victim, there's nothing you can do about it. I was watching Springsteen play, thinking about all this stuff, as one does, and I noticed a wonderful thing.

(I should declare, in the interests of transparency, that I've had the pleasure of playing with Springsteen, that I supported him a couple of times, that he once came to duet at one of my own shows, and that I have thus had the opportunity to wander backstage at his concerts, where a kindly roadie has given me used harmonicas that I have recycled and put back in action for my own act. So I know there are secrets, because all great magicians have secrets. But I am, in my own modest way, a fellow member of the Magic Circle, so I would never reveal anything from the wrong side of the curtain. No, what follows is something I noticed from my far distant and very poor seat at the Wachovia.)

At one moment during the Philadelphia show, Springsteen wandered offstage. From my oblique angle I could see him in the wings, shaking a bottle of water all over his jeans from the knee down. I immediately thought something along the lines of: "That's weird. His calves must be hot." A little while later, after his return to center stage, he took a long run-up and slid along the front of the platform. He slid a long way. He slid miles. He seemed to slide the breadth of the stage. His knees hadn't needed cooling down after all. The bottle of water was a prop, a simple, charming solution to ensure the longest, smoothest, most aesthetically pleasing slide in the world.

Later on, he ducked into the wings once more, shaking that same prop or its replacement over his hair (or perhaps he ducked his head into a bucket, I can't quite remember, but I could see). When he returned to the stage, while the light shone on him in a certain way during a particularly effortful solo, he shook his head, and thus his locks, and the water flew off in great arcs, reading not as water, but as sweat. No one, I think, in Row ZZ or Section 20001B, thought: "Oh, that's water." They thought it was sweat, and that he was working *that* hard for us. He *was* working that hard for us, but how else would we know? Springsteen simply doesn't sweat that much. No one on earth sweats that much. It was a show-business trick, a little fakery that reads well at the back of the room.

I told someone this, with enthusiasm, sometime later, theorizing that these things must happen at the same precise moment during every show on the tour. The reaction I got in return for my enthusiasm was: "That's lame." I understand this point of view (fake is wrong; rock and roll should be honest, otherwise you're Elvis in Vegas) but I don't sympathize with it. I think it's silly. To me, this is the very essence of Bruce Springsteen's genius. Rock and roll has always been a dirty business; the singer a cross between the snake-oil salesman and the televangelist that Bruce has so often, so successfully, pastiched during his shows. He clearly sees the link. Perhaps "honesty" is what makes all other performers—Peter Gabriel, Sting, and so forth—pale in comparison. (I don't know precisely who, or which think tank, comes up with these bits of business, or figures out how many creative uses a humble bottle of water can be put to; perhaps it is the Boss himself. Perhaps Penn and Teller work it all out. That isn't the point.)

Springsteen is the best live act in the world because he has taken the essence of his club show, famously the most powerful on the circuit, and used every means at his disposal, every trick in his bag (his wonderful songs, the intimacy of his banter, his dynamite band, bottled water) to re-create that up-close atmosphere in the faceless arenas and stadia that shrink most other acts. Whatever effects, whatever little bits of business he employs to bolster this illusion—the illusion that we are all together, in a small place, where we might be spattered with the performer's sweat, where one might be able to get from one side of the room to the other by sliding—are in the service of a much greater illusion: that rock and roll still matters, that it can take you away from your dull daily cares, that it can save you.

The truth is that, with a little sleight of hand, it can.

Springsteen proves it all night, every time he plays.

12

Twist and Shout

DAVID L. ULIN

I

Here's what I remember: We camped out for tickets. It was the only time I ever did. I was a nineteen-year-old college freshman living in a new city, Philadelphia, trying to find a way back into school after a year traveling cross-country, working in Texas and California before returning home via Amtrak, a long and looping journey east. On the train, I drank and played guitar and poker, smoked weed on the platform between cars. I met a woman, nineteen also, made out with her in a shared seat until some other passenger called the conductor to break us up. I felt like an adult—or no, not an adult but not a kid any longer. Let's say I was nascent, indefinable, in between.

Nascent. The word sounds so . . . calming, especially given what was going on that fall. It was 1980, and Ronald Reagan was in the white-hot moment of his ascendency. I remember the night he was elected president, turning on the television in my dorm room just in time to catch the end of Jimmy Carter's concession speech. It all happened so fast, like an accident: Turn away for a second and the world is changed. Three months earlier, in San Francisco, I had watched from a friend's apartment in the Marina as Reagan accepted the Republican nomination;

afterwards, I called my father, who assured me he would never win. "What now?" I asked, or might have asked, or should have asked, but as often happened, he had no answers I could use. This was the summer I discovered punk, local groups like Men in Black, Dead Kennedys, Jim Carroll Band, X from Los Angeles. I went to see them at the Old Waldorf, the Mabuhay Gardens, the Berkeley Square across the Bay, or at house parties, in garages and living rooms. At the same time, I remained a Deadhead, caught in the slipstream between generations, styles. Growing up in Manhattan, I had been obsessed with 1960s bands: the Beatles and the Stones, but also the Dead, the Velvet Underground, Jefferson Airplane. Of the bands coming up at clubs like CBGB, I listened (at first, anyway) only to Patti Smith. She shared those roots with me, her music loose, improvisational; I had seen her with Bob Dylan in a photograph. Once, a friend declared her the queen of rock and roll, suggesting, as king, another rocker from New Jersey: Bruce Springsteen. I knew Springsteen's music—was it possible, in New York in the 1970s, not to know Springsteen's music?—but I had long resisted him, or his mystique, even though I liked some of his songs. I started ninth grade the week *Born to Run* was released and he was simultaneously on the covers of *Time* and *Newsweek*; I heard him first one September morning, when "Tenth Avenue Freeze Out" came on the radio as I was getting dressed for school. If nothing else, the hype left me suspicious; I never bought an official Springsteen record until *Nebraska*, although I did have a double album bootleg of his August 15, 1975, show at the Bottom Line.

Philadelphia, in the autumn of 1980, was Springsteen territory. *The River* appeared in October and a national tour was scheduled, with three December dates at the Spectrum, across the parking lot from JFK Stadium and the Vet. I had been there once, with a kid who lived on my hall; we saw the Kinks, a band I recognized as influential although their music didn't speak to me. Do I need to say I felt similarly toward Springsteen? When his Philadelphia shows were announced, a plan was hatched to camp out in the Spectrum parking lot for tickets; I went along for the ride. Ever since *The River* had come out, I'd heard it constantly, pouring (or so it seemed) out of every dormitory, every open window on every street. It was a flashpoint of saturation, as if the city, the region, were in the midst of a fever dream. Philadelphia was just across the Walt Whitman Bridge from New Jersey; half the people in my dorm had been raised there. Growing up in Manhattan, I'd never given it much thought. The Turnpike State, I derisively referred to it, mocking the refineries, their sulfur smell. More exciting was the Dead's fifteenth anniversary residency at Radio City Music Hall; I already had my ticket to one of the shows. To camp out, then, for Springsteen tickets was a voyeuristic exercise . . . or no, not quite: Something to do for the experience, a lark. I rolled a few joints and filled a flask, bundled up a sleeping bag and snacks. Tickets went on sale at nine o'clock in the morning. Our group arrived after dark. The sky above South Philly was gray, hooded, diffuse in the glare of the lights of the parking lot. There was already a line. "Rosalita (Come Out Tonight)," "Independence Day," "Growin' Up," and "Badlands" blared from boom boxes as we sat cross-legged, drinking, waiting for the dawn.

I'm trying now to recollect the faces: a tall kid named Patrick about whom I recall nothing except for the curls tight on his head like a fright wig; my hall-mate from the Kinks show, with his sneaky laugh and white Nikes with a red swoosh. I had hair down the middle of my back and wore a hooded Guatemalan pullover, although this did not keep me from shivering in the not-quite dark. Did we sleep? We must have slept, but I can't tell you, just that around sunrise a few of us went for breakfast while the rest held our place in line. If I squinted, I could almost imagine I was in the parking lot at a Dead show, sipping coffee and passing a joint with a ragtag group of fellow travelers . . . except that here I was the odd man out. For every Springsteen track I loved—"Thunder Road," "She's the One," the magnificent "Adam Raised a Cain" (then, as now, my favorite of all his songs, for its explication of the impossible dynamics of the father and the son)—there were others I couldn't bear ("Tenth Avenue Freeze Out" was a prime example). It wasn't that I didn't understand his importance. It wasn't that I didn't want to see him live. It's just that, left to my own devices, I almost never put his music on. This was both a matter of taste and something more defining. Let's put it this way: in the fall of 1980, it felt to me a necessary act of resistance, as if to do otherwise was to capitulate to the status quo.

Status quo? Bear with me for a moment. It's hard, at this distance, to describe how much rock and roll meant to me in 1980, the extent to which I saw it as a battlefield. The bands I loved, they were not merely preferences, they were allegiances, offering a measure of belonging, a territory in which to stand. They represented a series of extrapolations, signifiers of who I wanted to become. John Lennon, Jerry Garcia, and (yes) Patti Smith with her word-besotted riffs of poetry; it was their sort of authenticity I sought. At nineteen, I already knew I wanted to be a writer, but I also understood the old forms weren't, couldn't be, enough. I imagined myself as a poet (the short lines, the pace of breath) but I was looking for a different sort of lens. I had begun to write songs that year, to think about the album as a unit of measure, not unlike a collection of verse. I had begun to think about sonic space, the interplay of words and music, or of the words (their textures, their intonations) as a kind of music in their own regard. Lennon's primal screaming at the end of "Mother" or Joe Strummer's yips and yowls on "London Calling" and "Death or Glory"—they spoke to an oral expression beyond mere language, in which the body, the voice, the mouth might become its own instrument. There was a chaos just beneath the surface, the idea that, in cacophony, we might find a path, a way to coalesce to deeper meaning, elemental, existential, something bigger than ourselves.

That was what Springsteen represented also, although at the time it seemed like a lot of songs about cars and girls. Still, what about those other songs, like "Adam Raised a Cain"? "All of the old faces," Springsteen growls at the top of the second verse, voice cracking like a snapped guitar string, "ask you why you're back." The line resonated for me the first time I heard it; this was what I was being asked also, every time I ran into someone I used to know. I had gone off to the West Coast as if it were an act of disappearance. Here today, then gone and see you later. That had been the point. I was tired of my community, of everybody always knowing everything; I wanted to be off the radar, to create a radar of my own. After my return, I was greeted, more than once, with astonishment, as if I were violating expectations just by walking the streets of my old neighborhood again. Now, I was in a new place, at the other end of the turnpike, with no real sense of where I was. This vigil for tickets, then, it might be read as an attempt to stake out a space for myself. Wasn't that what rock and roll had always promised? "Rock 'n' roll music," Springsteen would later write in his memoir Born to Run, "in the end, is a source of religious and mystical power." A testament, in other words, a source of transcendence and of awe. That was why I was here, that was what I wanted. Experience, yes, the opportunity to do something I had never done . . . but at the same time, something more. I might not be a Springsteen fan, and yet could I deny we spoke the same vernacular? Like him, like everyone in this parking lot in Philadelphia, I was looking to be found.

II

What I was really looking for that fall, what I really wanted, was *Double Fantasy*, John Lennon and Yoko Ono's first album since 1975. Everything about it intrigued me, especially those five years off. Lennon, after all, had done what I aspired to; he had walked away. He had taken his fame and chucked it in favor of domesticity. In a way, it was the ultimate fuck you. Even at nineteen, I was drawn to the notion that one could build the revolution a single household, a single family, at a time. This had been the point, hadn't it, since *Two Virgins*, with its nude cover portraits of the couple, front and back, that had to be sold in a brown paper bag? I had never blamed Ono for splitting the Beatles. I identified, or thought I did, with Lennon's need to escape. It was like high school, maybe even (I would find out, I guessed) like college. Who wanted to get stuck on that treadmill? It would be like spending the rest of your life going to class. "One has to completely humiliate oneself," Lennon told *Rolling Stone*, "to be what the Beatles were, and that's what I resent. I mean I did it, I didn't know, I didn't foresee; it just happened, bit by bit, gradually, until this complete craziness is surrounding you and you're doing exactly what you don't want to do with people you can't stand, the people you hated when you were ten."

This was the opposite of why we came to rock and roll, the opposite of what the music claimed to mean. The lure of rock was its honesty, its directness, its sparseness, its accessibility. As Lou Reed put it: "One chord is fine. Two chords are pushing it. Three chords and you're into jazz." That Reed was full of shit was part of the point (it was always part of the point with him) since he had broader aspirations; just listen to *Street Hassle* if you don't think so. At the same time, he was telling the truth. Lennon, too—his catalogue balanced the stripped-down textures of "Cold Turkey" and "Working Class Hero" with the baroque orchestrations of "I Am the Walrus" and "A Day in the Life." Then he disappeared.

I first learned he was returning in the spring, when I saw a picture of him in the studio in *Rolling Stone*. He was holding a strange guitar, expandable, no real body to it, just a neck and an adjustable bridge. It was hard to imagine how one might play it, but that only whetted my fascination. Part of the effect of Lennon's retreat (for me, at any rate) had been to provoke a certain anticipation, as if his return might recapitulate the form. That this was already happening just added to the fantasy; 1980 was an astonishing year for rock and roll. Every day, it seemed, a new record changed the way I listened, how I thought about listening: Pete Townshend's *Empty Glass*, Talking Heads' *Remain in Light*, David Bowie's *Scary Monsters*, Grace Jones's *Warm Leatherette*, Captain Beefheart's *Doc at the Radar Station*, the English Beat's *I Just Can't Stop It*, Elvis Costello's *Get Happy!!*, X's *Los Angeles*, the Clash's *Sandinista!*, Dead Kennedys' *Fresh Fruit for Rotting Vegetables*, Stevie Wonder's *Hotter Than July*. Given the mix, it made sense that Lennon was coming back. He was the avatar, the ur-figure, the father of us all.

Does that sound naïve? Well, yes, I'll admit it: I was nineteen. Just the same, these many decades later, nearly four of them, I still miss Lennon—as well as the younger version of myself who revered him so. I've gone from believing in heroes to not believing in heroes, an inevitable shift, I suppose, but one that feels like a loss. "When I met Yoko," he once told author David Sheff, "is when you meet your first woman, and you leave the guys at the bar, and you don't go play football anymore. Once I found the woman, the boys became of no interest whatsoever, other than they were like old school friends." What he was offering was a template for growing up. Not in the sense that I'd been taught to think of it—"Now I just act like I don't remember / Mary acts like she don't care," Springsteen sings in "The River," adulthood as a vice or a sentence, a weight from which it was impossible to escape—but in the sense that adulthood, true adulthood, meant a kind of freedom, or at least responsibility. This is what I'd learned in Texas, where I'd worked to support myself. This is what I'd learned in San Francisco, where I'd seen that photo of Lennon and his guitar. Possibility, that was the lesson he was teaching—as was Springsteen in his fashion. That it was a double-edged sword went without saying; the possibility or responsibility we were after couldn't help but cut both ways. Standing on your own, or up for your-self, could be a dangerous business. "Bigger than Jesus," the breakup of the Beatles, the decision to become a househusband, even his murder at the hands of an obsessive fan—it was safer to stick with the herd. Len-non brought it back around in one of his last interviews, when he was asked about Springsteen and *The River* (he was, apparently, an admirer of "Hungry Heart"): "And God help Bruce Springsteen when they decide he's no longer God. . . . They'll turn on him, and I hope he survives it."

Double Fantasy wasn't what I was expecting, although this too, I've come to realize, was part of the point. What do our artists owe us? Noth-ing, it's all projection, audience imposing itself on performer, seeing our image reflected back at us (or not). Like more than one reviewer, I thought Ono's songs were stronger: "Kiss Kiss Kiss," "Every Man Has a Woman Who Loves Him," "Hard Times Are Over." Of the Lennon cuts, only two, "Watching the Wheels" and "I'm Losing You," resonated at the level of his best work. When I'd imagined this record, it had been ground-breaking, "some kind of occult . . . jazz thing," to borrow a phrase from Kevin Barry's novel *Beatlebone*, in which Lennon is portrayed as seek-ing purity through solitude, although in the end this leads to madness, the madness of the isolated soul. "He wants to break the line and he wants to sing his black fucking heart out and speak at last his own true mind," Barry writes, and if I could have articulated a wish for *Double Fantasy*, it would have been precisely that. What I got instead was a record con-taining very little of that troubling darkness, leading me to confront the blurry line between reality and desire. It's not that I disliked *Double Fan-tasy* (it would have been impossible for me to dislike it). Later, after Len-non's death, I listened obsessively for months. If I scrunched my ears, I could almost hear what was beneath the surface. All the same, I often skipped around the album, zeroing in on a handful of songs.

In the meantime, that Springsteen show was coming up on us like a state trooper in the rearview. It coincided with the end of the term. I had bought four tickets and sold two, which covered my costs; the pair I kept were for myself and my best friend, someone I'd known a bit in high school and with whom I'd reconnected here. We went with that gang of others, the ones with whom I'd camped out, names and faces evading me like a flickering parade of distant ghosts. Yes, ghosts, and even the venue is a ghost now, torn down and replaced by another just like it, although with better amenities. And rock and roll itself has become another ghost, although, of course, it was ever thus. "What cultural revolutionaries do not seem to grasp," Ellen Willis wrote in 1969, "is that, far from being a grass-roots art form that has been taken over by businessmen, rock itself comes from the commercial exploitation of blues. It is bourgeois at its core, a mass-produced commodity, dependent on advanced technology and therefore on the money controlled by those in power." Here we see the contradiction at the center of, well, everything. "You think it's funny," Strummer sings in "(White Man) In Hammersmith Palais," "turning rebellion into money." Both he and Willis were getting at rock and roll's most fundamental tension: the quixotic desire to make revolution (cultural or otherwise) one product at a time. Think of Lennon, writing "Working Class Hero" from the comfort of his estate in Tittenhurst Park. Think of me, a child of privilege, responding to its lyrics ("As soon as you're born, they make you feel small") as if they were observations from my life. Think of Springsteen, performing blue-collar anthems each night to eighteen thousand paying fans. "I'm just a lonely pilgrim / I walk this world in wealth," he would later sing—one of the few instances I can call to mind in which a rock and roller shot straight with his audience about these ambiguities, these paradoxes.

III

The show, I don't recall so much. In that sense, perhaps, it represents one more, one final, ghost—as each, as every, story has to be. What I can tell you is this: It was the tour when Springsteen began those marathon performances, three and a half hours, four, like a Dead concert on steroids, hot and sweaty as a revival. On this night, he played thirty-four songs, fourteen in the opening and sixteen in the second set, plus a four-song encore, including "Detroit Medley" and "Santa Claus Is Coming to Town." I remember "Santa Claus" because I knew he'd play it; it was December, after all. I remember the medley because I loved "Devil in a Blue Dress," the driving beat of it, like a human pulse. As for the rest, I'm relying on the internet, that great Sargasso Sea of the imagination, where no piece of information ever entirely disappears. There it is, the set list, complete with album-by-album breakdown: seventeen from *The River*, five each from *Darkness on the Edge of Town* and *Born to Run*. "Independence Day," "The Promised Land," "Out in the Street," "The Ties That Bind," "Thunder Road." That's the data, the hard evidence, although it's very different in my memory. As for the latter, snippets of songs ripple across my synapses in snapshot glimpses, like the tatters of a flannel shirt ensnared by barbed wire. Red checkered flannel, the shirt I recollect Springsteen wearing as he played (or maybe that was another, later concert). Bandanna at his neck, white V-neck tee, jeans and boots, dervish of movement and of energy. We were behind the stage, high enough to see over the backdrop and the stacks of amps. Once in a while, he would turn and perform for us, a verse, a chorus, a guitar solo. I was disappointed that he didn't play "Adam Raised a Cain."

At the break, the house lights raised, my best friend and I surveyed the arena. All those seats, those faces: revival show again, rock and roll as redemption, as spiritual rite. That was the vibe of the performance, call-and-response, audience singing so hard it was as if the gig belonged to them. He was giving voice—not to the voiceless although maybe, but at least to those who felt they had been overlooked. I was wary of this, even as I wanted to embrace it; the voiceless he represented were in part responsible for Reagan's election the month before. At the same time, this was something Springsteen was addressing. "I don't know what you guys think about what happened last night, but I think it's pretty frightening," he told an audience in Tempe, Arizona, the night after the presidential vote. He was seizing the platform, trying to use his visibility. Like Lennon with "Give Peace a Chance": "We're trying to sell peace, like a product, you know, and sell it like people sell soap or soft drinks," he told David Frost in 1969. "The only way to get people aware that peace is possible, and it isn't just inevitable to have violence, not just war—all forms of violence." Now, as Lennon had recognized, Springsteen *was* the Beatles, or, to use Lennon's own words as they appeared in his 1973 song "I'm the Greatest" on Ringo's eponymous solo album: "the greatest show on earth, for what it was worth."

As we waited for the second set, we discussed other shows, other concerts, those we'd seen, those we wanted to see. Lennon was top of the list. I had missed him at Madison Square Garden on Thanksgiving night

1974, when he'd joined Elton John for a three-song encore: "Whatever Gets You Through the Night," "Lucy in the Sky with Diamonds," "I Saw Her Standing There." I'd had access to a ticket, but I was thirteen and my mother had refused to let me go. Now, there was a tour in the works, and we fantasized what that might look like, the songs he might perform. A lot from the new record, that was certain, as well as "Imagine," "Mother," "Come Together"—the hits. But what about the deeper catalogue? "The Ballad of John & Yoko," "I'm a Loser," "You've Got to Hide Your Love Away," all those songs, their searing vulnerability. Not to mention Yoko: "Don't Worry, Kyoko," "Air Talk," the legendary "Cut Piece." This could be a show that offered all the weirdness, all the uncontrolled expression, I had thought I wanted from *Double Fantasy*. I kept considering this as the lights went down and Springsteen came back. It felt so close, as if I were sitting at the edge of a portal, as if I could almost pierce the veil. Down on that stage, one hundred feet away, that was where we would see him, that was where he would perform. "Right in this space," I said to my friend, and we both grinned in satisfaction, as if it had already happened, as if all we had to do was dream it (*and we all dream on*) to make it so. Then, the second set got under way: "Cadillac Ranch," "Sherry Darling," and that Lennon favorite "Hungry Heart."

By now, we all know where this is going, don't we? I've delayed long enough. It's as if in going back to the moment, stretching it, extending it, I can somehow avoid the inevitability of what happens. That, though, is the problem with the past, with history, that it is immutable, no longer a matter of possibility but rather its opposite. So here it is: Springsteen played for four hours. The show ended at eleven. We were exhausted but also exhilarated. Even I, who was still not quite a fan. In the parking lot, there was an edge, an air of crisis; people gathered in small clusters as if something had gone wrong. "John Lennon's been shot," a kid shouted near the entrance to the venue. We told him to shut up, that it wasn't funny. Then we got in the car and every radio station was playing the Beatles, and we knew.

The next evening, Springsteen closed with "Twist and Shout," which has since become a staple of his set. This was after a preshow argument with Steve Van Zandt over whether the band should play at all. "It's hard to come out here tonight," Springsteen said at the beginning of the concert. "'Twist and Shout' was the first song I ever learned the chords to.

But sometimes you just gotta go on." I love the fact that, of all the music Lennon ever performed, "Twist and Shout" should have been Springsteen's tribute. It was, after all, a song Lennon did not write. First recorded by the Top Notes in 1961, it was covered by the Isley Brothers in 1962 and the Beatles the following year. Famously, that version was laid down in a single take, live in the studio, the last track cut during the all-day session for their debut album *Please Please Me*. "Twist and Shout" is a rave-up, two and a half minutes of propulsive R&B. Four chords—D, A, G, A7—all of them open. No wonder it was Springsteen's first song. Easy to play, if not to master, the essence of rock and roll in a single progression, and those lyrics, full of adolescent innuendo and lust. "Shake it up, baby / twist and shout / c'mon, c'mon, c'mon, c'mon baby / c'mon and work it on out." Even for an overthinker such as I was, it was impossible not to shake your ass and dance. This was the genius of it, both the song and Springsteen's decision to play it, the shared vernacular of the music once again. Everyone knew it, not just the feeling but the riffs, the words, the patterns. Everyone had heard it a million times. The only cover recorded by the Beatles to be a top ten hit, it caught, or evoked, the contradictions perfectly: transcendent and commercial at once. Like church, like a revival, like a Bible verse in a previous century: the fact that it was so familiar meant everyone could participate. The grief, the joy, it was all tumbled together, and Springsteen—Springsteen singing as both fan and star. What goes around comes around, all those overlapping generations and personas. I heard "Twist and Shout" on the radio the other day, and it still sounds like a hymn.

I wasn't at the Spectrum that night; I'd only gotten tickets to the one show. Instead, I was in my room, listening to *Double Fantasy*. Yes, and *Plastic Ono Band*, *Imagine*, *Walls and Bridges*, *Abbey Road*, *Revolver*, *Rubber Soul*. I was writing poems and songs. I was stunned and shocked and desperate for connection. Like Springsteen, like everyone in that arena in Philadelphia, I was looking to be found.

Works Cited

Brown, Bill. *Words and Guitar: A History of Lou Reed's Music*. Brooklyn, N.Y.: Colossal Books, 2013.

Cott, Jonathan. "John Lennon: The Last Interview." *Rolling Stone*, December 5, 1980.

Lennon, John, and Yoko Ono. *David Frost Show*, June 14, 1969. Transcript. www
    .beatlesbible.com/1969/06/14/television-john-lennon-yoko-ono-david-frost
    -show/.
Sheff, David. *All We Are Saying: The Last Major Interview with John Lennon and Yoko
    Ono*. New York: St. Martin's Griffin, 2000.
Willis, Ellen. *Out of the Vinyl Deeps: Ellen Willis on Rock Music*. Minneapolis: Uni-
    versity of Minnesota Press, 2011.

Part IV

Springsteen the Artist

Springsteen on Broadway. Springsteen's critically acclaimed show at the Walter Kerr Theatre in New York ran from October 12, 2017, to December 15, 2018, and consisted of 236 shows. It made a mint—$113,058,952 at the box office, according to *Broadway World*—but it was more than just a box office sensation. It was a poetic, spiritual, and, ultimately, transcendent show about family, death, love, self-identity, and the quotidian details of everyday life. Michael Hainey in *Esquire* called it an "epic dramatic monologue" while Springsteen himself described it in Whitmanesque terms: "It's me reciting 'Song of Myself.'" (June Sawyers)

13

Brilliant Disguise

✦

The Completely True Fictional Adventures of Bruce Springsteen

PETER AMES CARLIN

The first story I wrote about Bruce Springsteen was a short work of fiction I composed one cloudy Saturday in the fall of 1987. I lived in Portland, Oregon, as I do now, but the city and I have come a long way since those days of Spuds MacKenzie, perestroika, and the twin Dons of the apocalypse, Johnson and Henley. Back then I was only a few months into a shaky career as a freelance writer. And Portland, still a quarter century away from being the world capital of artisanal, farm-to-table quirk, was the hometown of Bruce Springsteen's wife.

The wife in question was Julianne Phillips, the actress Springsteen romanced at the very apex of the *Born in the U.S.A.* delirium in the mid-1980s. The couple's 1985 wedding incited a media riot in the bride's suburban neighborhood, but the hysteria faded as quickly as wedding day roses and after that the couple's visits played out quietly. But every so often you'd hear something. One Friday night Springsteen was espied shooting pool in a tavern on Macadam Boulevard. A couple of months later he was picking up a few pizzas at Angelo and Rose's on Barbur Boulevard and on a gloomy winter night he gassed up a rented Corvette near the west end of the Ross Island Bridge, grabbed a case of Budweiser inside, and paid with a hundred-dollar bill before zooming back into the soggy Portland night.

I never glimpsed Springsteen on the hoof, but when *Tunnel of Love* came out in 1987, the collection of songs about love, commitment, and the artist's overwhelming fear of the same hit me hard. I was in my mid-twenties. My friends were choosing mates and settling into apartments with sofas, nonstick pans, and an air of beginners' contentment while I continued reeling from one zipless calamity to the next. I knew something had to change, but I couldn't find a way out of my dismaying pattern until I got the hang of *Tunnel of Love.*

I usually don't seek personal advice from rock stars I've never met, but Springsteen's songs seemed to identify my desperation and catalyze a change. Electrified with feeling but unsure what to do next, I did the only thing I could: I tried to write something. A short story, I figured. Dropping the needle on "Ain't Got You," the opening song on *Tunnel of Love*'s first side, I thought about Springsteen's manifestations on my side of Portland and found an opening sentence: *I kept bumping into Bruce.*

From there I fell into a story about a Portland-based college graduate of my approximate height, weight, and hairstyle whose romantic crises propel him into several chance meetings with the rock-and-roll hero. Each time, Springsteen comes off as a thoroughly regular guy, but also just a little larger than life. When the narrator first encounters Springsteen at a Baskin-Robbins ice cream parlor in Lake Oswego, Springsteen recognizes the John Cheever story collection the guy is carrying and speaks authoritatively on "The Swimmer" and the surrealistic warp of the tale's suburban narrative. Months pass before our narrator meets Springsteen again. This time he's running on the Tryon Park trail in southwest Portland when Springsteen bolts up from behind, remembers him on sight, and chats effortlessly as the younger man all but ruptures a lung trying to match the rock star's blistering pace. When they arrive at a parking lot near Lake Oswego, Springsteen throws open the door of his mud-flecked Jeep Cherokee and offers to give the lad a ride back to his now-distant home.

A climactic fight with his girlfriend the next summer sends the narrator on a midnight journey over the mountains to the peak of Smith Rock, a rock-climbing mecca in central Oregon's high desert. His early morning ruminations are interrupted by Springsteen hoisting himself to the summit, the end of a solo sunrise ascent of the mesa's thousand-foot Morning Glory face. "Oh hey man," Bruce says, slapping the climbing chalk off his palms. By the end of the story, the young man and Springsteen are drinking beers on the hood of the musician's Jeep, talking about the quandaries of love and listening to Springsteen's home demo of a new song set on the northeastern edge of Oregon's Multnomah County, where Interstate 84 rolls alongside the Columbia River and where, as my imagined Springsteen sings, "That cold river rain washes your face / and the winds out of the Gorge blow your hair outta place."

I hoped the story would read as a gentle satire of the rock star's heroic reputation, but it turned out to be an unexpectedly accurate depiction of the real *Born in the U.S.A.*–era Bruce Springsteen. Long admired for his literate, deeply felt songs and for his wildly passionate concerts, his persona had expanded, along with his Captain America physique, to take in a working-class political consciousness and a rigorously egalitarian approach to stardom. When he wasn't blasting through another three-hour rock-and-roll blowout, Springsteen was speaking out for America's poor and for Vietnam veterans and against the corporate forces squeezing the life out of workers all over the world. And when he wasn't doing that he was folding his own underpants in hotel launderettes, helping stranded motorists change flat tires, and, for all we knew, working with the world's top astrophysicists to create swift and affordable interstellar transport from Earth to Mars and points beyond.

Or maybe he was just writing and recording a new batch of electrifying songs about the dark hearts of men, the morally conflicted nation, and ordinary folks' quest for a sweeter, more secure life for themselves and their children. Whatever he was up to, Springsteen seemed to do it with a focus, what my therapist would call an *intentionality*, that sprang from America's dreamiest dreams about itself. And if you didn't figure that out for yourself he'd put it out there at the end of his shows, the working man's Galahad lofting a sweat-stained Telecaster and the five words that distilled the essence of every word he had sung during the long evening: "Nobody wins unless everybody wins."

Compared to this, my Cheever-analyzing, six-minute-miling, solo-rock-climbing Springsteen barely measured up. How could he? The real Springsteen is the guy who invented his own heroic persona and then proceeded to animate it with real hurt, love, and yearning. But there's still a distinction between the majestic Springsteen we see on the stage and the all too human guy Bruce sees in his bathroom mirror every morning. And when it comes to the precise location of that line . . . well, even Springsteen doesn't seem to know for sure. "I come from a board-walk town where everything is tinged with a bit of fraud," he declared at the start of the one-man show he took to Broadway in 2017. He completed the thought through a confidence man's crooked grin: "So am I."

But that assertion is also a bit of a fraud, and not just because Springsteen actually comes from the landlocked village of Freehold, a good twenty miles west of Asbury Park or any other boardwalk town. And what does that matter when you compare it to the emotional authenticity at the heart of the man's best work? This is the essential paradox of Bruce Springsteen, art in general, and the transcendent flim-flam on offer at the little boardwalk house where Madam Marie can see your future written in the wrinkles of your palm. The imagination has its own story to tell. And sometimes it grasps truths that the facts could never touch.

Most of the world's introduction to the Bruce Springsteen legend came through the writing of Dave Marsh, the music journalist whose strik-ing 1978 *Rolling Stone* profile of the musician was a forerunner to the 1979 biography he titled *Born to Run*. I was in high school back then, a ner-vous teenager on the hunt for something, anything with a ring of truth. And Marsh's version of Springsteen was a veritable bell factory of ethi-cal, artistic, and moral authenticity.

Born into a struggling working-class family, Marsh's Bruce Spring-steen spends his childhood years in a series of houses that often lack essentials such as central heating and hot running water. While his mother supports the family with a full-time job as a legal secretary, Springsteen's father is constantly losing work due to the vicissitudes of a struggling economy and the triumph of corporate greed over tradi-tional notions of social responsibility.

Douglas Springsteen's professional frustration, compounded by the generational divide of the 1960s, makes him a stranger to his son, and a hostile one at that. Sometimes they fight about Bruce's clothes, some-times about the length of his hair, but always about the boy's disinterest in school and work and his all-consuming focus on his goddamned guitar. Theirs is a classic father-son struggle; the elder determined to instill discipline, the younger desperate for independence. The crucible of their conflict is the Springsteen's unlighted kitchen, where Douglas lurks during the evenings, filling the blackness with the vapors from his endless cigarettes and the beers he guzzles by the six-pack.

"He'd be tellin' me and tellin' me," Springsteen recalled in the dramatic recitations that identified the ghosts spinning him around the stage a decade later. "And I could always hear that voice. But I could never, ever see his face."

Rejected by his father, feeling cast away by his schoolmates, Springsteen puts every ounce of himself into rock and roll. He works incredibly hard, he encounters his musical soulmates. He struggles against a diabolical world and its cruel fates, but Springsteen holds tight to his hope and achieves success that eventually rockets him beyond his most fanciful dreams.

But it's what happens next that really matters. For the more successful he gets the more determined Springsteen becomes to personify the music he credits with saving his life. He suffers over the tiniest details of his recordings, as if human lives could be won or lost over the sonic depth of the kick drum. He plays marathon concerts that begin with hours-long sound checks to make certain that the music hits the most distant seats with the same clarity delivered to the lucky fans in the front row. He hurls himself into his performances aiming not just to entertain but also transform his fans by creating a small piece of the world where promises are kept, faith is rewarded, and spiritual transcendence can happen right here and right now.

Marsh, another working-class kid whose passion for rock and roll came out of his own emotionally impoverished childhood, recognized the truth when he heard it, and his first Springsteen biography is a masterpiece of advocacy journalism; you can measure the extent of his belief in his subject in the heat of his writing and in the breathtaking photographs that fill the original edition of the book. Many of the pictures are performance shots, frozen images of Springsteen in mid-strut, his fists thrust into the spotlight beam, his guitar hoisted over his head, and, in the most astonishing of them all, standing at a forty-five degree angle on the edge of the stage, his arms outstretched and his back to the crowd whose hands bear him up as if in resurrection.

Like every saint worth his halo, the Springsteen of Marsh's *Born to Run* can't bear the idea that he is anything more than an ordinary hard-working guy. Confronted by his own face on an immense Sunset Boulevard billboard the night before an arena show in Los Angeles, the rocker gathers some cans of spray paint, a few bandmates, and other friends and conducts a midnight raid on the offending advertisement, spraying the song title-cum-statement of purpose PROVE IT ALL NIGHT in five-foot letters with the signature E STREET added for good measure. Springsteen tells the story onstage the next night, receiving thunderous cheers, and later exults privately to Marsh: "I figured if they caught us that'd be great. And if we got away with it, even better."

Indeed, there is more than a trace of P. T. Barnum woven into the Springsteen mystique. Some of his best stories about the gloom and glories in his past contain generous exaggerations. A few others are what you might call total bullshit. But even the made-up stuff evokes deeper truths, and it also doesn't hurt that Springsteen is extremely good at what he does. For the first twenty years of his recording career it's like he can't put a foot wrong, moving effortlessly from the street-Dylan poetics on *Greetings from Asbury Park, N.J.* and the funky bard of the boardwalk on *The Wild, the Innocent & the E Street Shuffle* to the self-aware Elvis of *Born to Run* to the sadder-but-wiser voice of experience on *Darkness on the Edge of Town* and beyond with astonishing confidence and verve. In concert he sprints across the stage, leaps across the piano lid to the tippy-top of the amplifier stacks for three-plus hours each night, draining his emotional and physical batteries to the point where he can only drape himself over his microphone and howl that the power of the music has taken him over. "I am just," he screams, "A PRISONER OF ROCK AND ROLL!"

To have witnessed the three or four hours leading to that moment, with sweat coursing down your own back and a throat shredded from singing along, is to know, beyond a doubt, that he's telling the stone-cold truth.

As Marsh's first biography concludes just past the end of the *Darkness on the Edge of Town* tour in early 1979, the hero is on the ascent, but still not made in the shade. He can fill basketball arenas in some cities but plays to half-empty theaters in others. But, as Springsteen declares in the onstage shaggy dog tale that makes up the book's final paragraphs, he is certain that God is on his side. He knows this because the deity tells him so in a deep, dark New Jersey forest where Bruce and his sax-playing onstage foil and protector Clarence Clemons, aka the Big Man, go to find the secret of life. You see, God explains, Moses forgot to pass along His eleventh and most important Commandment. And what does it say? By this point thousands of ecstatic fans are poised to say it with him. Hands raised, faces aglow they scream at the top of their lungs.

"LET IT ROCK!"

If Marsh were a novelist that'd be a great place for his story to end. The working man's rock star figures out the journey is its own reward, finds himself a local girl, and settles down to raise his family and do his work among friends, family, and an audience that knows his joys and struggles as well as he knows theirs. But that's not where it ends. Not even close. And that's why *Glory Days*, Marsh's next Springsteen biography published just eight years after his first, stretches twice as long as the one that described Springsteen's first twenty-nine years on the planet.

Everything was a movie in those days. The white-hatted cowboy galloping to the White House across purple mountains, fruitful plains, and brave little frontier towns. The city on the hill. A nation full of picket fences, freshly cut grass, full houses, and cheerful, well-fed families. A dream of America as envisioned by Hollywood, from the Screen Actors Guild member in the Oval Office to the Soviet-free, USA! USA! USA!-dominated Los Angeles Olympics in 1984. But the real country, with its unemployed parents, hungry children, and damaged Vietnam veterans deserved its own hero. And Springsteen was waiting, newly expanded muscles throbbing, a guitar over his back, and hard truths pumping through his veins.

As the success of 1980's *The River* spread Springsteen's music across the planet, he leveraged his growing fame into a tool for social justice. After a brief side trip through the existential badlands of *Nebraska* in 1982 Springsteen returned in 1984 with *Born in the U.S.A.*, a record that was both the poppiest and most politically subversive album he'd ever made. The record launched half a dozen hit singles and nearly as many MTV-dominating videos. Now clean-cut enough to be the pride of Anytown, U.S.A., Springsteen became irresistible fodder for fan magazines and tabloid newspapers. Catapulted into the highest reaches of international celebrity, he was adored beyond measure and beyond reason, and when he fell from celebrity grace after a few years his eyes fairly glowed with relief. Half a decade of superstardom had left him, in his own words, feeling extremely Broooced-out. He got everything he ever dreamed of, and a whole lot more, but it had done nothing to shoo those tobacco-and-beer-reeking ghosts out of his head. His marriage to the actress Julianne Phillips ended quickly and scandalously. Settled at last with his background singer Patti Scialfa, Springsteen not only broke up his venerated E Street Band but also abandoned New Jersey for Los Angeles's celebrity-pocked Hollywood Hills, where he and the new Mrs. Springsteen made and raised their kids. He spent a few years in the creative wilderness, and eventually this began to bug him.

He missed his heroic self, and a significant percentage of the other people around the world felt the same way. He was closing in on fifty and what was he waiting for? As the twentieth century neared its end he called up those old E Street soulmates—actually he had his accountant do the calling with a low-ball offer they forced him to revise in short order—and concluded each night of Bruce Springsteen and the E Street Band's triumphant two-year comeback tour by declaring the "rebirth and rededication" of his band with a new song called "Land of Hope and Dreams": "Well, I will provide for you, and I'll stand by your side / you'll need a good companion now, for this part of the ride."

He meant it. The day the country was traumatized by the terror attacks of September 11, 2001, Springsteen heard a lone voice cry across a Jersey Shore parking lot: "We need you!" It was a call he had to heed. When the television industry broadcast an enormous telethon to soothe the nation's grief and raise money for the victims of the attack, the first face to appear on the candlelit stage was that of Bruce Springsteen, guitar-slung and harmonica-hung, singing a new song that described the wreckage of a shattered community and then exhorted the citizens to summon the strength to rise up, c'mon rise up.

That performance changed things. When Springsteen returned a year later with *The Rising*, his first E Street Band record since *Born in the U.S.A.*, the album hit the ground with the Richter-shaking kaboom of a new national monument, as if Springsteen, now in his fifties and flashing a little silver at his temples, had become the rocker laureate of the

United States; the official interpreter of the rank and file's values and visions in the twenty-first century.

All but etched in marble, Springsteen's older face gained a Rushmorean gravitas. His endorsement of Barack Obama during the presidential primaries in 2008 was, according to Obama's top advisor David Axelrod, the boost that helped Illinois's junior senator win the hotly contested race with Hillary Clinton for the Democratic nomination. After Obama won the White House that fall, Springsteen performed at his inauguration and became a regular guest of the president, whose visible excitement in the musician's company made it clear that he knew that when the Boss paid a visit, the leader of the free world had to settle for being the second coolest person in the Oval Office. Springsteen was honored at the Kennedy Center and awarded a Presidential Medal of Freedom. And when Hurricane Sandy devastated the Jersey Shore he choppered in with the president to examine the damage and do his part to launch the healing by submitting to a tearful bro-hug from the unrequited Bruce-lover governor Chris Christie, whose piggish sensibilities and bullying tactics had made him anathema to the trampled working class's most visible advocate.

Somehow all of these institutional laurels did nothing to compromise Springsteen's rock-and-roll credibility. On the contrary, Springsteen's appearance at the 2012 South by Southwest alt-culture festival earned him a new chorus of admirers among the indie music scene's most influential figures, many of them less than half his age. He continued to play three- and four-hour shows to stadia jammed with howling, reverent fans. No longer a prisoner of rock and roll, Springsteen became the form's very embodiment. A one-man animation of Apollo and Dionysus whose every roar is both an expression of his dark soul and a rigorously considered presentation of what he knows his fans crave the most: a fragment of the true cross, a spark from the burning bush, a drop of sweat from the brow of Elvis the King.

And he couldn't be happier when he's doing it. But when the show's over he still can't help feeling a little dubious about the whole enterprise. The first time I spoke to Springsteen for the biography I was writing in 2011, one of the first things he said was this: "When people talk about me like I'm perfect I feel diminished." On the telephone during the editing process he said something else: "If you've found out anything about me that you're not using because you think it might embarrass me or make me look bad? Put it in." The time for Bruce Springsteen fan fiction, even the kind he created for himself, was over.

Or was it? Can he ever really let it go? Would the rest of the world ever stand for it? Think again about the guy shouting from the car across the parking lot after 9/11: "We need you!" And we do. Just like Bruce needs to be the Boss.

When we finished the first of those conversations, Springsteen led the way to the parking lot of the bar we were in and unlocked the doors to the car he'd been driving. Usually Springsteen drives a Range Rover but on this day he had come in another car. Remember the Jeep Cherokee my imaginary Bruce drove in "Multnomah County Line" back in 1987? Twenty-four years later the real Bruce had come to pick me up in exactly that model and make of vehicle. *What*, I wondered, *the fuck?* I've been a journalist for my entire adult life. I'm as skeptical as they come. I'm also remarkably self-involved, which is more a Peter thing than a journalism thing, but may still be relevant here. Was it a coincidence? Had he some-how seen the story? Was this some kind of Bruce-the-trickster head-fuck? "So, uh, did you ever read . . ." I asked, and he didn't even look up from the highway. "I don't go on the Internet." Which wasn't the ques-tion I'd asked, but I was already too embarrassed to press the issue.

If you forked over the unfathomable amount of American currency it cost to attend the *Springsteen on Broadway* show and found your seat in the Walter Kerr Theatre on West Forty-Eighth Street, you might have passed a few minutes looking at the stage noticed just how raw the set design was. That's because it was created to have almost no design at all: just a microphone, a stool, a glass of water, a grand piano, a scattering of packing cases, the theater's brick rear wall, and that's it. At these prices, you might have thought, they could have thrown in a curtain or even a mirror ball, maybe one for each customer. But it was all a visual meta-phor, one that reminded us that every Bruce Springsteen concert, from the grotty little Student Prince club in Asbury Park to the huge stadium shows, has depended less on noise, lights, and fireworks than on the mind and music of this one guy. And tonight you'd see him as he really is, in the raw, bloody place behind his legend.

The house lights went down and Springsteen stepped onstage dressed in his now customary black jeans, black T-shirt, and work boots. He came with a black acoustic guitar over his shoulder, the central tool of his trade, and when the bovine chorus of Brooooooce-ing died down he got down to it right away, calling himself a fraud, saying that his life's work is really just a magic trick. He ridiculed himself for writing all those songs about cars and the freedom of the highway without knowing anything about automobiles and engines beyond how to put the key into the ignition and shift the thing into gear. The great advocate for Vietnam veterans dodged the draft without a thought about the less-canny teenager who had to go in his place. And you know what else? The spokesman for the American working class has never worked an honest job in his life.

This Boss thing, he said, is all an act. But then he'd stop talking and sing "Growin' Up," "Thunder Road," and the most furious version of "Born in the U.S.A." you'd ever heard, forcing you to understand that there's nothing phony about any of it. It all overflows with the anguish, anger, and back-to-the-wall desperation that is the stuff of life for everyone from the Boss to the ordinary folks who, as he has said, may not change the world but keep it spinning from day to day.

The Bruce Springsteen we call the Boss, the one we moo at—Brooooooce—like a herd of hay-deprived Guernsey cows, is actually a three-way creation. For rock critics he's the Elvis who followed that dream from adolescent hip shaking to intellectually engaged consciousness quaking. For fans he's a natural-born rock star, a moral beacon and avatar for their own better selves. And for Bruce this larger version of himself—the home run king, the heavyweight champion of the world, the Boss of them all—is even more crucial than that.

They never really got into a fistfight. Those stories of generational warfare between Springsteen father and son were a fiction meant to explain a conflict that was rooted in the old man's mental illness: in the dark spirits that tormented Douglas Springsteen throughout his life and made it nearly impossible for him to meet his son's gaze, let alone say that he loved him. "It wasn't what was said," Bruce growled at me one gloomy winter afternoon a few years ago. "It was what *wasn't* said." So Bruce thrust himself into the spotlight, sang his songs, and did the talking for both of them. What Bruce was trying to say to his father didn't become clear until he wrote about it in his *Born to Run* autobiography and repeated it in the *Springsteen on Broadway* show. And it is, for my money, the Rosetta Stone of Springsteen's deepest emotional, artistic, and professional impulses.

Just after Douglas died in 1998, Bruce had a dream where he and his father were sitting together in a packed arena watching Bruce-the-Boss Springsteen soar across the stage, in complete control as he bends twenty thousand fans to his vision and his will. After a time, his father leaned over to shout in Bruce's ear: "How do you *do* that?" Bruce shouted right back: "Don't you understand? That's who I think *you* are."

The Boss is the chosen one. The golem. The mammoth creature built from ordinary clay and the extraordinary hopes and fears of his community. He runs roughshod. He saves the day. He is the last bulwark between our fragile lives and the brutal world beyond the doorstep. "We need you!," the guy shouted through the smoke and ash of 9/11. Imagining the father he wished for but never quite had, Bruce cranked up his guitar and came galloping to the rescue.

A decade ago, my friend Ryan had an extraordinary run-in with Springsteen. It was the spring of 2008 and the *Magic* tour swung into the northwest for three shows, the first in Portland, the second in Seattle, and, after a night off, a concluding show in Vancouver, British Columbia. Ryan, along with two of his more feckless friends, made a road trip out of it, driving to Seattle after the Portland show, then motoring across the Canadian border to catch the third show. Springsteen's tour took a breather while the Foo Fighters played the Vancouver arena on the showless evening, and since one of Ryan's buddies is a pal of the Foo's drummer, Taylor Hawkins, they all got backstage passes to see what turned out to be the final show in the group's national tour. Heading to the side of the stage to watch Against Me!'s opening set, Ryan saw a couple of guys standing nearby having a chat. One of them was Bruce Springsteen.

A lifelong fan, Ryan waited until their conversation was over and then stepped over to say hi. Of course Bruce was happy to shake his hand. They spoke for a moment until Springsteen excused himself, saying he'd be right back. At that point Ryan figured that was it. He'd had his moment with Springsteen and it was swell. After all, it was the man's night off, he deserved a little time away from lunatic fans. Ryan turned back to the stage, but a moment later someone tapped him on the shoulder. Bruce had come right back. "What's goin' on, man?" he asked. So Ryan told him about the road trip, and how much he and his pals had enjoyed the shows, and how much they were looking forward to the next night. Springsteen beamed. "That's cool, man! Tell your buddies I said hi!"

The show was followed by a big end-of-tour party in the Foo Fighters' backstage lounge, and when it got deep into the wee hours and the party was winding down, Ryan stepped into the loading dock area to wait for his friends. And it was there that Springsteen, heading for the door, saw him and beelined in his direction. Did he have any requests for the Vancouver show, Bruce asked. Scrambled by the unexpected opportunity, Ryan could only summon one song title to his tongue: "None But the Brave," one of the lesser known outtakes from the *Born in the U.S.A.* sessions. Springsteen raised a brow. "*Ooh*," he said. "Tough one. Let me see what I can do."

The next night Ryan was with everyone else in the arena, taking in still another ecstatic concert by Bruce Springsteen and the E Street Band, when the star stepped to the microphone to set up the next song. "I met this fellah last night," he began. Then Springsteen told the whole story from his perspective, how he'd recognized Ryan from the Portland and Seattle shows, how he'd made the mistake of asking if he had a request, and how his new friend had come out with the name of an outtake so obscure he had never even tried to play it onstage. Springsteen continued, "But tonight we're gonna play it for him." He signaled the band and right there in Vancouver's General Motors Place arena the Boss made another fan's dream come true. And in so doing, he made everyone else's dream—the moment Elvis pushes through the blue TV screen and grabs your hand, the moment our impassive God speaks up to answer your prayer—come true, too.

I tell that story from time to time and am no longer surprised if the person I'm talking to ends up wiping away a tear. It really does capture something crucial in Springsteen's public essence. His open-hearted generosity, his way of showing, as he declared in "Land of Hope and Dreams," that prayers can be answered, that faith always wins, and not just in some pie-in-the-sky afterlife. Right here and right now. It felt like a huge deal; so huge in my eyes that it convinced me to invest the next three years of my life trying to write a book about Springsteen.

When I got a chance, I asked Springsteen about how he came to premiere "None But the Brave" in Vancouver in 2008. Did he remember talking to Ryan the night before the show? Why did he decide to take up the challenge and play a song he hadn't even liked enough to finish recording? He squinched up his brow. "I don't remember that," he said. "I mean, I do that every night. It's my job." He shrugged. "I make miracles happen."

Just like he'd done for the lost kid in my old "Multnomah County Line" story and just like he does every time he detonates another massive crowd of fans. It's his art, his magic act, his reason for living. The truth is a myth, but the myth is real. So real, he didn't even notice it anymore. Or so he'd said. But at the end of our last face-to-face interview for the book, Springsteen took one last pull on his Budweiser and changed the subject. Months had passed since he'd said he had no memory of Ryan and the "None But the Brave" incident in Vancouver. Now Bruce had another story to tell. "Remember how I said I didn't remember it? Well, I did remember that. I never forgot it."

He said it haltingly, eyes examining the empty pizza pan between us. Looking up after a moment he made another little shrug, a resigned kind of *whaddayagonnado*. Sometimes he forgets where one Bruce stops and where the other begins. It's all him, though. It's always been him.

I bumped into Bruce. He takes his tequila chilled and his Budweiser in the bottle. His clothes are a lot more expensive than they look. He swears *Moby-Dick* is a page-turner once you get into it. He's a hugger. He has a hitch in his gait and a nasty temper when he gets frustrated. He's great in a crisis and can be less than that on an ordinary day. He keeps his promises. He's okay with who he is. Most of the time. He's a nice guy. Most of the time. He wakes up each morning and spends the rest of the day doing the best he can.

Works Cited

Carlin, Peter Ames. *Bruce*. New York: Touchstone/Simon & Schuster, 2012.
Marsh, Dave. *Born to Run: The Bruce Springsteen Story*. Garden City, N.Y.: Doubleday, 1979.
Springsteen, Bruce. *Born to Run*, New York: Simon & Schuster 2016.

14

"The Welsh Springsteen"

✧

An Interview with Martyn Joseph
(by Irwin H. Streight)

A local promoter of folk music acts had put up posters around town advertising Martyn Joseph as "the Welsh Springsteen." Literary scholar Irwin H. Streight was curious to learn about Joseph's connection to Springsteen and arranged a backstage interview with him before his concert at the Octave Theatre in Kingston, Ontario, on April 16, 2016. The interview has been edited for this collection.

IRWIN STREIGHT: Why Springsteen?

MARTYN JOSEPH: When I give talks about songwriting, one of the things I say to people is "Try not to add to the noise out there." By that I mean that the basic pop song tends to lie to you. It fabricates a world that is not reality for most of us. Now it's important to have music that allows us to escape ourselves for a while, but people are hungry too. They're hungry for songs that deliver the truth, as much as it can be known, with passion and with integrity. For me, no one does that better than Bruce. He has the rare ability to bring about special moments through music when time and space, our struggles, our small victories, love and losses, and all that we know is transcended and the promise of possibility is present. You are made to feel like you are not alone in the world. For me that's the job of a great song. Springsteen can do that in a stadium as well as a small hall, and the experience is both personal and communal at the same time.

I also want to add that for me there is a spirituality to it as well. There are tremendous guitar players in the world, there are wonderful singers, amazing writers and artists that can do something very well. But I feel there is also something of a liturgical draw to Springsteen's work. For me that can't be defined, nor should it be, but my heart and soul are greatly moved by what he does and reminded of what's important in the world. And because of this, in the storm of life and all its beautiful contradictions, his songs shed a little light and we're able to make more sense of it all and find courage and strength to keep going—which is exactly what I try to do night after night in my 160 shows a year, albeit on a much, much smaller scale.

IS: How has Springsteen influenced you as a performer?

MJ: Bruce is a kind of elder to me and I'm sure to many of us. I try to emulate his stage ethos, whether I'm performing at a festival in front of thousands, or six hundred, or whatever it might be. Now it's usually just me and a bunch of guitars, but I want to bring that same commitment night after night. Even if it's twenty people in someone's front room, I still try to play like it's the last time I'll ever get the chance. Because I've never lost sight of the blessing that someone has bought tickets, stuck them on their fridge door, got a babysitter, and decided they would give me at least one night of their life. The responsibility of that weighs on me in a good way. So I want to make sure that they have a great time, make a deep connection. I want to draw alongside them, encourage and stand there with them in whatever space they currently find themselves in. I want the songs to meet them and say, "Come on, keep going." Sure some of it is driven by your own ego. And, yes, I'm still the little boy trying to prove himself to everyone. But when you see that commitment to something from someone it can be very affirming and occasionally life changing. Having listened to and observed Bruce for a big chunk of my life I have no doubt that's where a lot of that comes from. Also, you know, if I'm tired of the road, and perhaps feeling a little jaded about going out there one evening, well, I can take my headphones and lose myself in a few of those moments he has created, and, man, I'm good to go!

IS: You often include a Springsteen song in your live shows and have recorded an album of Bruce's songs. Are you giving back to Springsteen in some way by performing and recording versions of his songs?

MJ: I have absolutely no idea if I am giving anything back, and he certainly has no need for it, so I doubt it. I think I'm just saying "thank you." The idea behind the album [2013's *Tires Rushing By in the Rain*] wasn't mine. Through the years I have occasionally included a song of his amongst my own and people said, "I'd love to hear a recording of you playing that." And I would smile politely but not really entertain the idea of covering his songs on record. But after a while you realize there's a little more going on here than someone just wanting to have a copy of myself playing "If I Should Fall Behind." And I had this interaction with Dave Marsh who said that the covers were "respected" within "certain circles" (*laughs*). So I gave it a go.

IS: Why is it that we can listen to some artists and say that they are *covering* a song, and other artists we say are *interpreting*? Are you not interpreting Bruce?

MJ: I think I am in a sense. The interesting thing is I've had a lot of people come up to me and say, "I've been a Bruce fan all my life, but I never quite realized what that song meant until I heard your version." Now, I don't really want Bruce to hear that, and I don't think I want to hear it either because, well, that's almost blasphemous! But those are some of the comments I've had. So, whether I pronounce his lyrics a little clearer or something (*laughs*) or I'm giving them my version of what the song means to me and they get *that*—and Bruce meant something else—I don't know. When I occasionally break down "One Step Up" onstage to go a little deeper into the song, well, that gets a huge reaction, but I have no idea if that was what Bruce was thinking when he wrote it. I am trying to point out that this is more than just a bar love song. If you think it is just a nice little moving country song about a guy in a bar whose marriage has broken up, then, no, I think you're wrong: there is so much more going on. I think the song sums up the human condition. But Bruce might laugh at that suggestion. I have no idea. So, I guess in some ways I am interpreting. I'm putting my spin on the song, whatever it might be. I feel him so much when I observe Bruce's writing and performance. I would like to think that much of the truth of those songs is there in my versions of them. I was a little worried about putting that album out. I sent the recordings to Dave Marsh to ask what he thought. He said, "This is great!" and he ended up writing the sleeve notes for the record for which I was very grateful. In them Dave wrote kindly about me trying not to live up to the songs themselves but trying to use them to tell folks something about myself. I thought that was fascinating. We did a launch in London, and people turned up from all over Europe. Some people now regularly come to my shows having discovered me through my album of Springsteen songs.

IS: You chose to record a number of less familiar Springsteen songs, such as "Factory" and "Cautious Man," and of course "Happy." What determined your choice of songs? Were there particular song narratives that interested you? Or is there a narrative connecting the songs you chose?

MJ: Basically, I chose the songs that meant the most to me. I mean, the anthems like "Thunder Road" are there, and I loved "The Ghost of Tom Joad." But yeah, I wanted to find some of the lesser known titles from his amazing canon of works. But if you pin me down—and as someone who has been asked many times to list my top twenty Springsteen songs for websites—then the top song for me is "The Promise." That song pierces my heart and washes all over me and my ghosts. People say it's about this, it's about that. I don't know what it's about. I can only tell you that the lyrics echo and ring in my heart. The line about "carrying the broken spirits of all the other ones who'd lost" is like a familiar dream—all the narrative in that song is. When I saw the film of Bruce alone at the piano singing that song in New York City it just floored me. I thought, hell, he's singing about my life in the most intimate of ways. There I am, the people pleaser, being optimistic for everyone in the world except myself. I was struck in the same way years before by the line at the end of "Brilliant Disguise" when he sings "God have mercy on the man who doubts what he's sure of." Stunning poetry that carried weight and truth for me of the contradictions deep within. This revelation is the gift and grace of a great song, and they take on a private incarnation for the listener. I don't think any writer is allowed to own the absolute copyright of what a song is about. Because, well, who knows?

IS: You used a word in a previous interview in reference to Bruce that is quite interesting: *prophetic*. Is that a word that has some currency with you when you think of Springsteen? And what does it mean to say that a songwriter is prophetic?

MJ: I think I was speaking to that place where I see only a handful of artists operating, such as, say, U2 and Springsteen. They carry that artistic thrust that desires much more than the norm and the thirst for deeper understanding whilst recognizing that much of the spiritual realm is made up of mystery, not certainty. Within that we then look to them for inspiration, for guidance. So, I think that prophetic element is there in Bruce's work in that he stands in the gap for many and creates a vision, offers insight and a wisdom that is seldom, seldom seen in artists. Yet, he remains of the people, there is a lack of ego on parade. Quite frankly, the Rolling Stones are a great band, but would I mind if I never saw them play again? Probably not. But I think we need Bruce—especially in these days. Because he's always on the edge of our narrative and brings a bigger vision and version of ourselves, a bigger . . . theology of what it is to be alive, what it means to be in a relationship, what it means to be fully human, and how we save and protect that. When you find all that in someone's vision of their art then I think that it brings a form of prophetic voice, though something tells me the man himself might not be comfortable with that idea, which is actually part of what I'm trying to say. I've often said I am just glad he is in the world. I don't need to meet him, though would obviously love to if there was some sort of organic opportunity. I did have the chance once. We were in the same room when I was signed

to Sony Music and someone offered to introduce us, but I said
no, because I thought whatever I said to him would be wrong
and I would always regret it.

IS: What in you as a songwriter resonates with Springsteen?

MJ: Well, I think the Brits are very good at bringing you the latest
fashion in whatever it might be. So, the Beatles and the Stones
or the Arctic Monkeys—we tend to lead trends, though, of
course, a lot of popular music is birthed in America's history.
But, I don't think we are naturally good at showing sincere
emotion. We like to look cool and calm, though we know how
to make a lot of noise if needed. Thus, the British reserve. Now,
in the States they are not afraid to wear their hearts on their
sleeves and I love that, although it can get a little twee and
sentimental at times! As a ten-year-old, I can remember listening
to some of my grandfather's records, and he had an album by a
Welsh comedian / singer by the name of Max Boyce who is
renowned for his funny songs about rugby and its culture. But
Max also had a song called "Duw, It's Hard"—*Duw* being the
Welsh word for God. It was about his life and his father's life as
a miner. Even as a ten-year-old I would listen to this song and
was drawn to something of the sadness and story that was present. I don't know why—that's a whole other interview—but the
melancholy, a narrative, a story, I was drawn to that kind of
song. So, whilst I was listening to Led Zeppelin, I was also
listening to Glen Campbell. As I was listening to David Bowie I
was also listening to John Denver and of course Dylan and Paul
Simon. And whilst I was listening to all of these guys, I was
listening to *Born to Run*, the early Springsteen, this guy making
great music and also saying something really important through
it. It all seeped in, and I think I may have sold a lot more records if I had based myself in the States. I remember touring with
Art Garfunkel, who told me I should go live in Nashville.

I started writing songs at an early age. I look back at them
and cringe a little, of course, but they were obviously my teenage
perspective of the world, whatever it might have been. But I
wasn't really throwing much away. It all counted for something.
I was trying to tell some kind of a story within all that. I don't

know if I can say that was because of Bruce. But I think it came from the same spirit, the same place: that drive to try to make sense of the world by putting words down on a sheet of paper. You don't just pick that up; you get there by listening and observation. And then you make a decision about what kind of work you want to produce. That position of trying to tell your story but maybe somebody else's story too. There's a lot of those same themes in my work, so I have no doubt really that not only does it resonate but I have a lot to be grateful for in that Bruce and others were there to inspire and lead.

IS: Yes, as a songwriter you choose a narrator to tell a story.

MJ: Exactly. If you want to say something big in the world, just tell one person's story. By telling one person's story you tell ten thousand people's stories. And, if I might add, it's hard to write songs for guys.

IS: Expound on that. Because that is something that Springsteen does.

MJ: He does, and he does it so well. I don't want to say this and in any way sound disparaging, but it is easier to write for women because they are more willing to go to those places of emotion. And that's a strength, it really is. But men are told from an early age, "Don't you cry! Be tough, stand up for yourself!" So, there's all those things that shut down in us when it comes to emotion. And so it's hard to write that song that really gets at the soul of a guy. I have a song called "Cardiff Bay." I wrote it because I was touring the States a lot. LA, New York, Phoenix—all those towns seep so well into the psyche and fabric of the songwriter. Put a British town like Wolverhampton in and it doesn't quite sound the same. I thought, I'd love to write something that sounded like where I was from.

IS: That's a father-and-son song. It's your "My Hometown."

MJ: Well, yeah, I guess it is. But I didn't view it that way for a long time. I wrote it after walking around Cardiff docks with my son, just like my grandfather did with me, but I thought it was about Cardiff, my hometown. It was only as the years went by and I was loading out or hanging around after shows and some guy would come up and say, "Hey, thanks for the show. I really liked it." I'd say, "Well, thanks for coming." And then he would say, "That 'Cardiff Bay' song—I really liked it." And I would respond, "Thanks. What was it about the song you liked?" And he'd say, "Well, it sums up how I feel about my boy." And I began to realize that the song was actually about being a father, all that pain and beauty. Anyway, that sort of narrative Bruce does so well. He's able to break down those barriers for the guy. And you'll see it when you go to a Springsteen concert. You'll see guys wiping tears from their eyes. Very few other artists will have that effect, and it's because Bruce writes so intimately about the male narrative. Again, he has that wisdom because he has made the journey. He's been there and he is not afraid to put it down on paper in a way that the average guy can say, "Hey, he's singing about my life." And I want to do that, too.

IS: I've been to several of Springsteen's shows and have identified what might be called "the Bruce blessing." What is it about seeing Springsteen in concert that somehow lifts people up? Why do people at a Springsteen show feel like somehow they are part of a religious experience?

MJ: I think what you're talking about is his ability to make you feel more human. I think it's the collective good that is gathered at his shows. He touches that good in himself and he brings it out of those in the audience. People gather for a stadium show or an arena show, and, of course, we don't know the folks on either side of us. But after about forty-five minutes it becomes like a community hall. Because our lives are being laid bare before us through songs from the past—songs about the future, songs about what is going on, songs we fell in love to, cried to, lost to, whatever it might be. I think it's the sense that we, the audience, have become part of what is going on onstage. We become part of a world where we have each other, and little else. And Bruce allows us to recognize that in each other. We're a bunch of individuals, or a few groups, but at the end of the night as we walk out we are more than that sum. You see people hugging strangers. I don't find that a mystery. That's the way it should be. I once heard that the early Fathers of the Church described the glory of God as a human being fully alive. Bruce facilitates that experience.

IS: Bruce is soon to turn seventy. What do you think there is left for him to do?

MJ: Nothing and plenty. He has done more than enough, but there is so much more to come, I'm sure. I don't think the job of a songwriter is ever done. If you're a plumber, you go and fix somebody's pipes, they work well again and the job is done. But as a musician or writer you're never quite sure when that moment arrives. I think Bruce is a person who is driven by the need to write and communicate. He is aware that his work brings all of the joy we have spoken about. And I think that will drive him on for as long as he is able. He is not someone who is ever going to retire. And I certainly don't want him too. There is nothing for him to prove, no great mountain to climb, he's done it all. But he is still climbing the same mountain we are all on. He just happens to be the guy with the rope at the front pulling so many of us along behind him. And in terms of artists emerging, there's a lot of good stuff out there, but I don't know of anyone quite like him. And so, all I want him to do is to carry on playing and writing songs and being open and honest and passionate and surprising us and lifting us upwards and onwards, getting out there as long as his body and brain will allow. I fear the time when that can no longer happen. We are losing too much light these days.

15

This Train

✧

Bruce Springsteen as Public Artist

COLLEEN J. SHEEHY

Bruce Springsteen now inhabits a more expansive world than the label "rock star" can encompass. His soul-baring autobiography *Born to Run* follows no typical rock musician's narrative of struggle in obscurity, success, and debauchery, followed by stints in treatment and born-again sobriety. I've read many of those. Instead, his story mines the depths of historical trauma of the Irish working class, embedded in his father and passed on to a son who masked decades of depression with musical drive, art, and performance serving as antidote. Sublimation can work, but only so far, and Springsteen reveals his recurring depression and therapy, extending into recent years, with rare honesty. Springsteen's account of his first major hit of the deep blues while on a cross-country road trip with a friend left me with a hole in *my* stomach at his pain.

Born to Run, his best-selling memoir, was followed by the sold-out *Springsteen on Broadway*, a singular performance in which Springsteen strips himself down emotionally night after night (his first real job, as he jokes at the outset). Not focused on his own depression in the stage show, he tells stories of people who have made him who he is, using his own life and music to amplify the love and losses in all of our lives. Tears ensue on both sides of the stage lights.

In this context, on the occasion of Springsteen turning seventy, I argue that we reconsider him outside of the rock star label to recognize him as a "public artist," that is, as someone who performs a public address through his art, someone engaged with civic issues. But "public artist" is not just a political title. It refers to an artist who gives voice to the experiences and concerns of people living in a dispersed geography that come together spiritually around their music and physically at their performances. By vocalizing the concerns of his listeners, Springsteen binds his audiences into a civic imaginary: a public, a community. This is a position earned; it does not automatically come to all who step onstage, and it's earned by few musicians. As exemplified by his 2012 *Wrecking Ball* album of social commentary about the winners and losers in the Great Recession, his autobiography, his Medal of Freedom bestowed by President Barack Obama, and now his Broadway show, Springsteen has fully realized elements in his work that make him one of our best public artists. Springsteen's status is the result of his willingness to comment on social issues, to use his experiences as a means for others to reflect on their own lives, and his ability to build a devoted community of listeners around his music, performances, and ideas.

Amid the joy that Springsteen's concerts have provided to so many people, we must also recognize his long focus on sober social concerns and his call to his audience to attend to the misfortunate, people who became outsiders because of a society out of balance instead of personal failings. In some ways, this has been a staple of his music from the earliest days of his recording career, as illustrated by his large canon of Vietnam War songs. Starting with "Lost in the Flood" from *Greetings from Asbury Park, N.J.* and continuing into his *Nebraska* sessions with "Highway Patrolman," "Shut Out the Light," and "A Good Man Is Hard to Find (Pittsburgh)," and to, of course, "Born in the U.S.A." and then "Brothers Under the Bridge" in the mid-1990s. The songs came out of Springsteen's remembrance of Jersey Shore musicians who had been killed in combat, his involvement with Ron Kovic, author of *Born on the Fourth of July*, as well as Springsteen's work for Vietnam Veterans of America, experiences that made him question the morality of American wars and the nation's treatment of its veterans. From veterans issues to immigration to police brutality, Springsteen has taken his social convictions as a key aspect of his ideas about the role of the artist. He has exhibited a stirring bravery in putting those convictions into action and in commenting on injustices from the stage, and occasionally in public writings.

Though he commands a larger audience, Springsteen resembles those artists who work in the contemporary public art arena called "social practice." This approach has emerged as a dynamic and dramatic way for artists to use their talents to address a wide range of social issues, including poverty, racism, food justice, incarceration, disenfranchisement, and the environment. Social practice artists build relationships as an art form and support other people's agency to make connections and make change. Arising from a potent synergy of approaches forged in the 1960s and 1970s by feminist artists and artists of color, social practice has expanded in the contemporary art world since the late 1990s.

I find that Ernesto Pujol, a performance artist who works with communities to devise public ceremonies, best articulates some of the principles underpinning social practice that speak to Springsteen's public artistry. Pujol writes, "Art is a form of field research, a creative responsive method, an empathic useful aesthetic response." He talks about artists' roles, the fact that they need to work with intangible and invisible materials—emotion, spirit, memory. Therefore, it is required that an artist engage in deep listening, making him or herself open and vulnerable in what can be embarrassing acts of emotional exposure. Pujol aligns himself with the visionary German artist Joseph Beuys, reminding us of Beuys's belief that "art cannot call itself 'contemporary' if it is unable to reshape society, facilitating transformation." The artist helps gives visibility and voice to invisible experiences, in the process forming a community around their work.

Springsteen is one of these artists. When he talks of Freehold, New Jersey—in a book passage that he performed on Broadway and at the 2018 Tony Awards—he poetically acknowledges how sensory experiences united the townsfolk of his youth—the smell of wet coffee grounds from the Nescafé plant, the clanging sounds from the rug factory. More deeply, he sees all the people in Freehold struggling through life with the same challenges—to love, to make a living, to live with respect, "all doing their best to hold off the demons that seek to destroy us, our homes, our families, our town." In the Broadway show, this story leads into "My Hometown." The song recounts a touching personal memory from Springsteen's boyhood, when he drove with his father through the streets of Freehold. Yet by framing the song with broader themes of life's struggles, he gives voice to everyone in every place, every hometown where people are struggling.

While there are certainly models for Springsteen's use of music as public art, from Woody Guthrie to James Brown, Springsteen learned that each person could have a civic role from his mother, Adele, who worked in Freehold as a legal secretary. He writes in loving detail about how she would prepare herself for the world each morning as a matter of respect and dignity, going so far as to comment on the physical carriage in her walk to work as proof that she saw herself as an important part of a community. She provided a model of how to live as a public person, and she conveyed that everyone has a role and responsibility to society, a lesson her son absorbed.

If the stifling nature of Freehold made the young Springsteen's skin crawl, propelling him to want to escape, he went on to create his own musical community. This effort began in the Jersey Shore music scene and broadened over the years to include his fans. Few artists can claim the role Springsteen has in relation to his community. His special power was revealed vividly in the days after 9/11, a tragedy that struck hard in the communities around his New Jersey home, when a fan yelled to him, "Bruce, we need you now!" Bruce needed something too, and, prompted in part by one fan's declaration, he got busy writing songs that would become *The Rising*, his first album of new work in seven years. It remains a rare gesture in music and other art forms from that period, an expression of shock and mourning following national tragedy. In such moving songs as "Lonesome Day," "Into the Fire," "You're Missing," and "The Rising," he approached the subject from an emotional rather than political level. The album launched him on another worldwide tour, with new music that once again resonated with people's ragged emotions and uncertainty about the brave new world.

In the world of social practice art, conversation serves a crucial role in forming community and forging personal connections. In his memoir, Springsteen writes about rock and roll as a profound, ongoing conversation between musicians and audiences. The mutual dialogue between singer and audience comes poignantly full circle in Springsteen's stage show, when, at the end, he says to the audience, "Thanks for giving me so much joy." Through their applause, many audience members at the show I attended replied "Thanks for giving *us* so much joy!"

In song, story, and performance, Springsteen has created a public that follows him for both his joyful songs and his serious commentary. A group of people are not automatically a public. They need to be formulated into a public through the recognition of common connections. And books like Daniel Cavicchi's *Tramps Like Us: Music and Meaning among Springsteen Fans* document how Springsteen's music and Springsteen's concerts bring people together, allowing fans to form meaningful relationships with each other based on their shared appreciation of Springsteen's art.

"Land of Hope and Dreams," a song that has been a hallmark of Springsteen shows for two decades, exemplifies the expansive society Springsteen brings to life among his fans. A gospel song echoing Curtis Mayfield and the Impressions' "People Get Ready," "Hope and Dreams" was written in 1999 and performed on the Reunion Tour. The song expresses a renewal of his close community with the E Street Band but also a broader social contract. In describing the song, Springsteen writes, "I wanted something new to start this new stage of the band's life with. 'Land of Hope' summed up a lot of what I wanted our band to be about and renewed our pledge to our audience, to point the way forward and, once again, become a living presence in our listeners' lives." The song was finally released on *Wrecking Ball*, where he sings like folk hero John Henry, sounding like he has bellows for lungs. Now, he invites not only his lover to take off with him, but invites everyone to join "this train." The car from "Thunder Road" has become a train "rollin' down this track." Springsteen alters the song "Bound for Glory" by forefather Woody Guthrie by having his train open to all the fallen and imperfect. Guthrie sang:

> This train don't carry no gamblers, this train
> This train don't carry no gamblers
> Liars, thieves, nor big shot ramblers
> This train is bound for glory, this train

In "Land of Hope and Dreams," Springsteen embraces everyone, singing of a train that carries saints and sinners, whores, gamblers, and lost souls. Even more, he goes on to paint a vision of their destination in an inclusive, utopian society where "Big wheels roll through fields where sunlight streams / meet me in the land of hope and dreams." The song contains echoes of Springsteen's earlier work—"Born to Run" with its promise to "walk in the sun," and the claim "I believe in a promised land" from *Darkness on the Edge of Town*. But the message has changed over the years. Springsteen now believes in a community, not loner lovers.

In speaking of the aims of social practice art, Ernesto Pujol writes, "I believe the goal of lived practice is consciousness." He explains lived practice as an awareness of self and nonself, knowledge of the interconnectedness and interdependence of the tangible and intangible, of oneness. Springsteen, too, calls us to this state of consciousness and interdependence. This is crystalized in *Springsteen on Broadway* with a segment he added to the show several months after it opened. He talks about Martin Luther King Jr.'s famous statement, "The arc of the moral universe is long but it bends toward justice." Acknowledging the flagrant racism and bigotry on the rise in the United States, Springsteen adds, "That arc doesn't bend on its own. It takes all of us to bend it, day after day after day, to live with some compassion. Keep leaning on that arc." This introduction leads into "The Ghost of Tom Joad," his updated John Steinbeck story about migrants headed to California, a song from the mid-1990s with stinging relevance in the days of discussions of walls along the southern border. Springsteen reminds us of our responsibility to work together for that land of hope and dreams, lending our weight, our bodies, our spirits, to insist on justice. More than ever, Springsteen embraces a role speaking as our public conscience, urging us to care for each other. At the end of the Broadway show, he says, "This has been my service. This has been my long and noisy prayer." He has been praying not only for himself, but also for all of us and for the United States and for the world.

Springsteen calls us to be our better social selves and better Americans: to forge "consciousness," as Pujol would say. At the Broadway performance, Springsteen creates a public of disparate people gathered from all over the world. He performs a public prayer, makes himself vulnerable, and embarrasses himself with revelations of sorrow and mourning and redemption, love, wonder, and affirmation. This is a public role that few artists or politicians are filling today at a time of national political and social crisis.

In reflecting on the ways that Springsteen builds a public that is compassionate and principled, I'm reminded of a fan-made button a friend gave me in 2002 when the *Springsteen: Troubadour of the Highway* exhibit that I curated opened at the Weisman Art Museum. Likely from 1980, when Ronald Reagan was running for office, this pin resembled a political campaign button, declaring "Springsteen for President," with the singer's face in the center. I cherished the gift—but then gave it to Springsteen's mother Adele at the exhibition opening at Cranbrook Art Museum in Detroit. I had read that Bruce claimed his mother had the world's biggest Springsteen collection in her basement, and I didn't want her to be without this rare treasure.

Springsteen may have called Bob Dylan "the father of my country" when he inducted him into the Rock and Roll Hall of Fame, but now is the time for us to declare Springsteen "President of our U.S.A.," a place where I want to be born and live. Springsteen for president, indeed, "you just get on board."

Works Cited

Cavicchi, Daniel. *Tramps Like Us: Music and Meaning among Springsteen Fans*. New York: Oxford University Press, 1998.

Pujol, Ernesto. "The Art of Consciousness: On Sustaining the Embarrassing Practice of Perception." In *A Lived Practice*, edited by Mary Jane Jacob and Kate Zeller. Chicago: School of the Art Institute of Chicago and University of Chicago Press, 2015, 101–117.

Sheehy, Colleen. "Springsteen: Troubadour of the Highway." In *Springsteen: Troubadour of the Highway*. Minneapolis: Weisman Art Museum, 2002.

Springsteen, Bruce. *Born to Run*. New York: Simon & Schuster, 2016.

16

Born to Write

✧

Bruce Springsteen, Flannery O'Connor, and the Songstory

IRWIN H. STREIGHT

One of the popular Norton anthologies of literature on my office book-shelf, produced to service college and university English lit courses, includes the lyrics for Bruce Springsteen's "Nebraska." Springsteen's attention to poetic form has made his work attractive to such anthologies and to the discipline of English literature—currently anxious about its survival in the academy and often busy rebranding itself as cultural studies. It helps that those who edit such anthologies are usually late-middle-aged white American males. No doubt the fact that Springsteen is a pop music artist with exceptionally well-crafted lyrics and considerable cultural capital—the Boss—has also legitimized his inclusion in more than a dozen contemporary anthologies of literature I have collected. Springsteen's use of traditional forms of storytelling through lyric poetry in the ballad and dramatic monologue, and occasionally the elegiac mode ("My City of Ruins" and "My Hometown"), lends a literariness to his lyrics—a literariness that in the judgment of many editors deserves a place alongside the major works of both English and American poets, sometimes even trumping Nobel Laureate Bob Dylan as the lone writer in the anthology who publishes in song.

I'm bemused each time I open the alphabetically ordered slim poetry volume of the Seagull imprint that I regularly use in my introductory literature classes. Across the page from one of Edmund Spenser's famous *Amoretti* sonnets is Bruce Springsteen's "The River." August company, indeed! Editor Joseph Kelly includes "The River," as he remarks in a headnote, because it's "an excellent example of the contemporary ballad." In the aforementioned Norton anthology, the lyrics for "Nebraska" are offered as a contemporary example of the dramatic monologue. Here Springsteen is in the company of nineteenth-century British poet Robert Browning, who is credited with inventing the form in such poems as "My Last Duchess" and the creepy "Porphyria's Lover."

My interest in Springsteen evolved out of a connection indicated in a single footnote to the last line of the "Nebraska" lyrics in the Norton volume, as his Charles Starkweather character explains to a sheriff the motive for his multiple murders: "Well, sir, I guess there's just a meanness in this world." This line, informs the editor, includes an allusion to a bit of dialogue spoken by an escaped convict in a short story by southern author Flannery O'Connor. Setting aside the still-contentious issue of treating a song lyric as poetry and the question of whether Springsteen deserves to be included in the company of the great poets of the English-speaking world, Springsteen most certainly owes a debt to the gothic storyteller and literary genius Flannery O'Connor. Springsteen himself has spoken about his debt to the southern author. Indeed, a writer in the British fanzine *Uncut* once referred to Springsteen as "the Flannery O'Connor of American rock."

I can't recall how I was directed to the 1998 interview between Will Percy and Bruce Springsteen published in the now defunct arts journal *DoubleTake.* My abiding scholarly interest, now as then, is in all things related to Flannery O'Connor. At the time, I'd recently finished a dissertation on O'Connor's short stories—a close textual analysis of her often violent and mystery-infused fictions that sought, with the aid of some revelatory literary theory, to understand how her powerful prose worked its literary magic. Set in the postwar Bible Belt, stocked with shiftless white trash and vacant-headed, hypocritical good country people, and informed by her orthodox Catholic beliefs, O'Connor's stories are brilliantly crafted, puzzling, sometimes shocking, and both darkly and hysterically humorous. She is essentially a comic writer with a cosmic outlook.

In the interview with Percy, nephew of the late southern novelist Walker Percy, Springsteen refers to the "really important reading" that began in his late twenties, under the tutelage of his new manager Jon Landau, and how it has shaped his consciousness and craft as a songwriter. He singles out the fiction of Flannery O'Connor and remarks, "There was something in those stories of hers that I felt captured a certain part of American character that I was interested in writing about. They were a big, big revelation. . . . There was some dark thing—a component of spirituality—that I sensed in her stories, and that set me off exploring characters of my own." He comments that on his early records he'd been writing "big, sometimes operatic, and occasionally rhetorical things"—"Blinded by the Light," "Jungleland," and "Spirit in the Night" well fit this description. As he worked on songs for *The River*, and particularly the solo-recorded *Nebraska*, Springsteen was by his own admission "deep into O'Connor" and under the influence of her incredible storytelling gifts. He acknowledges that O'Connor helped direct him to "a more scaled down, more personal, more restrained way" of expressing his ideas in song. And in the interview he draws comparisons between songwriting and short story writing—both are "character-driven" and able to "present an entire life" in a few pages or in a few minutes of song. Dave Marsh, Springsteen's first biographer, confirms in *Glory Days* that reading O'Connor's short fictions had a transformative effect on Springsteen as a writer. He notes that Springsteen was impressed by the "minute precision" in her storytelling, "the way O'Connor could enliven a character by sketching in just a few details."

Just as Springsteen remarks that reading O'Connor's fiction was a "big, big revelation" to him as a songwriter, so reading the *DoubleTake* interview in which Springsteen extols O'Connor and discusses her deep and lasting influence on his songcraft and sensibilities was a big revelation to me. American rock icon Bruce Springsteen a Flannery O'Connor fan? I was surprised. As a devotee of Canadian folk music since my adolescent years, I had long been a passionate fan of that other *Brooooooce!*—Canada's Bruce Cockburn. I knew almost nothing about the life and works of Bruce Springsteen. So I came to Springsteen's songwriting very late—tipping into age forty—and listened initially to the O'Connor-influenced *Nebraska* and *The River* recordings as a curious literary critic and not as a newly awakened convert to the Boss's ministry of rock and roll.

Southern novelist Larry Brown once defined a good song as a short story written on a guitar. Springsteen's best narrative songs fit this description—even to the extent of following the classic short story structure of rising action to a climax or epiphany, and sometimes including the falling action of the novel. He often refers to himself as simply a *writer*, though his form is the song lyric. In fact, Springsteen once described his corpus of songs as "my ongoing novel."

"The Line" from *The Ghost of Tom Joad* is a good example of Springsteen's very conscious and necessarily compressed content and structure in what I've compounded to call a *songstory*. Carl, the song's narrator, deftly reveals his character and background in three detailed opening stanzas of first-person narrative: a recently widowed ex-serviceman, he has joined the California border patrol looking to put his life together and is doing his job well alongside an empathetic veteran, Bobby Ramirez. Then Carl tells of meeting Luisa in a holding pen waiting to be sent back across the border. They meet later that night and dance in a bar in Tijuana, and Carl knows what he will do the next time she tries to get through. Like Joe Roberts in *Nebraska*'s "Highway Patrolman," Carl lets the law of love trump the law: he picks up the illegally crossing Maria and her drug-running brother, drives them across the border, and faces off with Bobby Ramirez as the pair escape into the arms of America. The song ends with a patch of story six months after the event, as Carl recounts searching the bars and migrant towns in Southern California looking for Luisa, a beautiful black-haired woman who reminds him of something he has lost. A full short story is here: all the revelation of character and incident and the hope for human connection, told over a lightly strummed seesaw ascending and descending melody, in five minutes and twenty-two seconds.

A story, as Flannery O'Connor defines it, "is a complete dramatic action—and in good stories, the characters are shown through the action and the action is controlled through the characters, and the result of this is meaning that derives from the whole presented experience." Her axiom as a storywriter is that the *mystery* of the human is revealed through *manners*, our individual responses to moral circumstance. O'Connor's self-revelation about her own story art is expressed in a talk she gave a few months before her death in 1964 to an audience of college students and teachers who had gathered to hear her read "A Good Man Is Hard to Find," her most celebrated and confounding short story. O'Connor remarked, "I often ask myself what makes a story work, and what makes it hold up as a story, and I have decided that it is probably some action, some gesture of a character that is unlike any other in the story, one that indicates where the real heart of the story lies. This would have to be an action or a gesture which was both totally right and totally unexpected; it would have to be one that was both in character and beyond character. . . . It would be a gesture which somehow made contact with mystery." Like the "Good Man Is Hard to Find" story alluded to in the "Nebraska" lyrics, Springsteen's fictive songstories have a revelatory, dramatic emotional center. In the O'Connor short story, the central event is the grandmother's gesture of reaching out to touch the existentially distraught murderer to show her sympathy and kinship. In response to this touch of grace, as the author intends it, The Misfit shoots her three times point-blank. In a Flannery O'Connor story, a shot of divine love is sure to save and slay a character in a single motion.

Springsteen's less deadly songstories are nonetheless of a kind with O'Connor's literary stock in his ability to reveal the inner life of a character and the central truth of his narrative through subtly suggestive descriptive details. Billy Sutter's unexpected gesture in "Galveston Bay," for example, is the opposite of The Misfit's in terms of dramatic action, but it illustrates another kind of grace moment. Intending to shiv Le Bin Son in an act of retributive justice, at the last moment Billy chooses against violence and revenge. His act of restraint is the whole story: a little bit of light shone into a dark world of racially motivated violence. Springsteen writes in *Songs* that his Billy Sutter character "transcends his circumstances. He finds the strength and grace to save himself and the part of the world he touches." Billy does this simply, and with great effort, as he sticks his K-Bar knife back into his pocket. Charlie, the ex-con in "Straight Time," is a contrasting study. Though he has a menial job, he's married with a seemingly happy wife and young children and appears to be doing alright. Yet underneath, Charlie can still feel the itch to do evil; his "cold mind" has a will to cross that "thin line" between our better selves and our darker nature that so fascinates both Springsteen and O'Connor. Charlie allows his former meanness back in, and acts on it. We last envision him through an image that invokes Shakespeare's Lady Macbeth, trying to wash the smell of death from his hands.

The pumping pop rock anthems that set the stadium jumping and have made Springsteen's reputation as a performer are much less attractive to me than are his folk-style story songs. *Nebraska*, *The Ghost of Tom Joad*, and *Devils & Dust* form a subset of character-centered, narrative-style songs in Springsteen's discography and are the recordings I listen to most often. Songs on these albums are distinguished by the multiple narrators that inhabit the lyrics, the imagined characters who tell their stories. Few popular songwriters are able to do this so well or so extensively; it takes the literary skills and empathetic imagination of a fiction writer to create a fully believable character in the space of a song lyric and to tell his or her story in a complete dramatic action.

Springsteen is remarkable as a songwriter in his intention and ability to step inside someone else's skin, to see the world through their eyes, and to step back and allow his own voice, as he says of the *Joad* songs "to disappear into the voices of those [I've] chosen to write about." He adopts this first-person character style frequently. Five of the ten song-stories on *Nebraska* have fictive narrators; added to that Ralph ("Johnny 99") tells his own story in the last third of that lyric. Apart from the prosaically formatted third-person short story "Black Cowboys" and the hymn-like "Jesus Was an Only Son," the remaining ten tracks on *Devils & Dust* are narrated by imaginatively realized characters. In the requiem "Matamoros Banks," the twelfth and closing song on the recording, Springsteen speaks as much *for* as *about* the drowned male Mexican migrant on the bottom of the Rio Grande, and he describes his artistic method in a headnote to the lyric—giving a voice to the dead, as he will later do in the closing song on *Wrecking Ball*, "We Are Alive." All but four or five of the twelve *Joad* songs are voiced by Springsteen's fictive characters, depending on whether you think that's the artist / songwriter sittin' by the campfire doin' research while "searchin' for the ghost of Tom Joad," which I'm inclined to believe. In his autobiography, Springsteen writes about spending a lot of time in the small farm towns in the Central Valley of California and states that it "took a good amount of research to get the details of the region correct. I traced the stories out slowly and carefully. I thought about who these people were and the choices they were presented with." *Joad* is the only recording by Springsteen that includes a bibliography in the lyrics booklet listing his reading on his song subjects. This record picks up from where he left off with the O'Connor-influenced songs on *Nebraska*. Here as well he labored in a literary way to get the details of people's lives right and to further mine the vein of songstory writing that Springsteen acknowledges in his autobiography—and I wholeheartedly agree—is "the best" of what he does and stands for what he wants "to be about as a songwriter."

In a 2014 interview published in the "By the Book" section of the Sunday *New York Times*, Springsteen—now an avid reader of eclectic texts—is asked to name the "one book" that has had the greatest influence on him. He chooses the collected stories of Flannery O'Connor, likely referring to the National Book Award–winning *Flannery O'Connor: The Complete Stories*, first published in 1971, seven years after her untimely death from complications resulting from lupus. More than thirty years have elapsed since Springsteen's initial reading of her fiction influenced the form and content of his songwriting. O'Connor's stories "fell hard on me" Springsteen emphasizes. And his response to her stories is philosophical: "You could feel within them the unknowability of God, the intangible mysteries of life that confound her characters and which I find by my side every day." O'Connor is also mentioned at the end of the *Born to Run* autobiography as one of his models, an artist "who worked on the edges of society" and whose art had been "assimilated and become part of the culture at large."

"A story is a way to say something that can't be said any other way," wrote Flannery O'Connor. She added, "and it takes every word in the story to say what the meaning is." Songstories are by definition combined with music, which is more than just a hummable line to hang words on. The story in song lyric form is given force by the music, its dramatic tension expressed in tones and rhythm, sonic contrast and phrasing. Springsteen illustrates this in the *VH1 Storytellers* event while playing and explicating "Devils & Dust," moving between a major and a suspended chord that, as he remarks, sonically respond to the tension and ambiguities expressed by the narrator in the lyrics. As a teller of stories, Springsteen refined his craft by reading O'Connor's remarkable fictions. But he is a storyteller in *song*, and his medium in music is something that O'Connor was hopelessly unattuned to: she comically claimed to possess "the Original Tin Ear." So, listen well to the songstories of Bruce Springsteen: it takes every word and every note in a song to say what its meaning is.

Works Cited

"Bruce Springsteen: By the Book." *New York Times Sunday Book Review*, November 2, 2014, 8.

Marsh, Dave. *Glory Days: Bruce Springsteen in the 1980s*. New York: Pantheon Books, 1987.

Mays, Kelly J., ed. *The Norton Introduction to Literature*. Shorter 12th ed. New York: Norton, 2016.

O'Connor, Flannery. *The Complete Stories*. New York: Farrar, Straus & Giroux, 1971.

———. *The Habit of Being: Letters of Flannery O'Connor*. Edited by Sally Fitzgerald. New York: Farrar, Straus & Giroux, 1979.

———. *Mystery and Manners: Occasional Prose*. Edited by Sally Fitzgerald and Robert Fitzgerald. New York: Farrar, Straus & Giroux, 1969.

"Rock and Read: Will Percy Interviews Bruce Springsteen." *DoubleTake* 4, no. 2 (1998): 36–43.

Seagull Reader: Poems. 2nd ed. Edited by Joseph Kelly. New York: Norton, 2008.

Smith, Larry David. *Bob Dylan, Bruce Springsteen, and American Song*. Westport, Conn.: Praeger, 2002.

Springsteen, Bruce. *Born to Run*. New York: Simon & Schuster, 2016.

———. *Bruce Springsteen: Songs*. New York: HarperEntertainment, 2003.

17

Ten Great Springsteen Moments
(and Five Iconic Concerts)

✦

KENNETH WOMACK

Ten Great Moments

1. The Exuberant Lyrics of "Blinded by the Light"

With an unforgettable flourish, "Blinded by the Light" kicks Bruce Springsteen's debut LP into life, sending *Greetings from Asbury Park, N.J.* into a paroxysm of youthful ebullience. Years later, Springsteen would confess to writing his earliest songs with a rhyming dictionary on his lap. With "Blinded by the Light," he assaults listeners' senses with a fusillade of language and post-teenage angst: "Madman drummers bummers and Indians in the summer with a teenage diplomat / in the dumps with the mumps as the adolescent pumps his way into his hat." With songs like "Blinded by the Light" and "Spirit in the Night," Springsteen begins illustrating the windswept surfside terrain of the Jersey Shore, a moveable feast of con artistry and unforgettable characters.

2. Mad Dog's Drum Work on "Rosalita"

With *The Wild, the Innocent & the E Street Shuffle*, Springsteen's youthful abandon soars into full flight. For the budding songwriter, sharing his innermost dreams was nothing short of echoing the stentorian call-to-arms of the Animals' "We Gotta Get Out of This Place" writ large. In his own manifestations of the Animals' anthem, Springsteen nurtures the enduring dream that lives in the heart of his early twentysomething desires: the lusty notion of finally making his great escape—not merely from the Shore Points of New Jersey but from himself. In songs like "Rosalita (Come Out Tonight)" and "4th of July, Asbury Park (Sandy)," Springsteen makes good on this promise. For "Rosalita," he creates a boisterous narrative in which he entreats his bashful señorita to forsake her family ties and join him on a voyage into life's great unknown. As with the hyperbolic lyrics of his early work, "Rosalita" offers a panoply of vivid imagery and unquenchable boyish energy. But the sprawling, seven-minute song is ultimately driven by Vini "Mad Dog" Lopez's relentless beat, a steady percussion that keeps Springsteen's punchy lyrics and breakneck rhythms from spiraling out of control before the narrator and Rosie finally make their grand escape.

3. Roaring into the Future with "Thunder Road"

With 1975's *Born to Run*, Springsteen entered a vastly different artistic phase, having acquired a new producer and a (mostly) new incarnation of the E Street Band. But the most salient changes could be gleaned from his songwriting vision, which had slowly begun to discard the whimsy of youth in favor of the hard promises of his coming adulthood. With the slam of a screen door, "Thunder Road" erupts into being, finding Springsteen's narrator in the act of effecting his departure from the old life for places unknown. "Show a little faith, there's magic in the night," he tells Mary, his uncertain companion. She may not be a looker, but the narrow expectations of his younger days cease to matter in the longer game that he's now set on playing. For Springsteen, "Thunder Road" marks a turning point in which his characters are willing to bet on themselves and not on a stale nostalgia for the rose-colored past celebrated by their elders. Negotiating his way among the "skeleton frames of burned out Chevrolets," the singer has charted a new course—and there's no way, no how that he'll ever be turning back: "It's a town full of losers, and I'm pulling out of here to win."

4. The Big Man's Blistering Sax Solo on "Jungleland"

"Tenth Avenue Freeze-Out" hails Springsteen's musical transformation courtesy of Clarence Clemons's membership in the E Street Band. From *Born to Run*'s title track through "Meeting Across the River," the Big Man's melodic, dramatic saxophone affords the LP with an unforgettable terrain for Springsteen's carefully-honed storylines. But for Clemons, the album's pulsating climax in "Jungleland" makes for a career-spawning highlight. Springsteen's lyrics trace the heroics and despair of gangland run amok, but it is the Big Man's soaring sax solos that bring the narrative to life. "Outside the street's on fire in a real death waltz between what's flesh and what's fantasy," Springsteen sings as the song reaches its fever pitch. In Springsteen and coproducer Jon Landau's hands, "Jungleland" offers Clemons's instrument plenty of room to roam unfettered by time and space. As *NME*'s Talia Soghomonian observes, Clemons's solo on "Jungleland" is "surely the best sax solo ever, coaxing gracefulness and poetry from an instrument that generally struggles to convey either." *The best sax solo ever?* You bet. It's everything and more.

5. Max Weinberg's Sizzling Hi-Hat on "Candy's Room"

With the onset of his legal dispute with erstwhile manager Mike Appel, the protracted hiatus between the artistic and commercial heights of *Born to Run* and the release of *Darkness on the Edge of Town* may have been some of the most difficult years in Springsteen's career. But in the interim, he heightened his resolve. With his latest LP, he dedicated himself to bigger game than the dreams of your average rock star. "More than rich, more than famous, more than happy—I wanted to be great," he later recalled. But part of the musician's evolving greatness came with a knowing realization about the importance of letting his bandmates shine. With "Candy's Room," he does just that for drummer Max Weinberg. With the spotlight on his shoulders, Mighty Max plays a hi-hat solo for the ages, carving out the song's dark undercurrent of urgency and desire. "In Candy's room, there are pictures of her heroes on the wall," Springsteen sings. "But to get to Candy's room you gotta walk the darkness of Candy's hall." As yet more would-be heroes take aim at Candy's bedroom, Weinberg's drumkit lights the way.

6. Roy Bittan's Foreboding Piano on "Point Blank"

By the advent of *The River*, the E Street Band was working in lockstep with Springsteen's songwriterly vision. As Springsteen began to explore a postwar American dream victimized by the growing socioeconomic distance between the haves and the have nots, his latest album depicted this great divide with starkly drawn images of despair tempered by intermittent moments of love and whimsy. Roy "The Professor" Bittan's inventive piano sequences frequently serve as the backdrop for Springsteen's most despondent, heartbreaking narratives. For "Point Blank," he creates an ominous, smoky refrain for the singer's musings about the lingering darkness that awaits us all, particularly those on society's rough margins: "You wake up and you're dying," Springsteen croons and, worse yet, he cautions, "you don't even know what from." With the Professor's masterful piano figure punctuating the verses, Springsteen's lyrics take deeper, darker shades of meaning.

7. Getting to the Heart of the Matter in "Atlantic City"

With *Nebraska*, Springsteen takes a lo-fi, solo tour through the nation's backwaters, exploring the lives of the downtrodden and the lawless in equal measure. Famously recorded on a four-track cassette recorder, the songs examine the ordinary, workaday worlds of Americans punching a clock and desperately seeking out diversions. With "Atlantic City," he assumes the guise of a beleaguered everyman struggling under the weight of a brutalizing, unfair economy. "Well, I got a job and tried to put my money away" he sings. "But I got debts that no honest man can pay." With no recourse in sight, he cajoles his beloved into joining him for a night on the town: "Put your makeup on, fix your hair up pretty / and meet me tonight in Atlantic City." Springsteen's lyrics make for a powerful depiction of life in these United States for the working poor, who long for a taste of the good life wherever they can find it—even in America's gambling dens, where the house always wins. For Springsteen's browbeaten characters, losing at the gambling tables is just fine by them.

Beating the odds would be a dream come true. But when they inevitably lose, it will scarcely matter: they've been falling victim to the house, in one way or another, for as long as they can remember.

8. "Born in the U.S.A.," Perennially Misunderstood

With *Born in the U.S.A.*, Springsteen's reach went from arena-rock stardom to stadium-sized global onslaught. The album spawned seven top-ten hits and notched more than thirty million units on its platinum tour across the world's record charts. And while the LP's commercial appeal was apparent on nearly every track, the title track has emerged as one of Springsteen's most misinterpreted and confounding compositions. With the Professor's defiant synthesizer riff lighting the way, the singer contemplates the grim realities of the Vietnam War for its unwitting combatants. "Got in a little hometown jam so they put a rifle in my hand / sent me off to a foreign land to go and kill the yellow man." But in Springsteen's narration, the singer's circumstances become even more dire when he returns home, only to find himself shunned for his service. Knowing full well that blue-collar Americans overwhelmingly shouldered the war effort, Springsteen weaves a vexing tapestry in which his narrator adopts a faux patriotism, which, in keeping with the song's anthemic quality, renders his ironic stance even more powerful. From the earliest days of its release, "Born in the U.S.A." baffled its listeners, many of whom originally accepted it as an unvarnished paean to nationalism. But in so doing, they stumbled upon the song's deftest trick: by depicting the narrator's bitterness and abiding despair against a rousing musical backdrop, Springsteen reminds us about the pitfalls of wrapping ourselves in banners of patriotism to the detriment of our humanity.

9. Hitting Rock Bottom on the "Streets of Philadelphia"

While "Born in the U.S.A." revels in its contradictory, intentionally conflicting positions, "Streets of Philadelphia" works in brute, unflinching portraiture. As the Oscar-winning song from Jonathan Demme's 1993 film *Philadelphia*, "Streets of Philadelphia" finds Springsteen abandoning any sense of irony as he captures the dehumanizing essence of living with AIDS / HIV in a world that would rather remain ignorant of the ravages of the disease. In Demme's hands, *Philadelphia* acted as a significant, early effort to create a mainstream forum for the AIDS epidemic. Responding in kind, Springsteen crafted the song as a plain-spoken brief on existing among the afflicted and coming to terms with early death. As a masterwork depicting the narrator's stark recognition of his predicament, "Streets of Philadelphia" evokes its greatest moments of compassion as the singer contemplates his coming doom: "Ain't no angel gonna greet me / it's just you and I my friend / and my clothes don't fit me no more / a thousand miles just to slip this skin." Performed against the monotony of a staccato drum track, "Streets of Philadelphia" finds its greatest power in its narrator's relentless march toward a painful, lonely, certain death.

10. Rousing a Wounded Nation with "The Rising"

With "Born in the U.S.A." and "Streets of Philadelphia," Springsteen sought out glints of humanity in our darkest hours. By the advent of *The Rising*, he was confronted, like millions of Americans, with a moment of unexpected, galvanizing national crisis. The title track finds him wrestling with immediacy of the 9/11 terror attacks as he imagines a dutiful fireman climbing higher and higher into the World Trade Center: "Can't see nothin' in front of me / can't see nothin' coming up behind." As a nearly lifelong resident of the greater New York area, Springsteen witnessed the longitudinal nature of the nation's post-9/11 trauma as well as Americans' difficulty in escaping its long shadow. For Springsteen's narrator, a collective national victimhood evolved from the binding chains of the attack and its aftermath. But is the chain indicative of a sense of grief or loss or uncertainty? *Or does it connote all three*? "Come on up for the rising," he challenges the listener, framing his rallying call as an act of rebellion and defiance in the face of an irreconcilable void.

Five Iconic Live Performances

1. Harvard Square Theater, May 9, 1974

Not surprisingly, many of Springsteen's most defining performances occurred during his early, formative years on the road—a time when he was making his name among rock-and-roll stalwarts. On May 9, 1974, rock critic and *Rolling Stone* mainstay Jon Landau wandered into Springsteen's show at the Harvard Square Theater. Dejected by his lot in life and disenchanted with contemporary music, Landau found himself mesmerized by Springsteen's performance, a kinetic progression through rock, soul, and rhythm and blues. In a May 22, 1974, article in Boston's *Real Paper*, Landau reflected on the experience, writing that "I saw rock and roll future, and its name is Bruce Springsteen." For Landau, it had been a revelation: "On a night when I needed to feel young, he made me feel like I was hearing music for the very first time." "Springsteen does it all. He is a rock 'n' roll punk, a Latin street poet, a ballet dancer, an actor, a joker, bar band leader, hot-shit rhythm guitar player, extraordinary singer, and a truly great rock 'n' roll composer. He leads a band like he has been doing it forever." As history well knows, Landau shortly transformed his words into action. Within a matter of months, he would join forces with the musician and copilot his career in new and unexpected directions.

2. *Hammersmith Odeon, November 24, 1975*

With the tremendous stateside success of *Born to Run*, Springsteen's label was understandably ready to grow his reach. In November 1975, he arrived in London with Columbia Records' publicity machine working at full throttle. For Springsteen, the pressure to establish a European beachhead was immense, intensifying to a fever pitch as the twenty-six-year-old musician encountered the evidence of his record company's advertising campaign across the cityscape in the form of a poster proclaiming "Finally, London is ready for Bruce Springsteen and the E Street Band." Held at the Hammersmith Odeon on November 18, Springsteen's European concert debut has become the stuff of legend. Released years later as a concert film, Springsteen's London premiere depicted him in the act of wresting a time-eclipsing performance from his angst-ridden soul. But for many observers, including Springsteen himself, a second London show—performed just six days later after a quick swing through Stockholm and Amsterdam—proved to be even more triumphant, with Springsteen delivering an astounding *nine* encores to conclude his first European foray.

3. Capitol Theater, September 19, 1978

Springsteen's September 1978 concert at the Capitol Theater in Passaic, New Jersey, marks his most bootlegged performance—and for good reason. Having toured relentlessly behind the *Darkness* LP since May, Springsteen and the E Street Band were in top form. Broadcast live over WNEW radio, the show marked the musicians' exultant return to their home state. When they performed their set that night in the cozy eighteen-hundred-seat theater, the bandmates unleashed a show for the ages, charging through songs like "Badlands," "Racing in the Street," and "Prove It All Night" with unchecked intensity and abandon. By the time that the group cranked out their final encore—a spirited cover of Eddie Floyd's "Raise Your Hand"—Springsteen and the E Street Band had effected a spectacular climax to an incredible five-year run that had begun with their inception back in September 1972.

4. "Dream Baby Dream," 2005

Across nearly forty years of live performances, Springsteen had evolved a well-honed stage persona as a homespun preacher orating the soul-lifting gospel of rock and roll. By his 2005 *Devils & Dust* solo tour, he had elevated his presence further still, often acting as a progressive force promoting universal good. He self-consciously took to concluding his shows with a cover version of "Dream Baby Dream," which had been recorded in 1979 by the electro-punk band Suicide. In Springsteen's conception, "Dream Baby Dream" assumed even greater dimensions, emerging as a rousing, meditative anthem for a planet beset by vast socioeconomic inequalities as well as political and climatological uncertainty. With its plaintive Mellotron stylings, Springsteen's incarnation of "Dream Baby Dream" offered a glint of hope for a darkening world.

5. Springsteen on Broadway, 2017–2018

Inspired by the experience of writing his autobiography, *Born to Run*, Springsteen crafted a stage show in which he explored the vicissitudes of growing up and growing older with his own guitar and piano accompaniment. Across nearly three hundred performances, Springsteen's residency at the Walter Kerr Theatre became one of the hottest tickets on Broadway, at times rivaling Lin-Manuel Miranda's *Hamilton* for audience fervor. Writing in the *New York Times*, Jesse Green lauded Springsteen's theatrical run with unfettered praise. "As portraits of artists go," Green observed, "there may never have been anything as real—and beautiful—on Broadway." In many ways, Springsteen's Tony Award–winning show succeeded in bringing his life and magisterial career full circle, with his nightly orations taking him from his early days on the Jersey Shore as a son and fledgling musician to his later years as a husband, a father, and rock music's elder statesman.

Works Cited

Green, Jesse. "Review: *Springsteen on Broadway* Reveals the Artist, Real and Intense." *New York Times*, October 12, 2017.

Landau, Jon. "Growing Young with Rock and Roll." *Real Paper*, May 22, 1974.

Soghomonian, Talia. "Clarence Clemons's Five Best Bruce Springsteen Sax Solos." *NME*, June 19, 2011. www.nme.com/blogs/nme-blogs/clarence-clemons-five-best-bruce-springsteen-sax-solos-772777.

Part V

Springsteen, Sex, Race, and Gender

✧

"Thunder Road," Hartford Civic Center, Hartford, Connecticut, September 7, 1984. (Rocco S. Coviello)

18

Our Butch Mother, Bruce Springsteen

✦

NATALIE ADLER

When we say Bruce Springsteen is Dad Rock, what kind of father are we talking about? An average man made affable in retrospect? A bullseye for blame? A boss, a cop, a drill sergeant? Or better yet, a Daddy, suggestive of the erotic hidden behind the familial?

Though I know plenty of moms whose devotion to Bruce runs fiercer than any dad could know, there's a reason why we think of Springsteen as Dad Rock and not Mom Rock. The reason is that historically, over Springsteen's nearly fifty-year career, the dads have laid claim. In Springsteen, straight white dads of a certain age have seen their ultimate dad fantasy. In the words of Helena Fitzgerald, writing about Springsteen's ultimate "dadliness" in *Catapult*, "All a dad has to do to be a hero is show up." But not everyone shares that fandom. My broke, job-insecure generation of uncertain futures has little compassion for the Boomer nonsense of better days, especially when their nostalgia renders them fonder of their own childhoods than their actual children's futures.

That interpretation of Springsteen's fandom is limited by both generational and gender barriers. Behind the belief that his music speaks for the disaffected male, hard up and laid off, hides the assumption that class problems are either genderless or primarily a cis male concern.

Queer Springsteen fans see through that lie. Maggie Nelson has written about the "many-gendered mothers of the heart," a form of queer kinship that is both an intimacy and an identification. Springsteen has been our cis male Boomer dad for way too long. It's time to consider the possibility that he might be our butch lesbian mom.

I am not the first to note Springsteen's queer or even specifically lesbian appeal. If you are queer and the stereotypical Springsteen fan has always seemed to be the wrong side of Daddy to you, consider that tramps like us are *especially* born to run. He is not only for us, but also stands with us, from "Streets of Philadelphia" to refusing to play a show in North Carolina after the state passed legislation against trans people. In a fashion, he could even be one of us. The best male rock stars are many gendered and seldom straight: Prince, Bowie, Jagger. Consider Todd Haynes's biopic of Bob Dylan, *I'm Not There*, where the most convincing and curious portrayal of the star belonged to Cate Blanchett. And yet, Bruce (a butcher name there never was) is harder to claim as ours. Even if he shared a hot kiss with saxophonist Clarence Clemons at every concert, even if he wrote a song for Donna Summer to protest the racism and homophobia of the anti-disco movement, even if he sang a song called "My Lover Man," even if he admits in his memoir that his *Born in the U.S.A.* look of bandanas and muscles was "Christopher Street leather bar" gay, the ardent identification of the dads seems to disallow any other kind of desire for him. But in the same way you can know that you are gay before you know what it means, from a young age, I recognized Bruce Springsteen as the butch mother of my hungry heart.

Perhaps this is why, as a queer woman, I have never felt left out of his music—though I do feel left out of the fandom sometimes, in spite of my Central Jersey birthright—because the army of dads (and straight, white dads specifically) have claimed him so decisively. Much like Chris Christie on the beach, their fandom takes up all the space on what should be an abundant shoreline of possibility.

When I look at Springsteen, I might think Daddy, but the kind who wears a leather vest, not white sneakers and sweats. In the same way his protest song "Born in the U.S.A." has been misread as patriotic, his approach to masculinity has been misread as cis male, when it is in fact too performative to be anything but butch. To be clear, I am not claiming that

Bruce himself is queer. Showmanship, however, is a performance, as he reminds us over and over again in his memoir and Broadway show. His showmanship is genderqueer insofar as it is a performance of masculinity that draws attention to the distance between being identified as a man and identifying yourself as one.

Crowning a cis, straight white male as a butch icon is admittedly giving them more than their share—must *everything* be about them? As Hilton Als rightly asks in his review of *Springsteen on Broadway*, is it even "possible for straight white men to empathize with anything other than themselves"? But there is a disarming, queer playfulness in the art of labeling straight men as lesbians in disguise. It's a statement of protest that masculinity doesn't belong to cis men. The now defunct feminist website *The Toast* was once a great agora of declaring famous cis straight men, including Meat Loaf and William Shatner, as lesbian icons. But the fun isn't limited to snatching straight men from the strictures of heterosexuality. After the death of George Michael, Deb Schwartz paid her respects to our butch queen in pearls, may he rest in freedom.

It takes a certain amount of queer clairvoyance to sense a lesbian vibe from an obvious non-lesbian. The heart of butchness, however, is sometimes more literally worn on its sleeve. Als notes that Springsteen's "butch persona" allows him to reveal the smoke and mirrors behind the construct of masculinity. It also allows him a sense of empathy. As Walt Whitman wrote, "Agonies are one of my changes of garments / I do not ask the wounded person how he feels, I myself become the wounded person." And as with that other American poet, masculinity in Springsteen is as much a costume as it is a work uniform. Butchness is a way of wearing masculinity that plays on revealing and concealing emotion, an emotional identification as much as a sartorial choice.

The butchness Springsteen wears covers up hurt and vulnerability like a soft T-shirt under a leather jacket. Look at the cover of *Darkness on the Edge of Town*, the album that taught me not only how to dress, but how to stare. In his tight jeans, V-neck tee, and leather jacket, Bruce poses in front of a *floral wallpaper*, not a hot rod or a motorcycle. Add to that messy wavy hair, biker boots, and a flannel unbuttoned a little too far, and I had my look down. Fortunately for me, each of those items I inherited from my mother, who loved menswear and told me there were no rules for how to dress. I was free to believe that what looked hot on him would look hot on me, too, free to shrug off the old confusion of wanting him versus wanting to be him. Depending on my mood, I was prepared to be a soft butch by day and a hard femme by night. All I needed was my girl. You better get it straight, *darling*.

When I listened to Springsteen in my adolescence, I didn't switch the pronouns, and in turn learned something about the mutability of gender, the ease with which you could identify with the man singing or the woman to whom he sang, or even that there were more options than those two roles. There was possibility for me in these songs, a possibility of something that looked like equality for all expressions of gender, and permission that if I needed to feel like a gender different than the one I was told to take, I could. There is the possibility for those of us who do not identify as men to hear these songs about, allegedly, straight male desire, and still see something of ours in them. I've been listening to "Thunder Road" my whole life, for example, but it never occurred to me to identify with Mary. I was the aggressive one waiting with the car, making my butch plea to coax my closeted femme crush to run away with me. The song is beloved because the stakes are dire yet the win feels assured. Growing up without the omnipotent cultural promise of a happy romantic ending afforded to straight people, it was always hard to imagine what it would feel like to be promised a win. But perhaps in "Thunder Road," their happy ending is promised only so long as queerness remains subtext.

Sometimes queer love promises only disappointment, late nights wondering whether it is better to speak when you know it will turn out badly. Consider "I'm on Fire," a song that performs its gender roles to a T: "Hey little girl, is your Daddy home?" It's a song of butch torment and bad desire, of messing around with a straight girl with a boyfriend and knowing your love is futile, even if it runs hotter than his. This desire lashes out until you let it out: "At night I wake up with the sheets soaking wet / and a freight train running through the middle of my head / only you can cool my desire." Here's ancient Greek poet Sappho, from whom we get the words "sapphic" and "lesbian," in counterpoint: "You came and I was crazy for you / and you cooled my mind that burned with longing." It is hard to imagine straight desire feeling this *bad*, but if anyone can convince me, it's Bruce.

The butch/femme pair is a classic rock-and-roll dyad, with its shades of soft and stone. Unlike an imposed gender binary, the butch/femme pair inherits no violence and is based on adoration and complementarity rather than hierarchy. (The femme is just as much a take on femininity as butchness is to masculinity—it's not a catchall term for women.) The pair has roots in the postwar, working-class lesbian bars that probably bore some bizarro resemblance to the sort Bruce had to drag his dad out of, as he narrates in his memoir. In the novel *Stone Butch Blues*, Leslie Feinberg describes these bars as places of solace and rowdiness, safety and danger, considering the violent police raids to which such bars were always subject. When I first read *Stone Butch Blues*, it felt like a companion text to (or better, a dyke reboot of) *Darkness on the Edge of Town* or *The River*, insofar as it not only establishes queerness as a working-class concern but also traces the history of the queer struggle as concomitant with class struggle. Springsteen's own fraught relation to masculinity is inseparable from the class-related concerns of labor and exhaustion that all genders share, but experience differently. The will to fight against the desperation to leave, the urgency of repressed pain breaking through, the drive for survival that runs hotter than hope—all the familiar themes are there.

In *Stone Butch Blues*, as in Springsteen's music, intergenerational poverty and exploitation are the impediments to making it out alive, and in a body that feels like yours. The difference is, in the novel, the laid-off factory workers and union rabble rousers are not only cis, white, straight men. The protagonist, Jess, forges solidarity with the indigenous people of this country, with black civil rights crusaders, with sex workers, and, perhaps with the greatest difficulty, with her own burgeoning queer community as she tries on new words to describe her relation to gender and desire. Springsteen gives voice to these communities, too, but the voice of the dads who sing along loudest tend to drown out the others. The butchness that Springsteen wears becomes legible only through the queer love and class struggle that a writer like Feinberg describes. It's a toughness that gets forged by police beatings, pink slips, poverty, winter. A toughness that can protect love.

The stakes in a Springsteen song are nothing short of survival: "it ain't no sin to be glad you're alive." But survival isn't promised equally. Hanif Willis-Abdurraqib writes of going to the 2016 *The River* tour after making a trip to Ferguson, Missouri, and observes that the future Springsteen calls for, celebratory and forgiving, is so often stolen from black youths. It is for this reason that I feel compelled to wrest Springsteen's music from the tractor beam identification of the dads. They might be on their last chance power drive, but no one gets more chances than white men. The rest of us, and some more than others, are desperate for a future we can believe in, a future that looks like possibility, an open road leading to the horizon.

My actual mother is the one who taught me how to love Springsteen. Her stories of listening to his music when she was my age were different than my father's, less rosy: stories of staying home and crying and listening to "4th of July, Asbury Park (Sandy)" while her deadbeat boyfriend went to Point Pleasant for the Fourth of July without her. "Fuckin' Bob," she still shakes her head. We recently took each other to see *Springsteen on Broadway* as a Christmas present. Unsure of the dress code, I wore my biker boots, a leather skirt, and my *Darkness on the Edge of Town* T-shirt with the sleeves cut off. At one moment in his monologue, he listed local venues he had played with his first band, the Castiles, and mentioned Marlboro Psychiatric Hospital. In a stage whisper, my mother said to me, "Your grandmother was there." My grandmother, who died too young when I was eight, likely never saw Springsteen, in the hospital or otherwise. But I could imagine her, an inpatient of grief and alcoholism and bad luck, unimpressed with the young man and his guitar and his will to live. For a moment, I smiled at the thought of three generations of us at Springsteen concerts, but it passed, for the many-gendered mothers of my heart are not much interested in nostalgia. Better to keep your eyes on the road, on the future, roll down the window, and let the wind blow back your hair. Like Orpheus and Eurydice, let the men look back—let's get lost instead. Springsteen's music, taken to be emblematic of white male culture, expresses wisdom I've never learned from men. And because I did not so much interpret through a queer lens as I never thought any other way, I translated his masculine burdens into my butch virtues.

Toward the end of *Stone Butch Blues*, Jess finds a kindred spirit in her trans woman neighbor, Ruth. It's unclear whether or not their relationship will be sexual, but there is love between them, and desire, too, the kind Springsteen promises will greet you when you've honed your rough-ness into readiness. They discuss Ruth's painting of the sky: "It's not going to be day or night, Jess. It's always going to be that moment of infi-nite possibility that connects them." To me, this is the darkness on the edge of town, where the line between desperation and hope are obscured. Maybe it's always been easy for me to queer Springsteen songs because, as with queer culture, his yearning to *make it* seems so far from here, and yet possible. Queer theorist José Muñoz writes that "we may never touch queerness, but we can feel it as the warm illumination of a hori-zon imbued with possibility." The "we" he proposes is a community of those for whom the here and now isn't enough, who believe in a prom-ised land but know that that belief is hard won and hard kept, for the bad desire is just on the edge of the possible and survival isn't promised. My personal Springsteen anthem is "The Promised Land," queer for me every time I sing along: "Mister, I ain't a boy, no, I'm a man, and I believe in the promised land." (Not to mention the *drama*, my god: "Take a knife and cut this pain from my heart!")

You can argue that these themes are universal. *Everybody's* got a hun-gry heart, after all, even those who are never taught that their desires are bad. But saying that art speaks to everybody can easily erase par-ticulars and lose its bite in the urge to universalize. Springsteen might be the one true daddy, but Daddy doesn't mean the same thing to every-body. And anyway, the toughness he preaches reminds me of my mother and grandmother—tougher than the rest, sure, but a toughness that is only the leather exterior of vulnerability.

Works Cited

Als, Hilton. "'Springsteen on Broadway': Legends from a Life Story." *New Yorker*, October 30, 2017.

Feinberg, Leslie. *Stone Butch Blues: A Novel*. Ithaca, N.Y.: Firebrand Books, 1993.

Fitzgerald, Helena. "Bruce Springsteen: The Ultimate Dad." *Catapult*, January 18, 2017. www.catapult.co/stories/bruce-springsteen-the-ultimate-dad.

Kumbier, Alana. "How we got here." In *Because the Boss Belongs to Us*, edited by Alana Kumbier. Zine. Somerville, Mass., March 2011.

Masciotra, David. "Dear Straight Springsteen Fans: If You're Shocked That Bruce Can-celed His North Carolina Show, You Haven't Been Paying Attention." *Salon*, April 11, 2016. www.salon.com/2016/04/11/dear_straight_springsteen_fans_if

_youre_shocked_that_bruce_canceled_his_north_carolina_show_you_havent
_been_paying_attention/.

Muñoz, José Esteban. *Cruising Utopia: The Then and There of Queer Futurity.* New
York: New York University Press, 2009.

Rios, Carmen. "Playlist and Roundtable: We're Here and We're Queering Bruce
Springsteen." *Autostraddle*, January 14, 2015. www.autostraddle.com/playlist-and
-roundtable-were-here-and-were-queering-bruce-springsteen-268828/.

Schwartz, Deb. "George Michael Was an Over-the-top Butch Role Model." *The Cut*,
December 31, 2016. www.thecut.com/2016/12/george-michael-was-an-over-the-top
-butch-role-model.html.

Springsteen, Bruce. *Born to Run.* New York: Simon & Schuster, 2016.

Willis-Abdurraqib, Hanif. "A Night in Bruce Springsteen's America." *MTV News*,
February 17, 2017. www.mtv.com/news/2740249/a-night-in-bruce-springsteens
-america/.

19

Springsteen's Women

✦

Tougher Than the Rest

GINA BARRECA

I'm one of Bruce Springsteen's 5,441,231 (or so) fans, and while I haven't done the research, I suspect I'm not the only woman.

Springsteen looks like a guy who rose from the ranks, who didn't trade his work boots, jeans, and T-shirts for a leisure suit or a tux, and who didn't expect the women who accompanied him to change out of their T-shirts or leather jackets into gingham housedresses or matronly tweeds, either. He's known as the Boss, not the King; his fans don't idolize him but instead admire him. Springsteen's not even the Chairman of the Board as was that other singer from New Jersey, Frank Sinatra, because we like to think that Springsteen is not exactly part of the old boy's system.

Why do many of us, not only American women but also those from around the world, find Springsteen's music compelling? Is it because the female figures in his songs are not blank spaces on which to project male desire but are instead presented as human beings: flawed, passionate, fierce and smart, defiant, and daring even when damaged? Is it because, despite whatever difficulties they've faced, they remain intricately fascinating because of, not despite, their resilience? Is that why Springsteen's line "You ain't a beauty, but hey, you're all right" from "Thunder Road" remains a one-line anthem for the strong, defiant, and imperfect woman?

Yes.

Of all the lyrics ever written, even Julia Roberts chose that particular Springsteen line—"You ain't a beauty, but hey, you're all right"—as the one she believes most accurately represents her.

Imagine how the rest of us feel.

With lyrics focusing on what's abandoned, including abandoned factories, abandoned towns, and abandoned dreams, Springsteen also focuses on women with abandon: he writes about beer-drinking barefoot girls sitting on the hoods of cars, about factory girls who promise to unsnap their jeans, about girls who raise two kids alone in this mixed up world, about—in other words—tramps like us. Fifty years ago, Springsteen fans might have wanted to change their clothes, their hair, their faces, but instead they've—we've—aged together, unapologetically, not looking back at glory days except to mock our younger selves. If we're looking for partners, it's not for rescue or salvation but because we all need a companion for this part of the ride.

As a working-class guy from the boardwalk and not a rich boy from the beach, he seems not to see the world as marked "His" and "Hers" but "Theirs" and "Ours." You work for a living as a cook or a server, you have a chip on your shoulder the size of a boulder, you're as feral as you are housetrained, and you're willing to barter your safety for adventure? Male or female, or anybody in between, you're one of ours.

Springsteen's female fans, from Emmylou Harris and Taylor Swift to millions of ordinary people living somewhere between girlhood and death, hear him as a masculine narrator for an often decidedly feminized—and often feminist—story. Springsteen speaks not only to women but sometimes for women in a way that few men in rock and roll ever dared.

Who are the women in Springsteen's songs, the Marys, Marias, Sandys, Rosies, and Suzys? The mothers, the gypsies, the girlfriends, the pick-ups, the silicon-sisters, the ones who represent all that heaven will allow and the ones that'll be in your arms only once hell freezes over?

Shaped by mistakes too unintentional or innocent to be called sins, Springsteen's women go through life with scars deep enough to need sutures. They've been strung out and yet they've pulled themselves together, becoming more resilient because of their weaknesses. They bring their undainty, undaunted, and maybe unquenchable appetites for music, sex, love, anger, family, and the road ahead to Springsteen's stage.

And Springsteen brings the energy of his stage show to the women's movement. In 2017, he announced onstage in Melbourne his support for the Women's March in protest "against hate and division and in support of tolerance, inclusion, reproductive rights, civil rights, racial justice, LGBTQ rights, the environment, wage equality, gender equality, health care, and immigrant rights." Springsteen called the hundreds of thousands who marched in cities across the globe "the new American resistance."

The woman in a Springsteen song is familiar with resistance and issues of inequity and injustice. She's lived through them and that's one of the reasons she's usually generous, compassionate, and wise. Nobody's fool, she's also intuitive and, to a point, forgiving: as he writes in "Red-Headed Woman," she can "see every cheap thing that you've ever done" and yet she makes you want to "get down on your knees" and taste her. She can rotate your tires, metaphorically and probably literally, because she's been out there on the road long enough to know how stuff works.

In other words—and even if she might not use the word herself—the women in Springsteen's songs are feminists. Independent, loving, and courageous, she is nobody's object, property, or plaything. She's accepted the responsibilities of adult life whether or not she's been given the choice. If Bobby said he'd pull out but instead he stays in, she's the one who'll walk the floors night after night even though she's a young girl who misses the party lights, thinking that "her whole life feels like one big mistake."

But Janey only believes this until she realizes she can revise her own narrative. While the happy ending might not look like anything out of Disney, Janey's story, and her son's, will at least be their own. Made of spare parts and broken hearts, with lives that can seem like one long emergency, Springsteen's women are tough to categorize; like their male counterparts, they are tougher than the rest. They've also been around a time or two.

And, as Springsteen writes in his memoir *Born to Run*, the women in his life are survivors, knowing that they can "move on, with a heart stronger in the places it's been broken," and that they'll be able to "create new love, hammer pain and trauma into a righteous sword and use it in defense of life, love, human grace and God's blessings."

Worshipping at the darkened shrines of the boardwalk while admiring the gaudy spectacle of the church, his Marys aren't virgins and his hell is something you might just have to pass through before you leave this world.

In *Born to Run*, describing a time in the early 1970s when he and the E Street Band were recording *The Wild, the Innocent & the E Street Shuffle*, Springsteen introduces readers to a woman with whom he was living by saying she was "Italian, funny, a beatific tomboy, with just the hint of a lazy eye" who wore a "pair of glasses that made me think of the wonders of the library."

Julia Roberts could have played that role.

It's precisely the imperfections that make this character, briefly mentioned, memorable and endearing. Is it a surprise that a hundred pretty women are knocking down his door and that all the little girls want to tear him apart? I'm not even mentioning all the folks who want to kiss him and the gender-neutral implications of that line.

The man in Springsteen's songs says he wants to be our friend and we believe he wants to guard our dreams and visions. That guy understands he's nobody's bargain (needing a little touch up and a little paint) and also understands that he's no hero, since the only possible redemption he can offer comes from beneath a dirty hood. Whether the word "hood" refers to a car, a neighborhood, the hood of a sweatshirt, or the hoodlum wearing it, we're left to decipher for ourselves.

We're willing to accept his promise that what others may want for free—such as love—he's willing to work for, and that even though he can see the ghosts in the eyes of all the boys we sent away, we're the one with fire. (Confession: I've loved Springsteen's music since I heard "Blinded by the Light" in 1974 when I was seventeen. I wanted to be the girl in every Springsteen song as soon as I knew there was such a thing. I'd snuck, underage and over-eye shadowed, into the shady places Springsteen sang about. I knew about chaperones that stood in corners to watch young girls dance. But all I really wanted was to be standing next to a son who had the guts to tell his Mama that looking at reflections of light in order to stay safe isn't worth the protection it promises. Better to be blinded by the light than remain all your days hunkered down in the shadows of your old man's garage, your mother's failed dreams, the darkness of seaside bars, or, for that matter, Plato's cave.)

The long walk from the apparent security of conventional life's front porch to the adventure and challenge of his front seat might not be free, but if we make the bargain, we'll be free to let the wind blow back our hair and look into the sights of the sun. Because all of us are willing to sing along, we're the one. We see ourselves in Springsteen's lyrics as if the words were mirrors—compact mirrors, rearview mirrors, or funhouse mirrors—and locate ourselves in the landscape of his music. We look into his life as if it were a mirror as well, as we so often do with popular and beloved artists. I daresay we cheer, adore, and approve of Springsteen's second wife, Patti Scialfa, because she seems like one of us,

The breathtaking narcissism underlying such a reflection might be staggering, I'll admit that. But I don't believe it renders it inaccurate. I'm one of 5,441,231, remember. Surely I'm not the only one who can be thinking this—and while it doesn't explain how I respond to Springsteen's fifty years of writing music, I'm not going to leave it out.

Springsteen married Julianne Phillips in 1985. In my late twenties, I was living on Lafayette Street in the East Village that year, in an unhappy first marriage myself, with the line "I'm sick of sitting 'round here trying to write this book" from "Dancing in the Dark" written in red Sharpie on an index card taped over my desk because I was starting my dissertation. Not that I was bitter.

I wasn't the only one. I was not surprised that fans quoted in a *Rolling Stone* article laughed Springsteen's engagement to Phillips off as a mistake. Little girls in high school, women working on Wall Street, and married moms in suburban diners were equally disgruntled, as if Bruce—in this context, his first name was the only way to talk about him—betrayed them by choosing a literally picture-perfect twenty-five-year-old represented by the Elite Modeling Agency, a poster-child for the idealized WASP all-American feminine archetype. We heard Springsteen sing "There's a joke here somewhere and it's on me" and wondered.

In anybody's book, Phillips was a polished ingénue—and the world she represented was more Madame du Barry and less Madam Marie than we'd have liked. According to the New York *Daily News*, Phillips was "a young woman thoroughly comfortable in her own skin. Fair skinned and blue eyed, with a lissome figure and classic schoolgirl features, Julianne floated through Lake Oswego High School, waving the pom-poms with the cheerleaders on Saturday night and cutting a fine figure in her dad's MG roadster."

With daddy's car pulling into the hamburger stand, she probably forgot all about the library like she told her old man. Or maybe not; Springsteen's wish for all that heaven would allow sounded heartfelt enough. And yet as we listened to 1987's *Tunnel of Love*, we tried to decipher that first, brief marriage, where there were the three of them—him, her, and all the stuff they were so scared of—and figure out where they were headed.

In *Born to Run*, Springsteen describes his second wife and bandmate, whom he married in 1991, in radically different terms from his first. Scialfa, an inspiring, demanding, and complex woman, "did not live to make you feel safe. I liked all of this . . . I felt the risk of a formidable partner. When I started seeing Patti, she was deeply pleasurable, intelligent and exciting, but she scared me. I was putting my trust in her and despite her interest, I wasn't so sure she really wanted it." That's a fair balance, allowing for one step forward and two steps back for both parties. It's what permits a marriage, a duet, a partnership, and a life where people who think about such things and accept responsibility to be good companions for this part of the ride.

In a 2017 interview with *Variety*, Springsteen explained that he and Scialfa "developed natural boundaries. Some places we have a more professional approach, like if I walk into the studio while she's working. . . . When she comes onstage with the E Street Band she's an E Street Band member, and when we walk offstage we're husband and wife." He names two songs they've sung as duets for many years, "Brilliant Disguise" and "Tougher Than the Rest," as the ones that remain his favorite to sing with Scialfa: "Those are songs we've sung together for a lotta years, and they encapsulate our relationship in a very universal but personal way."

Universal but personal is how Springsteen has made his music feel to his fans for nearly fifty years, and women in his music are included in the universal, not marginalized by it. Those who fall from grace find in Springsteen's lyrics either a safe place to land or a sense of urgency to rise up, relying on a collective sense of shared power and contagious strength.

Of course Springsteen is a feminist. The women in his songs have always been human beings, with their own souls, wishes, nightmares, and achievements. They're not there for decoration or blind devotion; they're part of the music and a vital part of Springsteen's world. They're equally tough and equally vulnerable, as able to make their own decisions and chart their own courses as any man. And, like any man, they are able to fail.

But has the possibility of failure ever stopped a Springsteen figure, male or female, from doing a damn thing? Reminding us to show a little faith because there's still magic in the night, we listen.

Works Cited

Aswad, Jem. "Bruce Springsteen Talks Politics, Marriage and Why He Won't Write an 'Anti-Trump Diatribe.'" *Variety*, October 4, 2017. www.variety.com/2017/music/news/bruce-springsteen-politics-trump-marriage-1202576624/.

Carlin, Peter Ames. *Bruce*. New York: Touchstone/Simon & Schuster, 2012.

Ginsberg, Merle. "Bruce Springsteen: The Fans." *Rolling Stone*, June 25, 2018. www.rollingstone.com/music/music-news/bruce-springsteen-the-fans-55454/.

Margaret, Mary. "Julia Roberts: I'd Be So Lonely without Danny Moder." *People*, October 13, 2007. www.people.com/celebrity/julia-roberts-id-be-so-lonely-without-danny-moder/.

Springsteen, Bruce. "We Are the New American Resistance." *Brucespringsteen.net*, January 22, 2017. www.brucespringsteen.net/news/2017/we-are-the-new-american-resistance.

20

Shackled and Drawn

✧

LAUREN ONKEY

Pop quiz: Which song has Bruce Springsteen covered more times in concert: Woody Guthrie's iconic folk anthem "This Land Is Your Land" or Eddie Floyd's 1967 R&B hit "Raise Your Hand"?

The answer is "Raise Your Hand." But I suspect that most people would guess "This Land Is Your Land." His cover version of that song, first performed on *The River* tour in 1980, evokes Springsteen the American hero, the Kennedy Center Honor winner, the memoirist, the political voice. It's the Springsteen most embraced by scholars: the writerly Springsteen, who easily references books and films as influences and can command the stage at significant cultural events. But the throughline of Springsteen's career, from covering Martha Reeves and the Vandellas' "Dancing in the Street" with his early rock band Steel Mill to singing lines from the Cadillacs' "Gloria" on his solo (and writerly) *Devils & Dust* tour to his Broadway show where he passionately remembers listening to the radio as a child, has been Springsteen's assertion of the power and cultural significance of soul music to his own work and to the history of rock and roll.

I bought my first Bruce Springsteen record, the "Born to Run" single, in 1975, when I was twelve years old, and have been a fan ever since. In many ways, Springsteen shaped how I understood rock history. From the beginning, Springsteen himself has been somewhat of a rock-and-roll historian, covering surprising chestnuts from the pre-psychedelic era of rock and roll that were pretty out of step with 1970s rock (Harold Dorman's "Mountain of Love," the Crystals' "Then He Kissed Me," and the Dovells' "You Can't Sit Down," to note just a few examples); explaining genres and artists from the stage (like his 1978 tour jokes about the glories of "fraternity rock"); using his celebrity to reintroduce forgotten artists from the early 1960s like Gary U.S. Bonds, Ronnie Spector, and Darlene Love; and giving Rock and Roll Hall of Fame induction speeches. Springsteen's version of rock history reveres the girl groups and soul music that emerged after the first big bang of rock and roll. In 2012 at the South by Southwest Conference, Springsteen used his keynote speech to map out his version of what matters in rock-and-roll history, and soul music was at the center:

> And it was here, amongst these great African American artists, that I learned my craft. You learned how to write. You learned how to arrange. You learned what mattered and what didn't. You learned what a great production sounds like. You learned how to lead a band. You learned how to front a band. These men and women, they were and they remain my masters. By the time I reached my twenties, I'd spent a thousand nights employing their lessons in local clubs and bars, honing my own skills. I was signed as an acoustic singer / songwriter, but I was wolf in sheep's clothing.

Springsteen constantly dropped references to soul and girl group records into live performances, and I followed them like bread crumbs. Through Springsteen, I learned about Chris Kenner ("Something You Got"), Major Lance ("Monkey Time," the inspiration for "The E Street Shuffle"), and Patti Labelle and the Bluebelles ("I Sold My Heart to the Junkman," which Springsteen covered in 1974 and referenced on "New York City Serenade"). It became a ritual for me to find the original source of the cover (a more difficult task in the 1970s and 1980s than now) and learn about the story of the artists Springsteen worked into his repertoire. It felt like a service, like when a friend turns you on to a song they like. It shaped how I understood the history of rock and roll: it wasn't all guys, guitars, and albums. It was one-hit wonders, beautiful vocal harmonies, and perfectly crafted pop songs. It's a version of the music that felt inclusive: racially integrated, and with lots of women at the boys club.

In 1971, before he signed with Columbia Records, Springsteen assembled the Bruce Springsteen Band, a ten-piece ensemble with horn players and African American female backup singers. Inspired at the time by Van Morrison's sound on albums like *His Band and the Street Choir*, Springsteen seemed to be searching for a sound that would connect rock and soul in the tradition of the Rascals, Sly and the Family Stone, and the Isley Brothers. Such a large band was not financially sustainable in the early days of his career, and so he dropped the horns and singers after a few months. Occasionally, Springsteen has toured with these soul band elements—like the 1988 *Tunnel of Love* tour with a horn section or the 1992 tour with five backup singers—but they've rarely been front and center in his performances.

But then, for the *Wrecking Ball* tour that began in 2012, he assembled his biggest band ever, with a full horn section and backup singers—it hearkened back to the Bruce Springsteen Band. I loved this band, maybe best among all versions of the E Street Band I've ever seen, even more than the classic 1975 to 1981 lineup. The older I get, the more I understand the importance of soul music to my own life and identity—it's the sound I always return to, a docking station, a home. And so it's especially resonant for me how much it's come forward in Springsteen's music in the last fifteen years, live and in the studio. These sounds reflect the high-water mark of racial integration on the pop charts in the late 1960s and early 1970s. They carry with them gospel's hope that we can be better and blues' caution that we're not there yet.

Despite the soul and gospel in Springsteen's sound and his commitment to assembling integrated bands, his concerts attract virtually all-white audiences. This fact dilutes what can feel like the utopian community that is created onstage. We know this drill: when fifteen thousand white folks gather to look to black folks to represent soul and authenticity and emotion, psychic mayhem ensues. Our fractured, shared history shows itself in the arena, if we can face it. It can't just be a soul party. "We're baptized in these waters," Bruce sings on "American Skin (41 Shots)," "and in each other's blood."

On the *Wrecking Ball* tour, I felt this stutter step of emotion—joy and disappointment, physical release and deep reflection—during one of my favorite songs from the show, "Shackled and Drawn." It's a classic Springsteen trick: joyful noise with the blues buried inside. It's the story of a man whose lack of work is so devastating that it leaves him feeling shackled. But it's a whooping, hollering raver. With its *Seeger Sessions* mash-up of folk, country, Cajun, and gospel sounds, the song—especially the chorus—feels like a release. But the guy in the song is imprisoned; work gives him identity and purpose, keeping him free and far from the devil. "Shackled" is an old word. Musical and lyrical allusions to the American past run through many of the songs on *Wrecking Ball*, suggesting that the economic devastation that the characters experience, their disempowerment, is an old story, one imbedded deep in American capitalism itself. As Springsteen said in an interview when the record came out: "I use a lot of folk music. There's some Civil War music. There's gospel music. There are '30s horns. That's the way I used the music—the idea was that the music was going to contextualize historically that this has happened before: it happened in the 1970s, it happened in the '30s, it happened in the 1800s . . . it's cyclical. Over, and over, and over, and over again."

But "shackled" doesn't just reference a generic American past. It references the African American story specifically, where shackles were a way of life for enslaved people. Springsteen is often praised for writing about "the working man," the voice of the common man, yet when most people haul out that cliché, they mean a white working-class guy. The word "shackled" points us elsewhere.

The joy in the song comes from its propulsive rhythm and the passion and scale of the chorus. The album version features veterans of the Seeger Sessions Band: Patti Scialfa, Soozie Tyrell, Lisa Lowell, and Cindy Mizelle on vocals as well as Curt Ramm, Clark Gayton, Ed Manion, Art Baron, and Stan Harrison on horns. Lyrically, the chorus provides the singer comfort in community, even an enslaved one: despite the high times for the banking class up in the mansion on a hill, "down here below *we're* shackled and drawn." And in classic Springsteen style, he posits singing—and singing together—as the only way through it.

And then the song takes a twist, in the form of a reference to Lyn Collins's "Me and My Baby Got Our Own Thing Going" from 1972.

Collins, known as the "Female Preacher," was a member of James Brown's band and had her biggest hit with "Think (About It)," also from 1972. "Me and My Baby" opens in church, with male vocalists providing a bed of "yeah, yeahs" under Collins exhortations to the congregation: "I want all you proud sisters to stand up! I want everyone to stand up and be counted tonight! Brothers and sisters you know we got to pray together! I want you to stand on up!" The song itself is a horn-driven, up-tempo expression of a satisfied couple. It's a fun song, but it wasn't a hit—it just grazed the lower reaches of the pop chart when it was released.

In "Shackled and Drawn," Springsteen doesn't actually sample "Me and My Baby." Instead, the great Cindy Mizelle sings the preaching lines from the opening as "Shackled and Drawn" fades out: "I want everybody to stand up and be counted tonight! You know we got to pray together!" Heard initially on the album version, this reference to the Lyn Collins song in "Shackled and Drawn" is a small moment, one of a few musical samples on *Wrecking Ball*. The mash-up of genres and instruments along with the soul reference suggests an expansive and inclusive idea of American music. But it's not a random sample. Springsteen's use of this obscure track pushes us to ask about the meaning of Mizelle's closing vocal part in the context of the song's narrative. Her voice connects the plight of the white laborer to the voices in the African American church. It's a call to the community to come together, be counted, and pray.

In concert throughout the 2012–2013 tour, Springsteen made the Collins reference a key part of the song: Mizelle's voice moved to the center and the song expanded in length and incorporated a polyrhythmic, percussive opening, reminiscent of Joe Tex's "I Gotcha." Mizelle came down from the vocal line every night, sang and danced with Springsteen at center stage, and stole the show. "Shackled and Drawn" was the song that best showcased the rock and soul hybrid of the expanded E Street Band.

The performance mixed rhythm and politics. I heard it as a challenge to dance and think at the same time, to think about work and identity and race and music and how they are tangled together. As the song peaked, all the mobile members of the band—horns, singers, guitar players—stepped to the edge of the stage and danced it home. Every time I saw this song in concert, this moment made me feel great. And then one night I looked at Cindy Mizelle, an underrated musician who had become key to Springsteen's sound over several tours, and then at the fifteen thousand white folks dancing along (or looking at their phones and waiting for Bruce to play something a little less black, a little more rock, a little less political), and I got a chill up my back. In that space, Mizelle takes on a symbolic role as the embodiment of soul and passion for a white crowd, and that exchange has an ugly and complex history. We're still in a world where white listeners project their own joy and identity on the bodies and voices of black performers.

Bruce Springsteen's legacy around race is broader than his championing of soul music. But by arguing onstage and on record for the significance of a black musical legacy at the heart of rock and roll, Springsteen has done important work, asking us to redefine who matters in a genre now seen almost exclusively as skinny white guys with guitars. And at the same time, his work reveals that simply loving the music isn't enough. Fandom for African American music cannot be substituted for actually doing something to dismantle racism and white privilege. We need to live up to the potential and possibility of the integrated world the music offers, not escape in its joyous release.

Works Cited

Springsteen, Bruce. "Bruce Springsteen's SXSW 2012 Keynote Speech." *NPR*, March 18, 2012. www.npr.org/2012/03/16/148778665/bruce-springsteens-sxsw-2012-keynote-speech.

———. Interview at International Press Conference in Paris, February 2012. In *Talk about a Dream: The Essential Interviews of Bruce Springsteen*, edited by Christopher Phillips and Louis P. Masur, 406–420. New York: Bloomsbury, 2013.

21

American Skin

◆

Springsteen and Blackness

ELIJAH WALD

My introduction to Bruce Springsteen was the cover of *Born to Run*. The photograph promised the Bob Dylan of *Highway 61 Revisited* shoulder to shoulder with King Curtis, and in 1975 that was just what I was looking for. I was coming out of high school in the disco era and regarded current pop as a choice between sappy songwriters and dopey dance music. Parties were all about KC and the Sunshine Band getting down tonight while we danced the hustle, the bus stop, and the latest steps the cool girls copped from *Soul Train*. It was fun—unlike the white-bread balladry of Harry Chapin and Cat Stevens—but it wasn't my thing. I was into blues, folk, early soul, and oldies rock and roll, and *Born to Run* promised a return to those roots.

It was a few months before a friend who had the album invited me over to listen, and by then I'd read the press on Springsteen and was fully primed to be enthusiastic. But when the needle dropped, instead of a blast of bluesy, rocking soul I got middlebrow pop keyboards, a muddy wash of guitar and bass, and an occasionally audible saxophone. I liked Springsteen's voice and attitude and I wanted to like the record, but it had all the studio-slick faults of the mid-1970s major-label mainstream. The title track sounded like it would be good live, but there was no redeeming "She's the One," with finger-exercise harpsichord over thumping bass and the sax mixed down to sonic wallpaper. Which is to say, despite the cover, it sounded safely, blandly white.

I was a middle-class Jewish kid from Cambridge, Massachusetts, and had not in any way earned my contempt for that homogenized whiteness. But what was Springsteen if not a fantasy figure for kids like me? What was that cover photo if not a promise to fuse folk/rock Bohemianism with the soul of Wilson Pickett and Aretha Franklin?

Over the following decades I occasionally dipped into Springsteen's work, since people I respected thought he was the greatest. But I never saw him live and the recordings continued to fall short of the excessive praise and my enduring hopes. I only recaptured my first sense of excitement forty years later, when I read his memoir—once again titled *Born to Run*.

As a memoirist, Springsteen had exactly the perspective I'd wanted in his music. Describing his high school band, the Castiles, he wrote, "We were all little white boys with weak time and voices, but hey, that didn't stop the Stones, and the Stones were our Holy Grail and blueprint of cool." That is charmingly modest, but also shows a keen musical insight: rock critics have tended not to notice the Rolling Stones had weak time, because they compare the band to other British rockers rather than to American R&B outfits. Springsteen is declaring comradeship with "the world's greatest rock 'n' roll band" but also recognizing their limitations: the Castiles and the Stones were both, at bottom, "little white boys" doing their best in a style they loved but could never fully master.

For Springsteen, that insight was unavoidable: he was working clubs on the Jersey Shore, where black music ruled the radio and hot rhythm sections ruled the floor—in his words, "You had to get the girls dancing!" The one extant recording of a Castiles performance shows a competent dance band covering everything from mellow mainstream rock to gritty southern soul. Recalling those days, Springsteen takes particular pride in a 1966 gig at an African American club where the Castiles played an opening set and backed a hit R&B vocal group, the Exciters. The repertoire was "soul, soul, and more soul," and by the end, "We'd decently won over a black crowd suspicious of the white-boy hippies and backed the Exciters without embarrassing ourselves."

Springsteen was among the last major rockers to come up in that world, playing for audiences that wanted the current black dance hits.

By the time I was in high school, rock bands played for white kids who were listening rather than dancing, and white, black, Latino, and Asian kids all danced to records by black groups (and the occasional white guy like KC, who we thought was black). Instead of taking pride in their ability to get dancers on the floor and play the current hits, rockers took pride in playing their own material and wore "Disco sucks" T-shirts.

I saw the *Born to Run* cover as an attempt to bridge that divide, restoring the mythic fusions of early rock and roll: black and white, edgy and soulful, guitars and saxophones. Referring to that picture in later years, Springsteen would say, "I leaned on Clarence a lot; I made a career out of it in some ways." I read that as a confirmation of my response: I was attracted to Springsteen as a rocker who was trying to preserve the music's black roots, not only by playing styles grounded in blues and soul, but by working with black musicians. The problem was the often-recycled joke that a typical Springsteen concert had more African Americans onstage than in the audience—meaning Clemons, and only Clemons.

It wasn't supposed to be that way. Jon Landau, the critic who famously hailed Springsteen as the future of rock and roll (and a year later became his producer), had written eloquently about the problem of white rock fans turning their backs on contemporary black trends, and the group he celebrated in 1974 had three white members—Springsteen, Danny Federici, and Garry Tallent—and three black members: Clemons; Ernest "Boom" Carter; and David Sancious, who had played with Springsteen off and on since the late 1960s and whose mother's address in Belmar, New Jersey, gave the E Street Band its name.

That was the group that recorded the title track of *Born to Run*, but when Sancious and Carter left to pursue their own project, Springsteen replaced them with white musicians, Roy Bittan and Max Weinberg. For all but the earliest fans, this was the E Street Band. As a result, few recall the change with regret. Indeed, Springsteen is almost alone in suggesting it was a problem—and he only treats it that way when he considers the effect on Clemons: "He struggled living in the predominantly white world of our band . . . the loss of Davey Sancious and Boom Carter deeply affected him. For a long time he was alone, and no matter how close we were, I was white. We had as deep a relationship as I can imagine, but we lived in the real world, where . . . nothing, not all the love in God's heaven, obliterates race."

Sensitive as that passage is, Springsteen has never directly addressed his decision to hire two white players. He was in a difficult situation, under pressure to find top-flight musicians for a working band on the verge of a potential breakthrough but not yet in a position to offer huge salaries. If we leave race out of the equation, he was lucky to find such skillful and supportive sidemen, and the new lineup became one of the most popular bands in history. But it is hard to ignore the clashing messages as one looks at that iconic album photo, blazoning a racial balance the band had just lost.

Or rather, it apparently is not hard at all. Few chroniclers of Springsteen's artistic evolution bother to note the racial shift, and those few tend to mention it only in passing. One reason may be that having even one black band member is exceptional in a world of all-white rock groups—in white American parlance, "diversity" tends to mean mostly "us" with a few of "them," so we can feel good about ourselves without feeling threatened—and by that standard the new E Street Band was ideally diverse.

I can't blame people who discovered Springsteen after the shift for not highlighting the absence of band members they discovered only in retrospect. But it is harder to explain the almost complete critical silence about race when Springsteen broke up the E Street Band in the early 1990s and replaced all but one of his veteran sidemen with young unknowns. Critics debated the strengths and weaknesses of the new group, most describing it as both an artistic and commercial mistake, but very few even mentioned that seven of the nine new band members were black, and Dave Marsh—Springsteen's most assiduous chronicler—is the only one to treat that fact as significant.

Marsh knows Springsteen's music intimately, and he wrote that the racial shift changed it in interesting ways: The new rhythm section of drummer Zach Alford and bassist Tommy Sims "no longer concerned itself only with drive and dramatic accent, but with more subtle things," exploring and playing with the time in ways even expert rock drummers rarely manage; the crew of backing vocalists, all but one of them black, provided a gospel foundation; and Crystal Taliaferro, the singer and multi-instrumentalist who stepped into Clemons's role as Springsteen's center-stage partner, brought "commanding stage presence and unstoppable energy."

Marsh also noted the widespread negative reaction among critics and concert audiences and suggested "race had everything to do with why so many of the Big Bruce Fans disliked the Other Band." He diplomatically maintained that this was not racism, but rather a kind of conservative protectionism, preserving a white comfort zone in the age of hip-hop: "Rock and roll had come to signify whiteness and stability, a complete reversal of what it meant in the fifties and sixties, which was blackness and anarchy. . . . With his four-square rhythms, caution and dignity, emphasis on narrative and craft, reliance on sounds played by hands and not triggered by synthesizer patches, Bruce Springsteen became an icon of reassurance."

The distinction between racism and maintaining a conservative white aesthetic is tricky at best—the term "rockism" was coined for just this situation—and Springsteen was notably silent about the new band's racial composition. In a long 1992 interview for *Rolling Stone*, he discussed the sad state of American race relations and the challenge and excitement of working with his new musicians, but he never mentioned that most of them were black, nor does he mention this in his memoir. Perhaps he preferred to treat the racial makeup of the group as incidental, implying he just hired the best people for the job—the same explanation he has always given for choosing two white musicians in 1974.

For me, the race of the new band was significant not because it dramatically changed Springsteen's music, but because it didn't. As a deep, longtime listener, Marsh noted subtle differences, but to an outsider the new group still sounded like basic Springsteen. The visual symbolism of an iconic white rocker fronting an overwhelmingly black group was striking, but the music was still firmly in the rock mainstream. The only explicitly black element was the gospel-flavored backup vocals, which were already a cliché of white rock when Lou Reed referenced "the colored girls" twenty years earlier in "Walk on the Wild Side."

Indeed, Springsteen's description of the 1992–1993 tour suggests how removed he was from the world of his young sidemen. He writes, "Tommy Sims was all Ohio Players, Parliament Funkadelic and seventies funk, music I wasn't that familiar with." Along with the "Philly sound," which he also mentions in this context, that was basically the soundtrack of my high school years, and I was struck that someone who in the mid-1960s was playing dances featuring "soul, soul, and more soul" had so quickly fallen out of touch with black music.

Of course that disconnect was not unique to Springsteen—it was inherent in the shift from rock and roll to rock. The first term was promoted in the 1950s as a substitute for the racially coded "rhythm and blues," originally as a way of selling black music to white teenagers, but soon denoting an impressively integrated pop scene. Audiences might still be separated by race, but onstage and on television it became standard to see a mix of white and black hitmakers.

That was the world in which Springsteen grew up and honed his skills, and though still permeated by racism, it was a world in which crossing racial lines was a recognized mark of hip and cool. He and his friends shopped in black clothing stores and checked out music in black clubs. Garry Tallent even worked for a while in a black soul band—Little Melvin and the Invaders, which also included Clarence Clemons—and wryly recalled being treated as a novelty, the "funky little white boy."

Clemons similarly spent some time as the only black member of a white band, Norman Seldin and the Joyful Noyze, and likewise described this as unusual: "You had your black bands and your white bands and if you mixed the two, you found less places to play. . . . When he hired me, Norman did in fact lose some bookings. A few club owners were fearful that my presence would attract a Negro crowd and scare the white kids away."

Both jazz and rock historians have often framed their favorite music as a catalyst for social integration, but musical interchange need not include social mixing. In some periods, shared tastes encouraged black and white patrons to mix in clubs and on dance floors, but as styles evolved their audiences have often resegregated. If the first wave of rock and roll brought teenagers together, listening and dancing to the same bands, by the mid-1960s the rise of discotheques—dance clubs that used records rather than bands—made it easy for white kids to dance to black music without being in rooms with any black people. The British Invasion introduced some white listeners to older black styles (notably Chicago blues) but also separated rock from current black trends, and it became common for rock bands to play for non-dancing listeners while records by black artists ruled the dance floor.

Springsteen spent his early years moving back and forth between the new poles: after his stint with the Castiles, he formed a power trio playing what he recalled as "a repertoire of modern blues standards popularized by Clapton, Hendrix, Beck and the like." (Eric Clapton and Jeff Beck were both English, and although Jimi Hendrix was black, he arrived on the rock scene as an import from London with an English rhythm section.) Springsteen honed his skills at the Upstage Club in Asbury Park, where blues-rock was the common language, and recalled making a first splash with a guitarslinger version of "Rock Me, Baby," a B. B. King R&B hit that had become a rock standard thanks to Hendrix, Beck, and the San Francisco band Blue Cheer.

Virtually all the musicians in Springsteen's Jersey crew were Upstage regulars: Tallent, Danny Federici, Vini Lopez, Steve Van Zandt, Southside Johnny Lyon—and David Sancious, a unique black participant. Springsteen described Sancious as "a completely new presence on the scene," a black musician who had "the courage to cross the tracks and enter the primarily white rock world of the Upstage Club in search of musical adventure."

Sancious recalled, "I was nervous about it. It wasn't a place where black people went." He was pleased to find "a little sense of community," saying that despite the day-to-day racism he faced outside, "amongst that scene of people, especially the musicians . . . there was no funky racial vibe at all." Nonetheless, "the only black music being played in there was by white kids who were fans of black music and trying to learn how to play it."

Judging by what survives on tape, most of that "black music" was older blues recycled as blues-rock. Rather than playing current soul styles, Springsteen's next notable group, Steel Mill, is best remembered for an Allman Brothers pastiche called "Goin' Back to Georgia"—and the racial composition of the Allmans' group neatly presaged the classic E Street Band: white fans tend to remember it as interracial, while black listeners remember it as a white band with a black percussionist.

If Springsteen had evolved from that group into his singer-songwriter phase and on to *Born to Run*, this would be a straightforward story of a white rocker following a timely trajectory from rock-and-roll dance music through the Stones, Dylan, and the Allmans to a leading role in the wave of working-class rock he shared with Bob Seger and Tom Petty.

But unlike most of his peers, Springsteen made a few more stabs at playing black music, not only through lip service to "roots" but by working with black musicians.

In 1971 he formed a band with a trumpet and a saxophone and placed an ad in the paper for two "Girl Soul Gospel Singers," which was answered by Barbara Dinkins and Delores Holmes. According to later writers, his models at this point were Joe Cocker and, especially, Van Morrison—British tastes again—but judging by what survives from this period it was not that simple. In particular, there was an outdoor concert that July in New York's Damrosch Park where the band alternated guitar duels between Springsteen and Steve Van Zandt with Memphis-style horn arrangements and Dinkins and Holmes not only providing soulful backup but, in Dinkins's case, singing lead on two songs. Neither of these songs appears on any other Springsteen set list, and a third appears only on a couple from the same period: the self-explanatory "Dance, Dance, Dance." It is striking to listen to that performance, a year before Springsteen made his LP debut as a Dylanesque singer-songwriter with *Greetings from Asbury Park, N.J.*, and hear him singing music that was actually geared to the Asbury Park clubs, supported by horns and soul harmonies: "There ain't nothing to it, let your body go and / dance, dance, dance!"

Lyrics like that were standard in early rock and roll, but by the seventies they heralded the disco craze and Springsteen was moving in other directions. In career terms, and probably in artistic terms as well, it was a smart move, but he still sounds regretful when he talks about that group: "We had a lot of pretty good music," he told Peter Ames Carlin, but his audience expected "riff rock, prog rock . . . I realized that's what people like, and they didn't like rhythm and blues. So that was what I liked, but it tore my audience to pieces, and that was the end of that."

Except, of course, it was not the end. Springsteen is still going strong forty years later and has continued to perform R&B songs along with folk songs, classic rock, and old-time rock and roll. The band in Damrosch Park played more R&B than his later bands and gave more space to its two black vocalists, but it was not a great R&B band and I'm not arguing Springsteen's music would have been better—or that any of us would be writing about him today—if he had stuck with that style. Nor was that his blackest band in terms of personnel. Aside from the vocalists and Sancious on piano, it was a white band—Clemons joined more than a year later, by which point the singers were gone and Sancious was on hiatus, and the half black / half white "future of rock and roll" group with Boom Carter was still two and a half years away and existed for less than six months.

If I seem nostalgic for Springsteen's R&B roots and that evenly inter-racial band, it's not because I regret the reality of either, or equate them: Sancious, in particular, was as notable for his mastery of European clas-sical music as for his jazz or R&B skills. What I regret is the end of a time when the future of rock and roll seemed like it could be a continu-ation of the music's racially integrated past—a mythical time when being a rock fan meant caring about black music, black culture, and, at least aspirationally, crossing and attempting to erase the divisions of Ameri-can racism.

That is a lot of weight to put on Springsteen's shoulders, and I appre-ciate his attempts to carry it. My problem is not with him, but with a world of rock fans, critics, and historians who have forgotten or ignored the context in which Landau hailed him in 1974. When Landau imagined Springsteen and the E Street Band as "rock and roll future," he was using a different definition of rock and roll than most people use today, one that already marked him as an old-timer at age twenty-seven. That was the thrust of the article: ten years earlier, rock and roll had been Landau's life—meaning the Beatles, the Beach Boys, the Drifters, the Marvelettes, Wilson Pickett, Otis Redding, Bob Dylan, the Byrds, B. B. King, the Stones, and, above all, as a supreme touchstone, the Four Tops' "Reach Out I'll Be There." That mix was his "rock and roll past," and the point of his piece was that he feared it was gone until he saw Springsteen and realized it was possible as a future.

I was fifteen in 1974 and not hip enough to be at that show, though it was an easy walk from my house. I'd only caught the tail end of the rock-and-roll era, thanks in a large part to Sha Na Na—and I'll note that Landau worked them into his piece, describing Springsteen as "dressed like a reject from Sha Na Na." But I was holding onto a similar dream, and felt a similar shock of recognition and hope when I saw the cover of *Born to Run*.

Instead, we got the bifurcation of disco and punk or metal, the defi-ant blackness of rap, and the ironic whiteness of Americana. We got Prince, a lone black guitar hero updating the Hendrix persona, and decades of rock festivals that take their lack of black musicians for granted. Springsteen did not change that future, and I can't help feeling ambivalent about his story. I wish he had found some black musicians to replace Sancious and Carter in 1974; I appreciate his choice to form a majority-black band in 1992; I got chills watching him singing with Pete Seeger and a gospel choir at Obama's inauguration.

That last memory is key: it's not a great musical performance by Springsteen's standards, or by the standards of Little Richard, the Rolling Stones, or the Four Tops. I love it for what it symbolizes, for the vision not only of the artists onstage but of the audience, the most racially mixed assemblage to fill the Washington Mall since Martin Luther King's March on Washington. I wish Springsteen's regular audience looked like that, and one of the things I like about him is that I'm sure he does as well. But it doesn't—and Little Richard's did, and Prince's did, and Beyoncé's does. . . .

Because, for many reasons and for better or worse, black music has always brought Americans together across racial lines while white music has tended to divide us—and Springsteen, despite his roots in soul dance bands, despite the "future of rock and roll" band and the decades with Clarence, despite the 1992 band, despite "American Skin (41 Shots)," is an icon of whiteness.

I don't know if anything he could have done would have changed that, and I realize how unfair it is that more than forty years after *Born to Run* I still associate him with the death of a dream. It is particularly unfair because he has tried so hard to hold onto that dream, and in various ways to make it a reality. From my perspective, this essay is an attempt to honor him for that effort, and a reminder that he made it—and if it feels more regretful than celebratory, the reasons are bigger than Springsteen or rock and roll.

Works Cited

Carlin, Peter Ames. *Bruce*. New York: Touchstone/Simon & Schuster, 2012.

Clemons, Clarence, and Don Reo. *Big Man: Real Life & Tall Tales*. New York: Grand Central, 2009.

Henke, James. "Bruce Springsteen Leaves E Street: The Rolling Stone Interview." *Rolling Stone*, August 6, 1992. www.rollingstone.com/music/music-news/bruce -springsteen-leaves-e-street-the-rolling-stone-interview-172718/.

Landau, Jon. "Growing Young with Rock and Roll." *Real Paper*, May 22, 1974. www
.grubstreet.ca/articles/index/327/growing-young-with-rock-n-roll-early
-comments-on-bruce-springsteen.

Marsh, Dave. *Bruce Springsteen on Tour 1968–2005*. New York: Bloomsbury, 2006.

Springsteen, Bruce. *Born to Run*. New York: Simon & Schuster, 2016.

Statham, Craig. *Springsteen: Saint in the City: 1949–1974*. London: Soundcheck, 2013.

Wolff, Daniel. *4th of July, Asbury Park: A History of the Promised Land*. New York:
Bloomsbury, 2005.

Part VI

Springsteen and Aging

"My City of Ruins." Built in 1929, the Asbury Park Casino was once a beloved Jersey Shore cultural destination as well as a Springsteen hangout. During its heyday, the Casino and its accompanying arcade housed an assortment of amusements, most famously bumper cars, Skee-Ball machines, a skating rink, and a carousel. Springsteen has mentioned the Casino and the "ruins" of Asbury Park many times in his lyrics. (June Sawyers)

22

Summer's Fall

✧

Springsteen in Senescence

JIM CULLEN

Though it may be hard to remember—or believe—rock and roll was once a young man's game. Its dominant ethos was existential and antiauthoritarian, a lineage easily traced from the Who to punk rock by way of Neil Young. Even before their generation, this gospel was embodied by Elvis Presley, primal force run riot, a wayward shock of jet black hair swaying wildly as he banged a guitar. It's hard to keep that up: Elvis got old long before he died. But the keepers of the flame weren't only male. "You told me you'd hold me till you died," snarls the protagonist of Alanis Morissette's 1995 hit "You Oughta Know" at a faithless lover. But, she notes with incredulity as electric guitars rise to ride her rage, "you're still alive."

Bruce Springsteen has a somewhat odd, even strained, relationship to this live-fast-die-young tradition. To be sure, he is a direct heir of the Elvis bloodline, and much of his best music has the wild, Dionysian air that made rock and roll the thrillingly heretical force it was in the middle decades of the twentieth century. To this day, it's what many of his fans love best about him, and they turn out in droves to escape their workaday lives to hear and dance with him, long after most of them have lost interest in what he actually has to say. Yet even at his most wild and not-so innocent, there was always a sense that Springsteen was a dutiful rebel, one who lovingly evoked, borrowed, even resurrected his influences in countless covers, allusions, or acts of homage. The alchemy of albums like *Born to Run* was the way such concordances (an incantation of Roy Orbison here, a flourish of Bo Diddley there) never foreclosed his ability to write new verse for the canon. But he was always more Saint Paul than Prometheus.

In part, that's because Springsteen has long been among those rock artists who have chased a countercurrent in the rock tradition, one that has viewed the genre less as an escape from the deadening routines of everyday life than a means for grappling with them. This musical tradition emerged in the mid-1960s—the crucible of Springsteen's youth—in the work of Bob Dylan and the Beatles. They transformed rock and roll into *rock*, a musical idiom they sought to take beyond mere sensation into describing and embodying a fuller range of human experience through introspection, irony, and symbolism. A mere two years after Pete Townshend wrote "My Generation" in 1965, in which Roger Daltrey proclaims "Hope I die before I get old," Paul McCartney responded with "When I'm Sixty-Four"—a puckish ditty, to be sure, but one that hardly treated old age as a subject of contempt. There was pretense in rock's artistic conceits, and real losses too, ranging from an erosion of the vital life force of the music—hence the need for the bracingly brutish songs of the Ramones and their peers—to a tendency toward racial segregation of popular music in the 1970s that has remained with us ever since. But there's little question that it allowed the genre to grow and to last, much in the way that jazz and hip-hop did—and the way genres like ragtime and disco, seemingly preserved in amber, didn't.

Springsteen may well have been unique among his rock peers for the degree to which he remained connected with the vital sources of the genre, racial and otherwise. From the outset, however, it was clear that he was an artist committed to building a body of work, one that would chart where he and the characters who populate his songs were living at any given time. A consciousness of time's passing, and the growing sense of desperation that accompanied it, suffuses *Born to Run*, *Darkness on the Edge of Town*, and *The River*. But it was not until 1984's *Born in the U.S.A.* that his protagonists routinely began to actually carry the scars of aging, whether in the form of the PTSD-afflicted narrator of the title track or the divorced mother of "Glory Days."

While there was never any question that Springsteen was first and foremost a rock and roller, his musical choices reflected a maturation that led him in other directions. This was apparent in his relatively early fascination with Woody Guthrie, the folkish *Nebraska*, *The Ghost of Tom Joad* and *Devils & Dust* albums, and his deepening engagement with American roots music so vividly showcased in his Seeger Sessions recordings at the turn of this century. If such music cannot be described as timeless, it's very clearly multigenerational—not the product of a single moment, but an encounter to be reexperienced and reinterpreted as part of an ongoing dialogue between the living and the dead—a dialogue that's the subject of "We Are Alive," the closing track of Springsteen's 2012 album *Wrecking Ball*. While Springsteen's heart was always with the rebel without a cause, his art in effect made him a dissident among insurgents.

Then there were the rebels *with* causes. This is a yet another strain in rock history. If the live-fast-die-young strain was libertarian and hedonistic, and the rock-as-art strain was private and reflective, this activist one was more social and utopian—it celebrated collective emancipation and looked toward (and, at times, demanded) a better world. In the early years of the genre, this utopian impulse was focused most decisively in the realm of race relations, when rock and roll was at the vanguard of integration. Rock's role in political struggle was more implicit than explicit, expressed in music more than words—and, at times, was something to be taken at face value.

There was some overlap between these traditions, especially on the fulcrum of the late 1960s, that moment before years of hope became days of rage. You could hear it in songs like the Youngbloods' classic "Get Together" (1967) or Sly and the Family Stone's "Everyday People" (1969), which fused messages of pleasure, reflection, and solidarity. The counterculture was a broad coalition whose affinities seemed in harmony when the opponent was a still monolithic Establishment.

As rock and roll became rock, though, the impetus for social reform became simultaneously more focused, wide-ranging, and insistent. The Vietnam War in particular was a locus of protest (Edwin Starr's "War"), but one that could encompass broader social critiques beyond indictments of the war itself (Creedence Clearwater Revival's "Fortunate

Son"). Since the 1970s, it's been clear that rock could be a vehicle for engaging just about any political issue, from feminism (Carole King's "Will You Still Love Me Tomorrow") to the threat of the police state (the Clash's "Clampdown"—the Clash offering a political variant on the self-indulgent instincts of the Ramones, Sex Pistols, and other punk bands).

Significantly, Springsteen has performed all four of these songs. A man of his time, he absorbed the influences of his youth and has remained attuned to the popular music of his time ever since (he rendered a cover of Lorde's edgy class manifesto "Royals," in her native New Zealand in 2014). Ideologically speaking, Springsteen has spent his entire life on the left side of the political spectrum. His protest songs— like "Roulette," "Seeds," "The Ghost of Tom Joad," "American Skin (41 Shots)," and "Death to My Hometown"—are as politically scathing as anything this side of Rage Against the Machine. He has consistently positioned himself at the vanguard on issues such as LGBTQ rights and immigration.

And yet, here too, Springsteen has stood somewhat apart from fully embracing radical reform of any kind. In a way, there are opposing reasons for this: while he's too much the dutiful son to entirely live in the moment, he's too much the skeptic to fully embrace utopian hopes (his outrage tends to be intense but not programmatic). One searches his body of work in vain for a Springsteen equivalent of Sam Cooke's "A Change Is Gonna Come," John Lennon's "Imagine," or Crosby, Stills, Nash & Young's "Chicago," with its ringing assertion, "we can change the world." Springsteen's victories, when they come, are small, personal, and tinged with doubt.

The root cause of such tendencies is Springsteen's fundamentally conservative temperament. His orientation has tended to focus on preserving that which might otherwise die rather than articulate something entirely new. His great subject has been the vanishing white working class; his core means for exploring it has been a largely black musical idiom that African Americans themselves tended to leave behind and that white musicians also largely abandoned after the 1960s. His agenda has essentially amounted to keeping the faith—in a time when faith has become progressively less important, if not problematic, for the Baby Boomer generation and its successors. It's this, more than anything else, that's made him increasingly seem dated. But it's also likely to be the source of his durability.

Like God, we tend to make Springsteen in our own image—or at any rate, the image of whom we'd like to be. As with God, our experience of fandom is typically a matter of one-way communication, and the amount of information we receive from the object of our attention, affection, and, at times, reverence, is finite and incomplete. And so it is that we fill in the rest, which is typically a matter of hearing what we want to believe. When we don't, we usually move on. But the greatest artists find a way to challenge as well as confirm, to tell us what we need to know and pose compelling questions.

Over the course of the last five decades, Springsteen has been many things to many people: rock star, sex symbol, songwriter, to name a few. Such roles have overlapped; others have been more singular, even idiosyncratic. There's one that's been both highly specific and yet deeply resonant: Springsteen the Roman Catholic.

This isn't the right place to render a full narrative of Springsteen's complex (and, at times, tortured) relationship with his inherited faith. In part, that's because it's something that's already been done, at least for the first twenty-five years of his career. In part, too, it's because the outlines of the story are familiar: getting smacked by a priest for his clumsiness as an altar boy; getting stuffed into a trash can at his St. Rose of Lima parochial school by a nun who told him that's where he belonged; Springsteen's performance of the profane "If I Was the Priest" for John Hammond in 1972, who upon hearing it said he knew Springsteen could only be Catholic; Springsteen's triumphant return to St. Rose in 1996, where, to the dismay of his pastor, he celebrated the virtues of cunnilingus from the stage. For many cradle Catholics, to know the Church is to hate it, especially in the context of the liberating currents of the 1960s, when Springsteen came of age.

But that was never the whole story. Springsteen rendered the other side of it concisely in his 2016 memoir: "In Catholicism, there existed the poetry, danger, and darkness that reflected my imagination and my inner self. I found a land of great and harsh beauty, of fantastic stories, of unimaginable punishment and infinite reward. It was a glorious and pathetic place I was either shaped for or fit right into. It has walked alongside me as a waking dream my whole life." Noting the familiar truism that once you're a Catholic, you're always a Catholic, he noted his lapses and yet confessed, "I'm still on the team."

In the first half of his career, Springsteen's religious heritage typically functioned as a repository of terms and metaphors he deployed in his songs. Sometimes this was a matter of using spiritual language in a secular context ("Hey mister deejay, won't you hear my last prayer / hey ho rock and roll deliver me from nowhere," he croons in the final line of "Open All Night"). Other times it was a matter of endowing quotidian situations with biblical freight, especially in the titles of his songs ("Lost in the Flood," "The Promised Land," "My Father's House"). Springsteen's Catholic imagination was neither doctrinal nor moralistic, though there are cases when he deployed his heritage to depict spiritual crises of great psychological intensity, like the Dostoevskian criminal protagonist of "Stolen Car" who longs to get caught, or the agonized mother of "Spare Parts" who decides not to be like Jochebed, the mother of Moses who relinquished her infant son to float away on the Nile. The point here is that Springsteen's heritage was a religious means to an artistic (and largely secular) end.

This changed as he got older. The turning point was *The Rising* in 2002, whose very title depicted the resurrections of 9/11 victims in forthrightly Christian terms. "Into the Fire" was essentially a hymn in its invocations of hope, strength, and love. The most moving track on *Devils & Dust*, "Jesus Was an Only Son," is a meditation on the love of mothers for children—and one that really *is* rooted in doctrine, as most Catholics, unlike Protestants, maintain that Christ was an only child (the debate turns on the connotations of the word "brother" and "sister" in the gospels). Perhaps not surprisingly, Springsteen's religious heritage is something he increasingly invokes in an unselfconscious and unironic way as he's aged, his faith less mediated, deflected, or denied.

But Springsteen has not simply become an orthodox sectarian. His music engages subjects that are relevant for those who do not share his religious faith—or any religious faith at all. Which brings us back to the subject at hand: his relationship to his rock-and-roll lineage, a relationship that has both converged with and diverged from two of the most prominent streams in rock history: its self-indulgent tributary and its utopian one. That Springsteen has kept a foot in each stream reflects powerful facets of his personality as well as the specific historical moment in which he came of age. But to a degree that may well be unique among members of his Baby Boomer rock generation, Springsteen's body of work has also long exhibited traits that gave his music a specific character—and a durable appeal—that stand apart from either of these cultural strains and have shaped his work all along.

One of those traits is stoicism. The quintessential Springsteen protagonist from his golden triumvirate of *Born to Run, Darkness on the Edge of Town,* and *The River* is the angry rebel who declares his intention to get out while he's young. But Springsteen Village has long been inhabited by depressed fathers, apprehensive pregnant single girlfriends, and factory workers whose suffering is as palpable as their will to survive—a will often fueled by rock and roll itself. It becomes a reason to live, if not to believe.

Another important trait in Springsteen's body of work is moral ambiguity. His characters live in a world of sin, at times exhibiting contempt toward those who fail to understand this essential truth ("they made their choices and they'll never know / what it means to steal, to cheat, to lie / what it's like to live and die," says the protagonist of "Prove It All Night"). Even the most transcendent moments, like the birth of the child in "Living Proof," take place against a profane backdrop of a "world so hard and dirty, so fouled and confused."

It's in the nature of this particular form of cultural criticism that one could go on reeling off lyrics to illustrate the point. Perhaps a better way to proceed is to make a more sustained case with a particular piece of music that's simultaneously a snapshot of the aging Springsteen and a distillation of his lifelong essence. That song is "Girls in Their Summer Clothes."

Among Springsteen connoisseurs—about the only people who follow the music he's made since he dropped off the singles charts in the last century—his 2007 album *Magic* is widely considered as among his best. Perhaps more than any record since *Born in the U.S.A., Magic* was notable for the degree to which it was a straightforward rock album, one that wore its Bush-era milieu (and politics) lightly. At the very center of that album, track six of twelve, we find his most direct commentary on aging, "Girls in Their Summer Clothes."

Fittingly, "Girls" is an act of homage to a great band that, Brian Wilson's sonic innovations notwithstanding, seemed nostalgic from the moment of its inception: the Beach Boys. In the 2014 *Rolling Stone* list of the best Springsteen songs of all time, Jon Landau described the song as having "a *Pet Sounds* feeling mixed with the E Street Band." Ironically, Springsteen initially resisted putting "Girls" on the album: "I tip my hat to [producer] Brendan O'Brien for pushing for this song to be included on *Magic*," he notes on his website, adding that director Mark Pellington did an excellent job of capturing its spirit in the song's music video, which features girls of every age on a wintry Jersey Shore beach. "Girls" won Grammys for Best Rock Song and Best Solo Rock Vocal at the 2009 Grammy Awards.

The song begins with a lush, even caramelized, acoustic arrangement, Springsteen's voice filtered to a smooth sheen (he's no Brian Wilson, but then again, who is?). The lyrics have the feel of a benediction—at least at first, with its invocation of shining streetlights, a summer breeze, and happy couples, a tableau that unfolds on Blessing Avenue, no less. And then comes a jarring line: "Tonight I'm going to burn this town down." What's *that* supposed to mean?

Actually, the chill of these words makes the song's Beach Boy patrimony unmistakable in an entirely different way: by conjuring a snake in the sonic garden. Think of the minor-chord ache in Wilson's arrangement of the old folk song "Sloop John B," for example, or the strain of sorrow that runs beneath the loving daydream of "Wouldn't It Be Nice" ("it seems the more we talk about it / the worse it is to live without it"). Actually, the best analogy for "Girls in Their Summer Clothes" in this regard is "God Only Knows," in which a man dreamily expresses gratitude to a woman by raising the specter of suicide if she were to leave him: "What good would living do me?" Every breath she takes, he'll be watching her.

As with those Beach Boys narrators, Springsteen's, whose name is Bill, doesn't dwell on notes of unease, dreamily proceeding to the song's chorus, the key line of which is the song's title. Yet here again we bump into a discordant note: "The girls in their summer clothes pass me by." An innocuous expression of nostalgia, perhaps—one familiar, at any rate, to virtually every man over the age of about forty (and, one guesses, many women as well). But it's also more evidence of an unreliable narrator. Unselfconsciously talking about gazing at women might have been considered appropriate in 1967, but by 2007—and certainly ever since—subjecting females to this kind of male gaze had become, in the lexicon of our time, politically incorrect (Puritans of both the seventeenth and twenty-first centuries would deem this man guilty of lechery). But neither Bill nor Springsteen himself wants us to linger on this, because the words and music—a gently rising crescendo in the drums, like a wave breaking on a beach—reimmerses us in the song's idyllic village setting of bouncing rubber balls, porch lighting, and chiming bells. And then, once again, there's a dissonant note: "Things been a little tight, but I know they're going to go my way." *He* may know; the rest of us aren't so sure. Actually, on second glance, there are other intimations of unease lurking in the presumably sunny lyrics, passing mentions of gutters and encroaching darkness. (That chiming? It comes from a big bank.)

Yet once more we're swept along by the soaring harmonies, organ, and piano fills, which roll into the song's bridge. Bill has made his way to Frankie's Diner, mesmerized by its neon sign, which he compares to a crucifix. A waitress, Shaniqua, comes over to Bill and offers him a refill on his coffee, asking him what he's thinking. This is a quintessentially Springsteenian scenario: quotidian moments endowed with almost comic grandeur. Such working-class romanticism was his stock-in-trade years before he described an Exxon sign illuminating "Jungleland." But there was often also a spiritual overlay in such imagery, stretching from the roses and crosses Mary figuratively fingers in "Thunder Road" to the bones on Theresa's back resembling the stations of the cross on "I'll Work for Your Love" (another song from *Magic*). Bill's cross, stationed over a lost and found, offers a tantalizing promise of redemption—tantalizing, that is, before he proceeds to sabotage it: "She went away, she cut me like a knife / hello beautiful thing, maybe you could save my life." He winces; we cringe. At the very moment we sympathize (identify?) with Bill's unwitting rejection by a waitress, he responds by objectifying her in a mash-up of the sacred and the squalid: "beautiful thing." But the gentle tide refuses to stop rising, pulling us along once more: The girls in the summer clothes will keep passing by, and Bill will keep shadow-dancing with them. We may not approve of his behavior, but we recognize that we're subject to the same forces he is, inhabiting a dappled world of sin and love. Thirty-five years earlier, young Mary Lou of "Does This Bus

Stop at 82nd Street?" had it right: "The dope's that there's still hope." Our prognosis is terminal, but this drug will keep you alive. The side effects can be rough. But in the end, it's worth it.

Like the archetypal Baby Boomer he is, Springsteen spent his sixties in a death-defying fight against the ravages of time. In the last decade, he's released four albums, undertaken three international tours, published an autobiography (one he actually wrote himself), and made his first run on Broadway. He endured the aches and pains that come with age—sore knees, bad back, tendinitis from all that strumming—and had surgery to repair disks in his neck. And yet he remained a remarkable physical specimen (*New Yorker* editor David Remnick described his muscle tone in 2012 as resembling "a fresh tennis ball"). He appears to have taken to heart the biblical proverb that idle hands are the devil's workshop.

Springsteen has spent time in that hell. He grew up in the shadow of his father's clinical depression and struggled with it himself at different points in his life. It was nevertheless surprising—and, given all he has done, and the honors he has received, sobering—to learn that, as recently as 2014, on the eve of his sixty-fifth birthday, he found himself in a six-week stretch during which he could barely get out of bed, "an empty husk" who for the first time "felt I understood what drives people toward the abyss." Such a disclosure was, in an important sense, a gift—a reminder of his humanity and fallibility that keeps alive the possibility that even those whose lives are remote from our own may still be collectively engaged in the shared, hard, good work of growing old. "I work to be an ancestor," Springsteen writes at the end of *Born to Run*. Tomorrow's punks will slay him. But the world he conjured will be born again in another artist's imagination.

Works Cited

Carlin, Peter Ames. *Bruce*. New York: Touchstone/Simon & Schuster, 2012.

Cullen, Jim. *Born in the U.S.A.: Bruce Springsteen and the American Tradition*. New York: HarperCollins, 1997.

Hiatt, Brian, et al. "100 Greatest Bruce Springsteen Songs of All Time: "Girls in Their Summer Clothes." *Rolling Stone*, December 11, 2018. www.rollingstone.com/music/lists/100-greatest-bruce-springsteen-songs-of-all-time-20140116/girls-in-their-summer-clothes-19691231.

Remnick, David. "We Are Alive: Bruce Springsteen at Sixty-Two." *New Yorker*, July 30, 2012, 38–57.

Springsteen, Bruce. *Born to Run*. New York: Simon & Schuster, 2016.

———. "Video of the Week: Girls in Their Summer Clothes." *Brucespringsteen.net*, August 29, 2014. www.brucespringsteen.net/news/2014/video-of-the-week-girls-in -their-summer-clothes.

Wald, Elijah. *How the Beatles Destroyed Rock & Roll: An Alternative History of American Popular Music*. New York: Oxford University Press, 2011.

23

Work and Play

✧

Midlife Music

DANIEL WOLFF

She was in her mid-fifties; he was in his late fifties. They'd been married a little over a decade and a half. The oldest of their three children was seventeen, the youngest thirteen. They'd entered that point in a marriage when the primary job of raising kids was a little less demanding, the point when couples often stop to evaluate why they got together—and why they'll stay together.

Midlife.

They'd met through music. The spring she'd graduated from high school, he was already locally known. "I'd heard of him . . . I wanted to get in a good rock band. . . . He always had a great reputation and the best band." A decade later, she'd been to college for music and had a career as a backup singer; his reputation had gone national. In her early thirties, she toured with his band, was eventually invited to join, and started the relationship that led to their marriage. Music remained a bond.

He'd made some ten albums before they were married—and released another six since. They regularly charted in the top five. Her records were considerably less known. The first came out after she'd had two kids and was pregnant with a third. It reached the top twenty-five and might have done better if she'd toured behind it. "I had three little kids in diapers.

I was like 'Ok, let me just get my family together.'" A decade later, she released a second. "After working for other musicians and helping them tell their story, I wanted to tell my story. It's a celebration of my independence." Her tour in support of the record was cut short by commitments to his band.

It was three years later, in 2007, that she produced her midlife record, "about exploring the complexities," she said, "of a real, committed, long-term relationship [combined] with children and work." It reached ninety on the charts. The LP he put out two weeks later hit the top five in the United States and in nine other countries. His reputation was as a rock hero; hers was as a member of his band and his wife.

Her record opens with a song about a rock hero. After a jangly back-roads intro of slide guitar and harmonica, it finds the female singer at a crossroads. Somewhere, somehow, she's lost hope and faith. She's "looking for something to rock my soul . . . looking for Elvis." The music percolates along—both confident and questioning—until it reaches the bridge; then she carefully enunciates what sounds like an ultimatum. "You've got to work a little harder / sing a little louder / stand up and deliver / if you want my trust." That challenge hangs in the air for the rest of the record.

Two years later, he put out a response.

It wasn't really—or not overtly. But the two records engage in a kind of secret, unacknowledged dialogue. Both address the same subject: what becomes of the passion, the possibility of what she calls "All those Septembers / the pledges of allegiance / the prayers of trust." One is from a woman's point of view, one from a man's, but there are certain connections—even overlapping vocabularies. Separate midlife music made by people who've lived with someone a long time, both pondering what that means.

If she knew her audience was limited—that whatever she released, it'd most likely be heard by only a relative few—he knew he had a large audience that devoured his music and that came with expectations. He'd established himself early as an inspirational singer, creating out of rock-and-roll archetypes a character "born to run," perpetually searching, strung out on "streets of fire." While he'd worked to bring that music into adulthood, his audience made it clear both at live shows and in record sales that they wanted the sound of the guitar / drums teenage rebel.

When he tried to talk about his "brilliant disguise," there'd often be cries for "Thunder Road."

His midlife record opens with a spaghetti-western ballad about an outlaw trapped in his own image. As the rhythm of the string section builds, he sings in an uncharacteristically high, pleading voice. The outlaw marries, has a kid, but his reputation catches up with him. The repeated refrain, thrown out across the heavily orchestrated melody, is four words: "Can you hear me?"

On his record, the work of a marriage ("I swing my hammer") is about the construction of a dream. It dates from that "lucky day" when he first felt "the grace of your smile." For the sound of that dream, he's gone back to a stream of music from his adolescence: the soaring strings and meshed vocals of Phil Spector, Gene Pitney, Roy Orbison—songs of extravagant possibility. To that end, he's pitched his voice—famously used in the past as a rough, masculine shout—higher, almost out of his range. So that even as he declares his love, he sounds vulnerable, reaching for tenderness.

Her record has less of this high drama. Her voice is easily as distinctive as his, with a throaty vibrato and a tendency to extend phrases, but it stays comfortably in a mostly laid-back, low-key groove. If her arrangements also hanker back to 1960s rock and roll, she's more interested in the female side of history. When her backing singers throw in a "doo-lang," it evokes the long-ago innocence of what were once known as "girl groups." But her voice also carries the edge of twenty-first-century feminism. She may want to "cry, cry, cry, like any woman would," but she explicitly denounces the female rock music stereotype: she's "no beast of burden." In her take on the sexes, when "man swings the hammer," the world shakes. And that's not necessarily good.

What her record continually returns to is the difficulty of male / female communication—and the need for it. "You gotta work with me, baby," she half pleads over a gospel-like arrangement of organ and choir—as if that "work" were one of the ten commandments of living together. But the work doesn't, maybe can't, succeed. In any event, it never stops. In one song, she gives her address as "a town called heartbreak." In another, she insists she won't "jump through your little hoops of fire." She sees the conflict as primal, going back to Adam and Eve. Woman offers up her flesh and blood, but "you wanted my soul." And man responds, "No matter how hard I try/you ain't never satisfied." It's that difference, that tension, that fuels her songs.

His world—his record—is shaped by desire. In one histrionic, almost hysteric scenario, he gets a crush on a check-out girl in a supermarket. Suspended in the "aisles and aisles of dreams," he goes for the "cool promise of ecstasy." He declares himself "in love" with this stranger, the girl at the cash register: a love as unreal, as overblown, and as potent as the song's swelling, drum-smeared arrangement. As the strings (and his voice) keep rising, it can only end one place: with an apocalyptic explosion—immensely satisfying and useless. Here's what happens when you won't grow up, maybe can't grow up, maybe don't want to.

So when he vows in another song to set things right—vows that when their hope has "drifted in the wind," he'll show her "what love can do"— it's hard to believe. He seems to be promising not day-to-day, real-world love but a kind of heightened, cosmic, rock-and-roll drama. "A million suns cresting where you stood." Didn't she say she wanted him to sing a little louder? His is an inflationary record, pumping up emotion until it's larger than life.

Her record is much more down to earth. While his songs arch toward climax, hers tend to mistrust endings and answers. Where he piles horns on strings and mixes in a glockenspiel—as if these gorgeous baroque creations could prove the emotional work he's doing—she relies on a killer rhythm section and relatively sparse arrangements. The net effect is to question if more is really better. "You can sing for your supper," she declares at one point, "for the living and the dead/for the words you lock in silence/that you wished that you had said/or," she finishes, "you can sing to fill the emptiness/that's banging in your head."

It's not that she doesn't appreciate what her lover brings; she calls it "holy water . . . something to believe in." And it's as much sensual as it is spiritual. She's willing to be "spilled . . . like wine" across his lips and fingers, eager to share what she calls "sugar, sugar, sugar baby/bang-bang touch," the words doled out caressingly. But to her, that play has to be part of a larger something: the work. "You can play around," is how she puts it in another song, "but don't you play around with me."

On both records, this back-and-forth—the give-and-take of lovers over time—takes place almost entirely in an interior landscape. On her record, there's an occasional glimpse of the outside world: the Memphis road where she searches for Elvis, a woman racecar driver. And he sketches the Wild West, the supermarket, some railroad tracks by a water tower. But by and large, the songs operate in a sealed environment: no larger society, no children, the only work the emotional kind. Two people, locked into each other, entering the last part of their lives.

He called his collection *Working on a Dream*. Its center posts are three ecstatic, dreamlike songs of desire. In each, his lover is the trigger that sets off a string of visions. "As you slip into my car, the evening sky strikes sparks." "You were life itself, rushing over me." "With you, I don't hear the minutes ticking by." The rich orchestration and layered voices lean heavily on what might be called the Roy Orbison model. Orbison specialized in the long build, riding clouds of strings and guitar to a peak where his near-operatic voice would flash through. Often women are the key to that flash—and the cause of sorrow. *Working on a Dream* goes from one end of the equation—"With you I have been blessed"—to the other: "Why do the things that connect us slowly pull us apart?"

Again, the two records aren't explicitly connected, but there's a moment on his where he could be quoting from hers. He's announced that it's this life that matters—that walking through the fields, his jacket around her shoulders, "this is our kingdom of days." And then in the break, he declares his love, inadequately, almost inarticulately. "I love you I love you I love you I love you I do." And he has her whisper in response: "Then prove it, then prove it, then prove it to me baby blue."

He can't. Or, rather, his only proof is the music. He jumps to their two gray, wrinkled bodies lying in bed and cheers them both on: "Sing away, my darling, we'll sing away." But that sting of darkness, that endless need to prove it, remains. She may be his best hope "when I've lost all the other bets I've made," but it's still a gamble.

She called her collection *Play It as It Lays*. It's less about dreams than the reality of those prayers of trust. She doesn't believe the love, the marriage, can ever get it quite right. "Every perfect picture hides a mess or two," she sings on the title track: "Sometimes it's me, sometimes it's you." While she recalls—over a spare, hypnotic bass and drum—what the love once was, she doesn't expect the original glow to return. "If we lost a little along the way / that's all right / what's done is done." And when things go bad, she vows to "get back up to get it started again."

Her idea of love—the work of love—carries a heavy dose of pain. To evoke it, she goes back at one point to a 1963 hit by the Jaynetts, "Sally Go Round the Roses." Her throaty voice rises from a bed of female singers to quote the old song's chorus and describes being caught between "the cold hard truth and the soft warm lies." The last cut on her record is a quiet, almost private acknowledgment of a shared history: she's been down his "black ladder," he's been down hers. When she sings, "Tell me all my work is done," her whispering voice is too sorrowful, too knowing for a happy ever after.

Bruce Springsteen's *Working on a Dream* remains a triumphant attempt to evoke adult love by a man who admits he doesn't see the world that well with "my good eye to the dark and my blind eye to the sun." He seems incomplete on his own. Offstage, when the carnival's over, he's a "one-trick pony," a "one-legged dog." Patti Scialfa's *Play It as It Lays* is more than just its worthy companion. Her sweet-and-sour, probing investigation stands on its own as a master work. Grown-up, clear-eyed, beautifully melodic, her series of songs never resolves. It can't. Instead, it ends with a hard-earned midlife declaration: "I still care."

Works Cited

Katz, Larry. "E Street Detour: Patti Scilafa Leaves Hubby Bruce Springsteen at Home during Road Trip." *Boston Herald*, September 15, 2004.

Melanie B. "Patti Scialfa on How She Met Bruce Springsteen." *YouTube*, November 4, 2016. www.youtube.com/watch?v=s-Vuql182gg.

Stoynoff, Natashiya. "Rock & Roll Mama." *People*, September 3, 2007.

Part VII

Springsteen beyond Borders

"Springsteens Restaurant, Belfast, Northern Ireland." This Belfast eatery is expressly named after Bruce and features an American-style menu. (June Sawyers)

24

Bruce Springsteen's River in Dublin

✧

DERMOT BOLGER

You don't need to know the physical geography of Dublin, Ireland's capital city, to read this essay. Indeed, even if you were a regular visitor there or an inhabitant of one of Dublin's more affluent suburbs, it is still unlikely that you would be able to frame a mental picture of the specific location I have in mind: an isolated river road that I never traverse without thinking of one particular Bruce Springsteen song.

When I call this road isolated, I don't mean in the sense of it being a remote, picturesque byway. Certainly there was a period in my 1960s childhood when it retained a rustic visage and local families from the vast working-class neighborhoods of Cabra and Finglas—the two Northside suburbs separated by this river valley—would picnic here on summer evenings at a bathing spot called the Silver Spoon. Older boys stripped to the waist would jostle about, anxious to impress teenage girls while younger children waded in the water with cheap, tiny nets to catch pinkeen fish.

Today one side of the road is lined by the railings of a nondescript park that falls down to the river, on an incline too steep to build on. The other side is lined by small industrial units—timber and building merchants' providers, car parts suppliers, tire companies, electrical wholesaler trade providers, and a car wash for taxis. There are other anonymous small warehouses with poor signage that obscures their exact purpose from the casual passerby. Not that you find too many casual passersby on that river road after six o'clock when the steel shutters are pulled down. After dark it possesses such a desolate sense of being on the edge of town that few pedestrians venture along it and motorists never stop because they are simply passing by, speeding along this stretch of limbo on journeys invariably destined to end elsewhere.

It is a stretch of road where a young couple, with nowhere else to go, might sit undisturbed in a car to express their love and confide their dreams or perhaps, after dusk comes, slip through the drab railings into the steep unlit parkland where the River Tolka flows. I have no rational explanation for making this connection, but in my mind this roadway will always be the landscape of Bruce Springsteen's classic song "The River." On a geographical level this is nonsense. The Tolka is so insignificant a river that it would barely be noticed as a tributary to the actual river Springsteen had in mind when he wrote the lyrics of "The River": lyrics resolutely American in their setting. But those same lyrics remain resolutely universal in how they conjure up the fragile scenario in which young people's hopes are crushed by economic circumstances. The life story of his hurt and hurting protagonists seems, at a first listen, to be encapsulated in the two titles employed by Nadezhda Mandelstam when she chronicled the life of her husband, a Russian poet of genius purged by Stalin. Her book titles were *Hope against Hope* and *Hope Abandoned*. However, the more you live with Springsteen's lyrics the more you realize how—even amid the seeming economic and emotional implosion of their dreams—Springsteen's narrator still clings to what another poet, Leonard Cohen, called a "little wild bouquet" in refusing to allow his spirit to succumb to utter despondency. Even if all that buoys him up—on nights when home feels too lonely a place to return to—are his memories of first love once found by that river, the small flame of those memories remains a benediction that refuses to be quenched.

Therefore, despite the vast dissimilarity between the river that Springsteen had in mind and the Dublin backwater that his lyrics conjure up for me, I cling to the notion that my unexceptional river road of drab industrial units bordered by an unlovely park still retains the right to be counted as part of the true—if not literal—emotional landscape of his song. This is to say that it is as true an emotional landscape for "The

River" as are hundreds and probably thousands of other stretches of water across the globe that other listeners to that song immediately summoned up in their minds when they first heard its opening lyrics.

It is no small feat to write a good song about one particular place, but it is a far greater feat to write a superb song that, at its heart, could actually be about *any* place. A Dublin writer, Samuel Beckett, pulls off this same feat in creating a relatively anonymous location, or almost a dislocation, for his 1953 play *Waiting for Godot*. I have never seen any performance of that play without transporting it in my head to the Dublin Mountains where Beckett so often walked as a young boy. But, although a Dubliner, Beckett chose to write this play in French and then translate it back into English, adding to its oddness by initially forsaking his native tongue. Therefore, I know that a French audience will feel an equal emotionally territorial possessiveness in locating the setting of the play as being some remote crossroads in France. Indeed I have no doubt that Sri Lankan or Somalian audiences make similar mental readjustments in an effort to try to imaginatively enter Beckett's mindscape.

Of course "The River" is utterly different to Beckett's play in that while Beckett deliberately sets *Waiting for Godot* in a disconcerting landscape on the edge of nowhere (and therefore the edge of everywhere), Springsteen does not try in any way to clock the real physical setting of "The River." He has been upfront in stating how the song was inspired by early difficulties encountered by his sister and brother-in-law in starting out on their life together. It becomes a homage to their resilience and love while also offering a social critique of the human collateral damage of economic collapse and social inequity brought on by factors beyond the control of ordinary workers with no job security.

Therefore, the song is rooted firmly in the particulars of New Jersey life. Yet because it hones in so closely on the human tragedy at its heart, our emotional viewpoint focuses so tightly on the tense silence within the rooms where the protagonists try to cling to the last visage of fractured dreams that we find ourselves almost passing through that silence and reemerging out the other side. Listeners are transported from the particularity of one New Jersey couple into the universality of the millions of couples, past and present, whose lives and dreams have, at some time or other, been ensnared within the same familiar scenario. Not just "The River" but so many of Springsteen's other songs spill out from their origins to become infused with other lives and other places. They create an imaginative landscape where radically different people in radically different circumstances and, indeed, on different continents, can all simultaneously feel that he is somehow addressing them; that he is articulating the hopes, dilemmas, and realties of their lives; that somehow Springsteen has stood by the diverse rivers which his song conjures up and that he has captured the essence of emotions that his audience has felt in their lives.

This emotional response to his songs is different from imagining that we somehow have a nonreciprocal, parasocial relationship with their author. It simply means that something in their very essence rings true in our core and that, most especially when we are young, they become touchstones for articulating emotions that we may not as yet possess the vocabulary or emotional maturity to fully express ourselves.

I am a Dublin-born poet, novelist, and playwright from a city awash with a rich literary heritage: the city whose population has grown to over a million and a quarter in recent decades, but which was far smaller when it was the home of future Nobel Prize for Literature winners like Beckett, George Bernard Shaw, and William Butler Yeats (and more recently the adopted home of Seamus Heaney) and of world-famous writers who equally deserved this accolade like James Joyce, Oscar Wilde, and Seán O'Casey. Literature was always hugely important in the Irish national consciousness, not least because we endured a foreign occupation and gained our independence only following a series of armed upheavals during and after the First World War. When any small nation is forcibly ruled by a militarily stronger power, the center of political influence (and therefore the moneyed classes who become patrons of high art like opera, classical music, and portraiture) shifts to that foreign center of power—which, in Ireland's case until 1922—was the British Parliament at Westminster in London. However the two art forms that can thrive without such rich patronage are literature and popular music. This has made the articulation of the Irish experience by Irish authors and songwriters central to Irish people's awareness of their shifting identity.

All of this is to say that, when I was a young factory worker, making welding rods in the working-class Dublin suburb where I was born, Dublin's existing literary heritage was so vast that it might seem odd that I would need to look elsewhere for words to resonate with and echo the experience of life around me. Whenever I walked through the center of Dublin, I was always acutely aware of traversing the same streets through which James Joyce's all-too-human fictional creation, Leopold Bloom, walked during the tumultuous day minutely described in *Ulysses*. However the Dublin that I truly inhabited as a young man was not the Dublin of Joyce in 1904 or of O'Casey, whose plays brilliantly explore tenement life in the early decades of the twentieth century. Those great Dublin writers might have felt like ghostly forefathers on the shoulders of every young Dublin writer of my generation, but they could not describe our new world of factories and dual carriages and the sprawling new working-class estates in which some of us lived, simply because Joyce and O'Casey had not lived in this new environment that we were living through and in which we were all, in different ways, starting to find new ways to express our experiences.

The fact that a songwriter with the power of U2's Bono and a novelist with the power of Roddy Doyle both lived only a mile or two away from me and were both among a whole generation starting to explore the imaginative boundaries of our shared world means that it would be a matter of a few years before the Dublin of my generation did indeed find its fresh and original voices to articulate its experiences.

But such local voices were still only starting to develop when, aged nineteen in 1978, I commenced my first job doing shift work in a welding rod factory and celebrated getting my first small brown wage envelope—it was cash in those days as not everyone had bank accounts—by purchasing Bruce Springsteen's recently released *Darkness on the Edge of Town*. Some musical moments on that album felt a tad bombastic and overblown, as if their emotion was unearned. But other, more stripped down moments seemed to speak directly to me and my experiences in a way that, as yet, the words of Joyce and O'Casey did not. Even today I still rarely hear one track from that album, "Factory," without remembering how I would often play it in the early morning when I returned home at seven thirty from a night shift. Looking back now, I can even see how its imagery influenced one passage in my long-out-of-print debut semiautobiographical 1985 novel *Night Shift*, which was based on my time working in that welding rod factory.

I call the novel semiautobiographical because it describes many of my own experiences as someone in their late teens who was suddenly thrust into the very adult world of factory life, where a shop steward was organizing a very bitter protest action about working conditions and I found myself laboring alongside grown men who were twice or three times my age. However some of the experiences that happen to the novel's central character were most definitely not my own. This is because they borrowed from the real-life experiences of one of the few other young workers in that factory. Although only a year older than me, this young man found himself already married after his girlfriend became pregnant and he did what was perceived to be the decent and expected thing in those days, which was to get married before the bump of his bride-to-be grew too pronounced. I didn't know him well, but some other young workers in that factory often talked about how, when they went courting with their girlfriends, they occasionally sought out isolated stretches of the River Tolka that afforded some privacy for youngsters with nowhere else to go.

Two years later, in early December 1980, I had left that factory and was working in a different job when one night I found myself with some of my fellow workers invited back, after a night in the pub, to a house in another working-class Dublin suburb. Our host was a young van driver whose wife was in bed, their child asleep. But his young wife woke up and came downstairs to sit and drink and chat with us as he took out a new double album that he had just purchased and wanted to play for us. It was, of course, Springsteen's *The River* and, as the title track of the album started, he said quietly, "This song is my life: this song is about me." He wasn't long in this new job, and, as that night was the only occasion when I ever visited his house, I do not even recall his name now. Therefore I have no knowledge of which circumstances within the song he most identified with. I just remember all the chatter in the room dying down, so that the ten people there were suddenly all intently listening to Springsteen's lyrics. In that moment there was a sense that the song was simultaneously addressing all of our lives or the lives of people whom we knew closely; that we were all visualizing different stretches of rivers in different locations in our mind, none of which Springsteen had never set foot in, but all of which had suddenly been brought to life by his lyrics.

For me, the location of that song instantly became the Tolka and its protagonists became that welding rod factory worker who was barely older than me whom I had worked with two years previously: a young man who had married his childhood sweetheart with love but also with haste. I have no idea how their lives panned out, no more than I have any notion of what happened to the van driver who first played me the song—on the very night, by sheer coincidence, when John Lennon was shot and we all woke on a living room floor to hear "Imagine" being played constantly on every radio station. Looking back across the years, I wish those people nothing but happiness, but all I know about them for sure is that they—like thousands of others in thousands of other places—probably still pause for a moment and reflect whenever the opening chords of "The River" get played on the radio.

Needless to say, Bruce Springsteen did not make me a writer, although his lyrics opened up ways in which I could imaginatively address my own experiences. From the age of fourteen, writing was all that I ever did and even if I had not published fourteen novels since then and seen over a dozen of my plays performed, it is something that I would still be doing every day after coming home from whatever job I worked. This is because writing is my way of making sense of my world, my way of creating my own space where I am not a consumer but an individual. It is the most intimate sphere where, whether alone with a pen and paper or the blank screen of a laptop, I know there is nowhere for me to hide from what I really feel inside.

But what Springsteen did in those hugely influential early albums was write songs that seemed to speak directly to me; songs in which he seemed to validate my life experiences and the life experiences of people I worked with. His songs helped me to an understanding that my world of Dublin factories and working-class estates was as much the source of literature as Greek mythology or the dreary snobbish Bloomsbury set.

Springsteen was by no means the sole influence in helping my teenage self find the confidence to write about my own life. I drew similar inspiration from someone like Phil Lynott of Thin Lizzy, in whose lyrics I heard my hometown mentioned for the first time in rock music. Today, young Dubliners grow up with a whole different musical legacy to draw inspiration from, starting with the vast oeuvre of U2. Today,

I also understand enough about life to have assimilated my own literary heritage of Joyce and Beckett whose words have turned my native city into a universal landscape of the imagination.

But I have never forgotten how those Springsteen albums were such important stepping stones. I have never met Springsteen and never expect to do so. But I know the two words that I would say to him if I did, because I have witnessed the depth of experience and emotion that these two simple words can convey. Irish music was revolutionized in the 1960s by a group of bearded Dublin men who took the ballads of their people and injected new life in them, in the process becoming almost the Irish punks of their time. This group, who for decades became internationally famous, were called the Dubliners. I count myself extremely fortunate to be a friend of their last surviving member: the great fiddle player and composer John Sheahan. I was walking with John late one night when we passed a rather rough bar where a number of smokers were clustered on the steps. I heard one man shout loudly and begin to walk after us. I felt that I was in one of those knife-edge situations in any city where you do not know whether to stop and confront your pursuer or walk quickly on. But John knew what to do. John quietly stopped and turned to face the man who, although down-at-heel in appearance and the worse for wear from drink, drew himself up to his full height and held out his hand to shake John's hand. Speaking with dignity and obviously summoning what the decades of listening to John's music had meant to him, this man said the two words that summed up all that needed to be said before he turned and walked away. The two words I'd say to Bruce Springsteen: "Thank you."

25

The Boss in Bulgaria

✦

RICHARD RUSSO

I almost didn't make the trip. My Boston flight was delayed and then delayed further and finally canceled altogether. Like so many overseas flights these days, this one was full, which meant that hundreds of passengers would have to be accommodated on other flights, and since ours was one of the last scheduled out of International Terminal E, that wouldn't happen until morning. If I conceded defeat right then, I might catch the last bus back to Portland, Maine, where I lived. Whereas if I joined my fellow passengers at the thinly staffed customer service counter, that sensible option would vanish, and I'd be stuck in Boston overnight. Worse, even if I was lucky enough to snag an early morning flight to Frankfurt, I would've already missed my connecting flight to Bulgaria. There wouldn't be another until the following day, and there was no guarantee I'd get a seat. Worst-case scenario, I'd be stranded in the Frankfurt airport without my luggage, unable to get to Bulgaria and, if flights back to Boston were full, powerless to return home for who knew how long. Why run that risk?

I had a cell phone number for Elizabeth Kostova, whose foundation organized the annual conference I was attending. The problem was that she and many of her colleagues and the other American writers, all departing from other cities, would already be in the air, so in fact there was no one from whom I could get advice, though, to be honest, it wasn't really advice I was after so much as permission to bail. Because this Bulgaria writers' conference fit rather snugly into the category of "good deeds," didn't it? Sure, I was being paid, but the real reason I'd agreed to participate was my fondness for Elizabeth, a writer whose books I admired. Each year her foundation brought together a contingent of American and British authors with Bulgarian ones in the hopes of encouraging, after decades of communism, their own national literature. Good, necessary work. On the other hand, what did I have to do with Bulgaria or it with me? Such self-serving questions generally don't occur to you when things are going smoothly, only when they unexpectedly pivot and head due south, when what was supposed to be easy suddenly becomes difficult. Standing there with my haggard fellow travelers and feeling like a bait-and-switch victim, I wanted out, so I looked in the folder containing my travel instructions and contact phone numbers and found one—for a foundation staff person with whom I'd been corresponding—that wasn't a cell phone. Maybe I'd be able to reach someone there. It was too late to make such a call, but if the person I was trying to reach was already on a flight, I rationalized, no one would pick up, right? I could leave my message—*Flight canceled. No good options. Sorry. I tried my best*—and hang up, inconveniencing no one. Imagine my chagrin, then, when a sleepy-sounding man with a thick accent answered on the second ring. When I identified myself, he seemed to know who I was. "Yes! Yes!" he said.

"My flight's been canceled," I told him. "It doesn't look like I'm going to be able to make it. I'm sorry."

"But, you . . ." he said, pausing to locate the right expression in English. "You are the star!"

My impulse was to deny this, to tell him there were several excellent writers on the trip, and that of course the real star was Elizabeth herself. But I knew what he meant. Yes, this was her conference, but she participated every year. This year, like it or not, mine was the marquee name. Since winning the Pulitzer a decade earlier, I'd become increasingly ambivalent about celebrity, an attitude I probably wasn't entitled to. After all, wasn't fame simply a by-product of what I'd worked so hard to achieve for so long? Add to that the fact that the message I intended to leave—*I tried my best*—wasn't really true, was it? "Okay," I told him. "I'll see what I can do."

Well, shit, I thought, hanging up and noting the time. There was a good chance I'd already missed that last bus to Portland. Apparently I was going to Bulgaria. Or at least to Frankfurt. There were still about seventy-five people ahead of me in the customer service line. The man at the front had been talking to the lone agent for the last fifteen minutes. Nothing to do but hunker down. At some point I realized that an old Moody Blues song I'd heard on the radio earlier in the day was running through my brain. Dear Lord, when was the last time I'd thought of them? In the run-up to this conference I'd been sent a questionnaire by the producer of a television talk show on which I was to appear. They had a copy of my most recent book but wanted background information on its author. Who and what were my cultural influences? Could I list some of my favorite books, artists, musicians? I'd mentioned Dickens and Twain, Edward Hopper, and Springsteen, of course. Though I'd liked them well enough as an undergraduate back in the seventies, there were probably five hundred bands I would've listed before the Moody Blues, but it was their lyric that was now running through my head on a loop: "I'm just a singer in a rock and roll band . . . I'm just a singer in. . . ."

Except I wasn't. Assuming I got to Bulgaria, I would be a literary rock star of sorts for the next week. Home. My own bed. Work. These were what I wanted. What I always wanted.

The annual conference was a big deal there. Its serious work—a week's worth of workshops, lectures, and individual conferences—took place in Sozopol, a resort town on the Black Sea, but for publicity reasons it always began and ended in Sofia, the capital. Thanks to my travel delays I'd missed both the orientation activities and the first full day of the conference. Now we were off to Sozopol, a five-hour bus ride.

My seatmate was the well-known biographer Elizabeth Frank, who'd done the conference before and could help me interpret what I was seeing out the windows. I'd been surprised by how vibrant Sofia was, its cafés and coffee shops full of young people flush with freedom and hope after the fall of communism. In the countryside, Liz explained, things were very different. Out here, many people remembered communism fondly. Maybe there'd been no food in the markets, maybe there were times when it seemed like everyone might starve, but at least back then all and sundry were in the same boat. Now the stores were full of food, but it was unaffordable, so how, they wondered, was this better? While some of the Bulgarian countryside looked well tended and prosperous, especially the vineyards, there were also long stretches of fallow, weedy poverty. According to Liz, what prosperity there was came from outside, EU money streaming in and buying up everything on the cheap. Asked how such a thing could happen, the old-timers had a ready explanation: *It's the Jews.* "Seriously?" I said. "*This* again?" "Right," Liz sighed. "This again."

At some point our conversation turned more personal, and Liz told me a story that I would think about often in the days to come. When she was a little girl, living with her family in New York City, she was sometimes awakened late at night by loud voices. One was her father's; the other belonged to his writing partner. They were TV comedy writers, and what they were arguing over so passionately was whether a line from this week's show *was* or *was not* funny. To Liz, getting woken up by their ardent bickering was both comforting and inspiring. If good writing was worth arguing over, like politics, it must be important. Maybe she'd be a writer herself one day.

Hearing this story left me feeling strangely bereft, because as a kid I, too, had been awakened in the middle of the night by loud voices, my mother telling my father to keep his voice down, because their son was asleep in the next room. *What is wrong with you,* she always wanted to know. And his response: *Okay, Jean, how about you just kiss my ass?* And then one day all that stopped because he was gone. Years later, when I told him I wanted to be a writer, he didn't try to discourage me, though to him it was clearly a puzzling ambition. But it must've seemed as natural to Liz's dad as it later did to Liz herself that she would become a writer. He was, she told me, her first mentor, and for the rest of his life he remained one of her most faithful readers and champions. My own father would die before my first novel was published, leaving me to wonder, with each new book, what he would've made of it all.

In Sozopol we writers took over a small hotel built on a bluff overlooking the Black Sea. To get to the beach, you had to wind down through narrow one-way streets. Across the bay several modern condo developments had sprung up, and others were being built—more EU money—and this new construction offered a startling contrast to the quaint, almost fairy-tale architecture of the old town. Everywhere you looked, you saw the confluence of cultures—nearby Greece, Turkey, the former Soviet Bloc. I found myself wondering what in all this, after centuries of conquest and subjugation, was actually Bulgarian?

The teaching was challenging. Many of the Bulgarians spoke some English, though for the most part we communicated through translators. Mornings, the Bulgarian- and English-speaking faculty and fellows had separate writing workshops, but in the afternoon the lectures and panels were translated, Bulgarian into English and vice versa, and at meals every effort was made to combine the groups, in part so the food, mysterious to us foreigners, could be explained. ("Really? You're supposed to eat these tiny deep-fried fish head and all?") The Bulgarians were all singers and serious drinkers, and after dinner they congregated on the hotel patio for long nights of song and cheap red wine. (I'd forgotten how much of the brutal, hangover-inducing wine we'd drunk as graduate students—back when I was just a singer in a rock-and-roll band—came from Bulgaria.) Not wanting to be unsociable, we Americans and Brits would join in for a while, but we had our morning workshops and afternoon talks to prepare, so one by one we drifted away. My room was on the third floor, its balcony overlooking the patio below, and I was awakened several times each night by singing that became more boisterous as the hours lengthened. Bulgarian folk songs came first, though at some point those segued into American rock and pop. There seemed to be a special fondness for Bon Jovi, and that first night, when I heard them bellowing "Oh! We're halfway there. Oh-oh, livin' on a prayer," I went out onto the balcony and peered down into the dark, thinking a few Americans and Brits had rejoined them, but no, the singers were all Bulgarian.

Was that how it seemed to them, one brief generation after the fall of communism? That they were halfway there? And how they felt as artists searching for their voices after decades of enforced silence? Did the Anglo-American presence contribute to their buoyant optimism? One thing was for sure: none of the singers in the courtyard below had ever been woken in the middle of the night by a parent arguing over whether something was funny or not. I suspected their fathers were more like mine than Liz Frank's. While they wouldn't want to stand in the way of their children's dreams, neither would they comprehend why, with so many needful things in the world, their kids would want to tell stories, write poems, paint pictures.

Near the end of his life, battling Alzheimer's, the novelist Ross Macdonald wrote to Eudora Welty, "I think you may understand . . . how hard it can be to speak after a lapse into silence." Indeed. The human voice, like any other instrument, needs to be used. What do you say if you haven't spoken all day? All week? All year? What if you haven't been allowed a voice your entire life? What if the same was true of your parents, even your grandparents? Would everything you've been wanting to say for so long come gushing out? Probably not, actually. Or so it seemed of my Bulgarian writers, whose manuscripts I read in translation. Most of them were talented and, yes, anxious to enter the literary conversation from which they'd been excluded for so long. They wanted not only to write but also to start magazines and publishing houses for their stories and poems to appear in. They wanted all these things at once. But again, how? Do you go directly to the big subject—what life was like under totalitarian rule? If so, should that be treated as serious drama? As satire? Are you allowed to forget all that? Giddy with freedom, are you allowed to be happy? Devout? Sure, you're now free to say anything you want, but what should you say first? These seemed to be the unspoken questions lurking behind the Bulgarians' manuscripts. Or, to put it another way, how do you sing alone, on the page, in the light of day, like you do collectively, at night, at the edge of the Black Sea? Where do you find the confidence necessary to create a voice uniquely your own? Halfway there? Perhaps, but isn't it also possible that you're just beginning? And here's an even more alarming thought: *What if there's no you yet?* What if your writerly identity has to be invented before speech is possible?

How sweet and generous (and perhaps naïve?) it was of these Bulgarian writers to imagine we could help them. How intently they listened to us when we told them what we liked best about their stories and plays and essays, what we thought was working, and where their tone shifted unexpectedly, wrong-footing us. How good-naturedly they endured our probing personal questions: How did they feel about what they were reporting? What emotion motivated the telling? In a sense, coming from the other side of the world to advise a group of writers whose experiences of life were so different from my own seemed arrogant, but then again the problem of locating the right voice with which to speak is pretty universal. Black writers often feel the need to address their blackness, women writers their gender, gay writers their sexual orientation. No doubt they would all love the privilege blithely assumed by white male authors: the complete, unfettered freedom that derives from being unshackled from unfair expectations.

Yet as Melville's Ishmael once asked, "Who ain't a slave?" Even the most blessed writers encounter obstacles. We all shoulder burdens, even if they aren't equally heavy. Wouldn't it be wonderful, we can't help thinking, to simply set them down and walk away? Shouldn't that be an option? Consider a writer like Kenneth Millar, who grew up in Canada, moved to Southern California, and there invented the aforementioned Ross Macdonald, who in turn invented Detective Lew Archer as well as the city of Santa Teresa (his fictional Santa Barbara). More than anything, it was Archer's tough, world-weary voice that anchored that brilliant series of detective novels. But to read Macdonald's dazzling correspondence with Eudora Welty in *Meanwhile There Are Letters* is to understand that while Archer's voice might be Macdonald's, it certainly isn't Millar's. Ken Millar was no wise-cracking tough guy. The voice we hear in his letters to Welty is educated, intellectual, sensitive, at times almost effete—the quiet voice of the bird-watcher he was: indeed, it's the voice of a man whose experience of life could not have been further removed from that of his detective hero. Whatever Millar's burdens might have been, he seems to have set them down and walked away.

As a young writer I vividly remember trying to achieve just such a metamorphosis in my graduate writing program in Arizona, a place as far from my home in upstate New York as Millar's California was from his native Ontario. While I would have loved to write books like Macdonald's, and even tried my hand at detective stories, such a radical metamorphosis simply wasn't possible for me, so in the end I had little choice but to return, at least imaginatively, to my heart's home and be who I was, who I'd always been and, it appeared, I was meant to be. I had come to realize that I'd inherited a patch of dirt about the size of Faulkner's and had to figure out how to be content with that. At the time, though, my inability to invent a new, improved self felt like nothing so much as defeat.

But what of my Bulgarians? Who should *they* be? Should they embrace their burdens, as I did, or toss them off like shackles, as Millar was somehow able to do? This was what they seemed to want me to tell them: who they were, what they should value most, how to get from where they were to where I was. And so each night I carefully read their manuscripts, looking for clues to their identities. And every night, in the courtyard below, they sang, first the unknowable songs of their country, then the songs of my own. Night after night they insisted they're halfway there.

Back in Sofia, the conference winding down, I geared up for my TV appearance. One of the benefits of having been a teacher for so long, as well as a veteran of many book tours, is that I generally don't get nervous about public appearances, though I was a bit anxious with this one. It was live, not taped, and I was to be the last guest on the ninety-minute show, which meant that any anxiety I might be feeling would likely intensify as I watched the other guests from the wings. Naturally, I'd be working with yet another interpreter, and nothing is more lost in translation more quickly than humor, my strong suit. But never mind, I told myself. What happens in Bulgaria stays in Bulgaria.

The program was clearly modeled on American and British talk shows, its host an attractive woman who was seated at the center of a horseshoe-shaped piano bar. Her cohort—combining the duties of Ed McMahon and Doc Severinsen—was a young fellow at the piano, who would sometimes banter with the host but mostly just noodled at the keyboard as she talked with her guests, all of whom entered the studio—I kid you not—through a haze of dry-ice smoke.

When it was finally my turn, I climbed aboard the last remaining stool at the piano bar, and my translator nestled up close, whispering the host's first question in my ear, something about how it felt to win the Pulitzer Prize, and my heart leaped with gratitude. I knew the answer to *this* one! Not in Bulgarian, of course, but still. I'd been warned to keep my answers short, a challenge since I like long answers. They keep the next question, which you may not know the answer to, at bay. But guess what? I knew the answer to that one as well, so I gave it confidently, even risking a mild witticism, at which the host threw back her head and laughed, and the pianist did a comic little arpeggio on the keyboard. I was a hit! Evidently, even on the other side of the world I was a funny guy.

More questions. More answers. More noodling at the piano. At some point, though, I became aware of movement in my peripheral vision and noticed the other guests glancing in the direction of whatever was going on behind me. Was it my imagination or had the noodling on the piano, atonal a moment earlier, begun to resolve itself into a melody, a tune I knew? What was it?

Stay focused, I told myself. My segment couldn't have more than three or four more minutes left. Apparently I was going to survive. Indeed, the host was now grinning like she was about to award me a second Pulitzer right there. *What was that damn tune?* "Well, Richard Russo," said the English voice in my ear, "we understand you're a fan of Bruce Springsteen, who is very popular here in Bulgaria, so this is our way of saying, 'Welcome to Sofia, and please do come again.'"

Rotating on my stool I saw there were now three more musicians—bassist, guitarist, and drummer—and when they joined in I suddenly recognized the song. When the guitarist stepped up to the mic, I heard the lyric in my brain a split second before his voice reached my ear: *Grab your ticket and your suitcase / thunder's rollin' down this track / well, you don't know where you're goin' now / but you know you won't be back / well, darlin' if you're weary lay your head upon my chest / we'll take what we can carry / yeah, and we'll leave the rest.* The singer had a pretty good voice. Not like Bruce's, of course, but not bad either. What I couldn't tell was if the words were being sung phonetically, or if the singer actually understood them. *Yeah, this train, carries saints and sinners / this train, carries losers and winners / this train, carries whores and gamblers / this train, carries lost souls.* Did the singer comprehend that he was singing a great American anthem, maybe the greatest written in my lifetime, by the greatest storytelling songwriter of his generation? Did he understand it was Springsteen's voice that had helped a weary nation through the bitter end of the Vietnam War, the AIDS epidemic, the attack on the World Trade Center? I couldn't tell, and somehow the possibility that he *didn't* know the meaning of those words caused my throat to constrict. *Well big wheels roll through fields where sunlight streams / oh, meet me in a land of hope and dreams.* Dear God, I thought. I'm about to break down sobbing on Bulgarian television. And if I do, it will not stay in Bulgaria. *I said this train, dreams will not be thwarted / this train, faith will be rewarded / this train, steels wheels singin' / this train, bells of freedom ringin'.'*

I will draw the curtain here, leaving it to the reader's imagination whether I maintained some semblance of dignity and decorum or wept like a child on the far side of the world, wept for pride in Bruce and the nation that spawned him, with a welling up of admiration, too, for every singer, poet, and artist lucky enough to find, against all odds, a voice and the courage to raise it, and of deep empathy for the many more who try and fail. And yes, yes, profound admiration for my Bulgarians who sang and drank the night away in the conviction they were halfway there, which you have to believe or you'll never catch that train, the one carrying saints and sinners and lost souls, the one headed for the land of hope and literary dreams, which is neither here nor there but, rather, in each of us who chase it.

26

We Take Care of Our Own

WAYNE SWAN

June 2018

The offices in Australia's Parliament House share a relatively similar format, leaving the members of Parliament (MPs) who occupy them only limited room for self-expression.

For most MPs, the walls are adorned with family photos, indigenous artwork, or certificates of appreciation from their local communities. The bookshelves are typically stuffed with hefty volumes of Hansard (the printed proceedings of the Australian Parliament and its committees), political manuals, or a few too many publishers' copies of the member's own books.

My office is a little different. Hanging next to the photo of my three children is a framed poster that never fails to draw comment from the first-time visitors and dignitaries who drop by. The poster advertises Bruce Springsteen's 1980 show at the Nassau Coliseum; the iconic picture of the Boss, first taken for the cover of *Darkness on the Edge of Town*, stares intently back at its viewer.

Just below the poster, in the corner of my bookshelf, is a small stereo. A modest scattering of CDs surrounds it—Neil Young's *Harvest* and a compilation from the Australian rockers Cold Chisel get regular airplay. But at the top of the heap are the Springsteen staples—all the albums from his first decade of recording, released during my first decade of adulthood. They have never left me.

May 1974

Springsteen Begins Recording Born to Run, *the Album That Would Catapult Him to International Fame*

In May 1974, I was nineteen years old. Like Springsteen, I'd come from a working-class family, though I was lucky enough to get opportunities that many of my parents' generation were denied, but their talents deserved.

One such opportunity was to attend university. For many of my peers, a university education would have remained out of reach if it weren't for the election of Gough Whitlam's reforming Labor Party government, which abolished university fees in 1974.

The Whitlam government had swept to power in the Australian summer of 1972, snapping our nation out of the torpor of twenty-three years of conservative, Liberal Party rule. Whitlam, the new prime minister, was a modernizer, but he never forgot the working-class roots of the Labor Party he represented.

Among a litany of achievements, his government abolished conscription for the Vietnam War, introduced universal health care, substantially raised social security payments for older Australians, and established a sewage system in the outer suburbs of Sydney.

Whitlam inspired many young Australians to engage more deeply with politics. In May 1974, I was one of their number, joining the Labor Party at the University of Queensland. I'd come to study in Brisbane from Nambour, a small town in Queensland's Sunshine Coast Hinterland. Before I came to university, I'd had no contact with politics or politicians—just a role model in my father, who was a staunch Labor voter.

While at university, I lived in a five-bedroom bungalow that was party central and Labor Party central rolled into one. My housemates and I, as typical university students, regularly treated our neighbors to some timeless music well into the early hours of the morning. The eternal riff from "Layla" by Derek and the Dominos. The pre- and post-electric incarnations of Bob Dylan. The swooping, searing, screaming vocals of Robert Plant. In music, as in politics, it was a great time to be alive.

By the end of 1975, the world that we had enjoyed as university students would change forever. On November 11, in an unprecedented act of political treachery, the governor general abruptly dismissed the Whitlam government, using his nonpartisan position to remake national politics. An election was called, and, from the stairs of Parliament House, the deposed Gough Whitlam urged the assembled throng to "maintain your rage" at the system that had viciously ejected his government.

The rage and enthusiasm sparked in our rambling university quarters by what became known as "The Dismissal" was exemplified by one album that had recently risen to high rotation for us—and for our forbearing neighbors. *Born to Run* was the soundtrack to that summer.

Born to Run captured the spirit of youthful freedom and sweeping change that we'd glimpsed all too fleetingly as students. Its title track carried the warning that big, daunting responsibilities were just around the corner.

But more than this, the album transmitted from New Jersey the same sense of accountability, responsibility, and affinity that we as young activists in Australia felt for the working people we'd grown up with. When Springsteen sang about the desire to escape a deadening manufacturing job, he was singing about people we knew.

The first time I saw the Boss perform live, many years later, his spoken introduction to "Born to Run" would transport me to that university residence, where it seemed like he was speaking to the fundamental reason that my friends and I had first chosen the political life: "Nobody wins unless everybody wins."

Looking back, I shouldn't be surprised that Springsteen's influence, which took root during my earliest days in politics, would accompany me for the next four decades.

September 2008

*In the Midst of the Worst Financial Crisis to Hit the
United States in Eighty Years, Springsteen Abandons Plans to
Record a Gospel Album and Turns His Attention to the
Economic Devastation Confronting Working Americans; the
Album He Writes Will Become* Wrecking Ball

In mid-September 2008, the global economy stood on a knife edge. The
world's fifth-largest investment bank, Bear Stearns, had collapsed
in March, to be taken over by J.P. Morgan in a deal brokered by the
Federal Reserve. Mortgage giants Fannie Mae and Freddie Mac, their
books saddled with bad loans, were bailed out by the U.S. government.
And in what would become the watershed event of the Great Recession,
financial services firm Lehman Brothers filed for bankruptcy.

The crisis would exact an enduring toll on Americans. Nearly nine million jobs were lost during the Great Recession and nearly nine years passed
before the same number of jobs returned. And when the jobs came back,
they generally came back with lower pay and less security. While countless working Americans have suffered, the salaries, bonuses, and job security of the Wall Street executives who were among the architects of the
crisis have only increased. Not one Wall Street executive was jailed.

It's often the case that great artists—people like Bruce Springsteen—
tend to pick up the rumblings of profound social change long before the
economic statisticians notice them. Crises start well before they become
statistics.

If you listen to the albums that came out after *Born to Run*—albums like
Darkness on the Edge of Town, The River, Nebraska, and *Born in the U.S.A.*—
you can hear Springsteen singing about the shifting foundations of the
American economy that economists took much longer to detect, and
which of course everyone was talking about after the Great Recession.

For instance, from the track "Atlantic City" on the *Nebraska* album:
"Now I've been looking for a job, but it's hard to find / down here it's just
winners and losers / and don't get caught on the wrong side of that
line." Or from "My Hometown" on *Born in the U.S.A.*, which describes
a town where the stores have closed down, main street is shuttered,
and where "They're closing down the textile mill across the railroad

tracks / foreman says these jobs are going boys and they ain't coming back." Springsteen saw that for ordinary people life wasn't getting any better; other people were grabbing all the gains. As he put it, the sense of daily struggle in his songs kept growing. And he responded with an abiding question: when are ordinary people—the people who look after their families and who get up in the morning and go to work each day—going to get a fair go?

Nothing has fueled my own public life more than this question.

I was first elected to Federal Parliament in 1993. Australia was emerging from its deepest recession since the Great Depression, but the long shadow cast by high unemployment and underemployment meant that some Australians who were laid off during the recession would never work, or work fully, again. In my first speech, I acknowledged,

> I was fortunate enough to be born into a privileged generation that took full employment for granted. It is an awesome responsibility to enter this Parliament at a time when unemployment exceeds 10 percent and long-term unemployment is approaching half a million. The social cost of unemployment places enormous responsibility not just on politicians in this House but also on academics, industrial leaders and everyone in our community not to tap the mat and say, "There is nothing we can do." We should never resort to the pathetic bleating that we sometimes hear from sections of our community that there is nothing that can be done.

By the time Lehman Brothers collapsed in September 2008, I had been appointed Treasurer in a newly elected Labor government. Many members of our cabinet had also been brought up in working-class families. All of us had witnessed the devastation wrought by the recession of the early 1990s. So, when the crisis reached our shores in 2008, we were determined to protect the jobs, homes, and livelihoods of the millions of Australians who had put their trust in us in the voting booth just months earlier.

Australia's experience of the Great Recession was vastly different than that of the United States. Our response to the crisis, with its centerpiece of stimulus payments to low- and middle-income households, was motivated by the same ethos that had guided most of us into politics. We believed—we believe—that working people are an engine of economic growth. They're not an afterthought, or a consequence of growth. They are vital to it.

Although Australia avoided recession in 2008 and the massive loss of jobs and human potential that it otherwise might have entailed, discontent was never too far below the surface.

March 2012

Springsteen Releases Wrecking Ball, *to Wide Acclaim; It Is His Tenth Album to Reach Number 1 in the United States*

By March 2012, I had been Australia's Treasurer for four and a half years. Our economy had weathered the Great Recession and was the envy of our neighbors. But although Australia had avoided a crisis—or perhaps *because* we had avoided a crisis—conservative voices and corporate elites had been emboldened to call for an all-out assault on our government's plans to introduce a new tax on mining profits and a price on carbon emissions.

The blatant self-interest at the core of their campaign to derail these progressive reforms was nowhere more evident than in the infamous billionaires' protest. Within a year of America's 99 percent occupying Wall Street to demand greater equality in the distribution of income and wealth, representatives of Australia's top 0.01 percent, including two mining billionaires, took to the back of a flatbed truck in Perth, Western Australia, to demand that the proceeds of the country's once-in-a-lifetime resources boom be distributed solely to them, the billionaires.

Prior to the release of *Wrecking Ball*, I had been listening again to *Darkness on the Edge of Town*. A fragment from "Badlands" remained lodged in my mind. Although it had been written in North America more than three decades earlier, the song seemed to speak directly about the affluent protestors Down Under:

> Poor man wanna be rich
> Rich man wanna be king
> And a king ain't satisfied
> Till he rules everything

In March 2012, I penned an essay titled "The 0.01 Per Cent: The Rising Influence of Vested Interests in Australia" for a national magazine. The essay made a simple point, which the brazen billionaires had helped bring into sharp relief: if we don't grow together economically, our community will grow apart.

It was a lesson that the plutocratic elements of the business community could claim not to have learned from the economic crisis, because in Australia there had been no crisis to speak of. Nevertheless, these plutocrats seemed intent on fomenting a crisis on their own terms. There was no small irony when one chief executive claimed that it was "almost a shame . . . we didn't have a deeper downturn to wake us up [to] the heavy lifting we're going to have to do."

When *Wrecking Ball* came out that month, I was struck not just by how attuned Springsteen had remained to the people and the subjects he had written about almost forty years earlier, but also by how the message and the warning that underscored his music still applied just as strongly to Australia as it did to the United States.

The message is that to build a better society we have to ensure the fruits of economic growth reach everyone. And the warning is that if we don't include everyone and don't listen to everyone, the social discord that follows will put our prosperity at risk. This is what Springsteen is speaking out against. "Wherever this flag is flown," he sings on *Wrecking Ball*, "we take care of our own."

We take care of our own. It's a powerful message, which has enormous relevance in Australia. It's the same egalitarian version of patriotism that gets us out of bed in the Labor movement, that cuts us to the quick and stirs us into action when we see attempts to diminish it in the name of unashamed self-interest. It's the message that inspired me and a generation of my peers to enter politics and fight for the working people we grew up with.

If I could distill the relevance of Bruce Springsteen's music to Australia it would be this: Don't let what has happened to the American economy happen in Australia. Don't let Australia become a Down Under version of New Jersey, where the people and the communities whose skills are no longer in demand get thrown on the scrap heap of life. Don't let this be a place where ordinary people's views are drowned out and only those with the most expensive megaphones get a say.

Nobody wins unless everybody wins.

June 2018

In 2018, I announced my retirement from Federal Parliament, twenty-five years after I was first elected. As I repeated to countless media outlets at the time, "I might be getting out of Parliament, but I'm not getting out of politics." The sense of accountability and responsibility that had first encouraged me to seek higher office still burned as strong as ever.

Although I wasn't going to run in the next election, I decided that I had one good run left in me. So I announced my candidacy for the National Presidency of the Australian Labor Party—a role that oversees the direction of the party, ensuring that its interests remain aligned with those of the working people who first formed the party and who remain its base today.

The night that my victory in the presidential ballot was announced, my office was flooded with parliamentary colleagues and staff who brought well wishes, drinks, and song requests. My small stereo and modest office CD collection couldn't hope to appease the room's wide and, in some cases, highly questionable music demands.

While some colleagues contemplated a building-wide search for a more accommodating set of speakers or a broader variety of CDs, these plans were quietly laid to rest as the familiar warm warble of the Boss's telecaster filled the room, just like it had in that university house in 1975. Now, as then, just one album, one song, and one artist could truly encapsulate the moment.

ACKNOWLEDGMENTS

In completing this book, we racked up debts no honest editors could pay. Thanks first and foremost to Peter Mickulas, our editor at Rutgers University Press. Peter has been a tireless advocate for this collection for over two years, and he served as a constant source of guidance, encouragement, and enthusiasm throughout the editorial process. We could not have completed this book without him. Our gratitude also to the entire team at Rutgers, including Jennifer Blanc-Tal, Courtney Brach, Dana Brach, Jeremy Grainger, Brice Hammack, Micah Kleit, Karen Li, Elisabeth Maselli, Vincent Nordhaus, and Gina Sbrilli. Thanks also to Lou Masur for suggesting we publish with Rutgers and keep this book in the Garden State.

We owe a huge thank-you to Ken Womack. Ken was an early supporter of this project and, through the Bruce Springsteen Archives and Center for American Music at Monmouth University, secured crucial funding to help bring it to publication. Though his heart will always be with the Beatles, this book and the entire field of Springsteen studies owe Ken a debt of gratitude.

Thanks also to all of our contributors for being so easy to work with. It can be difficult to edit pieces that authors have been pondering for a long time and that hold personal importance, but our essayists were understanding and helpful every step of the way. Special thanks to Irwin Streight for helping us shape the scope of the collection, allowing us to publish the interview with Martyn Joseph he had initially intended for publication in *BOSS: The Biannual Online-Journal of Springsteen Studies*, and for being a trusted friend and colleague before, during, and throughout the editorial process. Thanks also to Cheryl Hirsch; to Mona Okada for her help securing permission to quote from Patti Scialfa's and Springsteen's lyrics; to Rocco S. Coviello and Frank Stefanko for providing our cover and section-break photos; and to Caitlin Flanagan for her assistance identifying and contacting prospective authors and for providing logistical aid in the early stages of the project.

In addition, June Sawyers would like to thank all of the contributors, including those who expressed an interest in being a part of the collection but, for various reasons, were unable to follow through. I would also like to thank Jonathan Cohen for his magnificent editorial skills and for going above and beyond the call of duty. Jon kept everyone on their toes, including his co-editor, dotting every "i" and crossing every "t" along the way. What's more, the students in my 2017 Springsteen class at the Newberry Library—especially Theresa Nugent and Linda Odegard—helped me see Springsteen's life and career in a new light. And, as always, thanks to Theresa Albini for just being there. Over the years she too has become a huge Springsteen fan.

Jonathan would like to thank all the mentors who have supported his interest in Springsteen and Springsteen studies over the last decade, including Thomas Jundt and Leonard Moore at McGill University; Grace Hale, Matthew Hedstrom, Brian Balogh, and Karl Hagstrom Miller at the University of Virginia; as well as Irwin Streight and Roxanne Harde. My endless thanks to June Skinner Sawyers for working with me, for her level-headed guidance, and her vision that formed the original basis for this project. Thanks to Joey Thompson for his well-founded skepticism that Bruce Springsteen matters and to Bill Wolff as well as the Boston funshop group (Danielle Deluty, Daniel Gastfriend, Raffi Grinberg, and Cary Snider) for providing comments on the introduction. Thanks also to Charlotte and Judah Grinberg and the Boston board game crew (Ben Lang, Sarah Trager, and Sarah Smith) for giving me something to look forward to every week and to my friends in the UVA History Department for letting me blast "Dancing in the Dark" once in a while. My appreciation to the Jefferson Scholars Foundation and the Mellon / ACLS Dissertation Completion Fellowship program for their financial assistance while completing this collection. None of my work, or any of my accomplishments, would be possible without the love and support of my parents, Miriam May and Shaye Cohen, or my siblings, Ava and Josh, Ezra, and Hannah, who always keep me grounded. Finally, the biggest thanks to Shayna, my own Jersey girl, for her humor, her sincerity, her affection, and her willingness to tolerate Springsteen playlists on long road trips. She is my beautiful reward.

Jonathan D. Cohen, Cambridge, Mass.
June Sawyers, Chicago, Ill.

ABOUT THE EDITORS

JONATHAN D. COHEN received his PhD from the Corcoran Department of History at the University of Virginia. He is the coeditor of *All In: The Spread of Gambling in Twentieth-Century United States* and his writing on American gambling has appeared in the *Washington Post*, the *Hill*, *Vox*, *Commonwealth*, *Public Seminar*, as well as the *Journal of Policy History*. His writing on Springsteen and rock music has appeared in *New Jersey Studies*, *Intermountain West Journal of Religious Studies*, and the collection *Bruce Springsteen and Popular Music*, edited by William I. Wolff. He is the managing editor of *BOSS: The Biannual Online-Journal of Springsteen Studies*.

JUNE SKINNER SAWYERS has written and lectured extensively on Bruce Springsteen. Her books include *Racing in the Street: The Bruce Springsteen Reader; Tougher Than the Rest: 100 Best Bruce Springsteen Songs*; and the e-book *Workingman: The Faith-Based Politics of Bruce Springsteen*. She appears in the documentary *Bruce Springsteen under Review 1978–1982: Tales of the Working Man*. Her essay "Endlessly Seeking: Bruce Springsteen and Walker Percy's Quest for Possibility among the Ordinary" appears in *Reading the Boss: Interdisciplinary Approaches to the Works of Bruce Springsteen*, edited by Roxanne Harde and Irwin Streight, and "Weeping Willows and Long Black Veils: The Country Roots of Rosanne Cash, from Scotland to Tennessee" in *Walking the Line: Country Music Lyricists and American Culture*, edited by Thomas Alan Holmes and Roxanne Harde. Her other books include *Cabaret FAQ: All That's Left to Know about the Broadway and Cinema Classic; Bob Dylan: New York; 10 Songs That Changed the World; Read the Beatles: Classic and New Writings on the Beatles, Their Legacy, and Why They Still Matter;*

and *Celtic Music*. Her work has appeared in the *Chicago Tribune, San Francisco Chronicle, Stagebill, Scottish Tradition, Common Review,* and *Third Coast Review,* among other publications. She teaches humanities courses at the Newberry Library in Chicago.

ABOUT THE CONTRIBUTORS

NATALIE ADLER is a writer living in New York. She has a PhD in comparative literature from Brown University and was a first-generation college student. She works in disability advocacy and leftist organizing in the Bronx and Upper Manhattan. Currently, she is completing a novel about queer feminism. The most Jersey thing about her is the expertise with which she orders at a crowded Italian bakery.

ERIC ALTERMAN is Distinguished Professor of English and Journalism, Brooklyn College, City University of New York. He is also "The Liberal Media" columnist for the *Nation*, a senior fellow at the Center for American Progress in Washington, D.C. and the Nation Institute and the World Policy Institute in New York, as well as former columnist for the *Daily Beast*, the *Forward*, *Moment*, *Rolling Stone*, *Mother Jones*, and the *Sunday Express* (London). He is the author of ten books, including the national best seller *What Liberal Media? The Truth about Bias and the News*. He has been called "the most honest and incisive media critic writing today" in the *National Catholic Reporter* and author of "the smartest and funniest political journal out there," in the *San Francisco Chronicle*. A winner of the George Orwell Prize, the Stephen Crane Literary Award, and the Mirror Award for media criticism (twice), he has also been a Media Fellow at the Hoover Institution at Stanford University, a Schusterman Foundation Fellow at Brandeis University, and a Fellow of the Society of American Historians. He received his PhD in U.S. history from Stanford, his MA in international relations at Yale, and his BA from Cornell. Previously, he taught at Columbia, NYU, and Hofstra. His book, *Trouble with the Truth: Why Presidents Lie and Why Trump Is Different* will be published by Basic Books in 2020. His forthcoming history of the Israel/Palestine debate in the United States is also under contract at Basic. He lives in Manhattan.

GINA BARRECA, author of ten books and editor of eleven others, is a Board of Trustees Distinguished Professor of English at the University of Connecticut and the winner of UConn's highest award for excellence in teaching. Hailed as "smart and funny" by *People* magazine and "Very, very funny. For a woman," by Dave Barry, she was deemed a "feminist humor maven" by *Ms. Magazine*. Novelist Wally Lamb said "Barreca's prose, in equal measures, is hilarious and humane." Her weekly columns from the *Hartford Courant* are now distributed internationally by the Tribune Co. and her work has appeared in most major publications, including the *New York Times*, the *Independent of London*, the *Chronicle of Higher Education*, *Cosmopolitan*, and the *Harvard Business Review*. She is a member of the Friars Club and an honoree of the Connecticut Women's Hall of Fame. She is the author of *If You Lean In, Will Men Just Look Down Your Blouse?* which was an ELLE Reader's Prize selection. Her earlier books include *It's Not That I'm Bitter, Or How I Learned to Stop Worrying about Visible Panty Lines and Conquered the World*; the best-selling *They Used to Call Me Snow White but I Drifted: Women's Strategic Use of Humor*; *Babes in Boyland: A Personal History of Coeducation in the Ivy League*; and the edited collection *Don't Tell Mama!: The Penguin Book of Italian American Writing*.

NANCY S. BISHOP retired in 2012 after over thirty years in corporate marketing and public relations, working for two large professional services firms. She is editor and publisher of *Third Coast Review*, a Chicago-centric arts and culture website, where she and over a dozen other writers publish reviews of theater, film, books, music, games, art, and food. She is a theater critic, a member of the American Theatre Critics Association, and a 2014 Fellow of the National Critics Institute at the Eugene O'Neill Theater Center. She holds an MA in journalism from Northern Illinois University and a BA in journalism from the University of Missouri. She believes that any life event is better with a Bruce Springsteen song.

DERMOT BOLGER is one of Ireland's best-known writers. His fourteen novels include *The Journey Home, Tanglewood, The Lonely Sea and Sky, The Family on Paradise Pier*, and *An Ark of Light*. His first play, *The Lament for Arthur Cleary*, received the Samuel Beckett Award. His numerous other plays include *The Ballymun Trilogy*—charting forty years of life in a Dublin working-class suburb—and an adaptation of James Joyce's *Ulysses*, staged by the Abbey Theatre, Ireland's National Theatre. His *That Which Is Suddenly Precious: New & Selected Poems* appeared in 2015. He devised the best-selling collaborative novels *Finbar's Hotel* and *Ladies Night at Finbar's Hotel* and edited *The Vintage Book of Contemporary Irish Fiction*. A former Writer Fellow at Trinity College, Dublin, he writes for Ireland's leading newspapers and in 2012 was named Commentator of the Year at the Irish Newspaper awards.

PETER AMES CARLIN is the author of *Bruce*, the biography of Bruce Springsteen published by Touchstone / Simon & Schuster in 2012. He has also written books about Brian Wilson, Paul McCartney, and Paul Simon, worked as a senior writer at *People* and a TV critic / columnist for the *Oregonian* newspaper, and published work in the *New York Times Magazine*, the *Los Angeles Times Magazine*, the Atlantic.com, and *American Heritage*. He lives in Portland, Oregon, with his wife and family.

JEFFERSON COWIE holds the James G. Stahlman Chair in American History at Vanderbilt University, where his research and teaching focus on how class, inequality, and work shape American politics and culture. He is the author of *Stayin' Alive: The 1970s and the Last Days of the Working Class*, which won a number of awards including the Francis Parkman Prize for the Best Book in American History. His most recent book is *The Great Exception: The New Deal and the Limits of American Politics*. His writing appears in a number of popular publications from the *New York Times* to *Foreign Affairs*; his thoughts on Springsteen have appeared in *Dissent*, *Reviews in American History*, and *American Quarterly*.

JIM CULLEN teaches history at the Ethical Culture Fieldston School in New York. His books include *Born in the U.S.A.: Bruce Springsteen and the American Tradition* and *The American Dream: A Short History of an Idea That Shaped a Nation*. He is currently writing a cultural history of the 1970s sitcom *All in the Family*.

JOEL DINERSTEIN is the author of three books on race, popular music, and American identity—*The Origins of Cool in Postwar America*, *American Cool*, and the award-winning *Swinging the Machine: Modernity, Technology, and African-American Culture*—as well as the article "The

Soul Roots of Bruce Springsteen's American Dream" in *American Music*. He has served as a consultant for popular music for the NEH, Putumayo Records, and HBO's *Boardwalk Empire*. He is Professor of English and American Studies at Tulane University.

GILLIAN G. GAAR is the author of *Boss: Bruce Springsteen and the E Street Band—The Illustrated History*. She has written over fifteen books, including *She's A Rebel: The History of Women in Rock & Roll; Entertain Us: The Rise of Nirvana; Return of the King: Elvis Presley's Great Comeback*; and *Green Day: Rebels with a Cause*. She has also written for numerous publications, including *Mojo, Rolling Stone*, and *Goldmine*, and served as project consultant for Nirvana's *With the Lights Out* box set. She lives in Seattle.

DEEPA IYER is a South Asian American writer, lawyer, and activist. She is the author of *We Too Sing America: South Asian, Arab, Muslim and Sikh Immigrants Shape Our Multiracial Future*. She lives in the Washington, D.C., area.

MARTYN JOSEPH is an award-winning singer-songwriter. With a career spanning over thirty years, thirty-two albums, over half a million record sales, and thousands of live performances, his music touches genres of folk, rock, soul, folk funk, and Americana. In 2013, he released *Tires Rushing By in the Rain*, an acoustic album of Bruce Springsteen songs, to great public and critical praise.

GREIL MARCUS is the author of *Mystery Train; Lipstick Traces; The Dustbin of History; The Old, Weird America; The History of Rock 'n' Roll in Ten Songs*; and other books. With Werner Sollors he is the editor of *A New Literary History of America* and with Sean Wilentz of *The Rose and the Briar*. He was born in San Francisco and lives in Oakland.

LOUIS P. MASUR is Distinguished Professor of American Studies and History at Rutgers University. A cultural historian, he is the author of *Runaway Dream: Born to Run and Bruce Springsteen's American Vision* and co-editor, with Chris Phillips, of *Talk about a Dream: The Essential Interviews of Bruce Springsteen*.

PAUL MULDOON was born in County Armagh in 1951. He now lives in New York. A former radio and television producer for the BBC in

Belfast, he has taught at Princeton University for thirty years. He is the author of twelve collections of poetry including *Moy Sand and Gravel*, for which he won the 2003 Pulitzer Prize, as well as *Selected Poems 1968–2014*.

LAUREN ONKEY is Senior Director of NPR Music in Washington, D.C. Prior to that she was Vice President of Education and Public Programming at the Rock and Roll Hall of Fame and Museum in Cleveland, Ohio. She is the author of *Blackness and Transatlantic Irish Identity: Celtic Soul Brothers* and many articles on popular music, cultural studies, and women's studies. She holds a PhD in English from the University of Illinois at Urbana-Champaign and was an Associate Professor in the English Department at Ball State University.

RICHARD RUSSO is the author of eight novels, most recently *Everybody's Fool* and *That Old Cape Magic*; two collections of stories, with *Trajectory* published in 2017; and the memoir *Elsewhere*. In 2002 he received the Pulitzer Prize for *Empire Falls*, which like *Nobody's Fool* was adapted to film, in a multiple-award-winning HBO miniseries; in 2016 he was given the Indie Champion Award by the American Booksellers Association; and in 2017 he received France's Grand Prix de Littérature Américaine. He lives in Portland, Maine.

A. O. SCOTT is a film critic at the *New York Times* and the author of *Better Living through Criticism: How to Think about Art, Pleasure, Beauty, and Truth*.

COLLEEN J. SHEEHY has long been concerned with the role of art and artists in our civic lives. As Director of Education at Weisman Art Museum for fifteen years, she organized *Springsteen: Troubadour of the Highway* in 2002, which toured nationally. She also published an essay examining the complex meanings of the album cover image for *Born in the U.S.A.* in a collection of essays on album cover art, *Coverscaping: Discovering Album Aesthetics*, edited by Asbjorn Gronstad and Oyvind Vagnes. Her interests in popular music as an art form and popular musicians as contemporary artists have underpinned several projects and exhibitions. She organized the symposium and edited (with Thom Swiss) a volume of essays, *Highway 61 Revisited: Bob Dylan's Road from Minnesota to the World* and, with graduate students at the University of Saint

Thomas, organized *Musicapolis: Scene and Seen, 1965–2005,* for the Minnesota Center for Photography in 2005. She served as Director and CEO of Plains Art Museum in Fargo, North Dakota, from 2007 to 2015, and since then has been President and Executive Director of Public Art Saint Paul, an organization that commissions and produces public art, community engagement, and social practice.

WESLEY STACE is the author of four novels. He makes music under the name John Wesley Harding.

FRANK STEFANKO is a world-class photographer most noted for his work with Bruce Springsteen and Patti Smith. In addition to his celebrity and rock-and-roll photography, he enjoys making landscape photographs in places that have not yet felt human footprints. His work has been shown in several museums, and he is represented by galleries in the United States, the United Kingdom, Italy, Sweden, and Australia. He is the author of three books of photography: *Days of Hope and Dreams: An Intimate Portrait of Bruce Springsteen; Patti Smith: American Artist*; and, most recently, *Bruce Springsteen: Further Up the Road*, which encompasses his photographs working with the artist over the last forty years.

IRWIN H. STREIGHT is Associate Professor in the Department of English, Culture, and Communications at the Royal Military College of Canada, in Kingston, Ontario. He is co-editor with R. Neil Scott of two major reference works on American author Flannery O'Connor: *Flannery O'Connor: An Annotated Reference Guide to Criticism*, which won a Choice "Outstanding Academic Title" award, and *Flannery O'Connor: The Contemporary Reviews*, volume 16 in the American Critical Archives series published by Cambridge University Press. With Roxanne Harde, he co-edited *Reading the Boss: Interdisciplinary Approaches to the Works of Bruce Springsteen*. His forthcoming book *Flannery at the Grammys* explores O'Connor's deep influence on a suite of well-known singer-songwriters and, more broadly, her presence in popular music.

WAYNE SWAN served as the Treasurer of Australia for nearly six years, including three years as Deputy Prime Minister. He was elected eight times as the Federal Member for Lilley between 1993 and 2019. He was one of the longest serving finance ministers in the G20 and in 2011 was awarded Euromoney Finance Minister of the Year for his "careful stewardship of Australia's finances and economic performance" during the global financial crisis. He is a commissioner on the Independent Commission for the Reform of International Corporate Taxation. In June 2018 he was elected National President of the Australian Labor Party.

DAVID L. ULIN is the author or editor of ten books, including *Sidewalking: Coming to Terms with Los Angeles*, shortlisted for the PEN/Diamonstein-Spielvogel Award for the Art of the Essay, and the Library of America's *Writing Los Angeles: A Literary Anthology*, which won a California Book Award. He has received fellowships from the Guggenheim Foundation, the Black Mountain Institute at the University of Nevada, Las Vegas, and the Lannan Foundation.

ELIJAH WALD is a musician, writer, and occasional academic whose dozen books include *Escaping the Delta: Robert Johnson and the Invention of the Blues; Dylan Goes Electric*; and *How the Beatles Destroyed Rock 'n' Roll: An Alternative History of American Popular Music*. He lives in Philadelphia and is currently researching a book on borders and immigration.

DANIEL WOLFF's writing includes "Patti Scialfa's Passionate Gamble," *4th of July, Asbury Park: A History of the Promised Land*, and the introduction to *Born to Run: The Unseen Photographs*, by Eric Meola. His latest book is *Grown-Up Anger: Bob Dylan, Woody Guthrie, and the Calumet Massacre of 1913*.

KENNETH WOMACK is Dean of the Wayne D. McMurray School of Humanities and Social Sciences at Monmouth University, where he also serves as Professor of English. He is the author or editor of numerous books, including *Long and Winding Roads: The Evolving Artistry of the Beatles; The Cambridge Companion to the Beatles*; and *The Beatles Encyclopedia: Everything Fab Four*. More recently, he is the author of a two-volume biography of Beatles producer George Martin, including *Maximum Volume: The Life of Beatles Producer George Martin (The Early Years,*

1926–1966) and *Sound Pictures: The Life of Beatles Producer George Martin (The Later Years, 1966–2016)*. He serves as editor of *Interdisciplinary Literary Studies: A Journal of Criticism and Theory,* published by Penn State University Press, and as co-editor of the English Association's *Year's Work in English Studies,* published by Oxford University Press.

INDEX

Page numbers in italics refer to photographs.